Blackstone's Leadership for Sergeants and Inspectors

Blackstone's Leadership for Sergeants and Inspectors

Second Edition

Bryan Boon

OXFORD
UNIVERSITY PRESS

OXFORD
UNIVERSITY PRESS

Great Clarendon Street, Oxford, OX2 6DP,
United Kingdom

Oxford University Press is a department of the University of Oxford.
It furthers the University's objective of excellence in research, scholarship,
and education by publishing worldwide. Oxford is a registered trade mark of
Oxford University Press in the UK and in certain other countries.

First Edition published in 2015
Second Edition published in 2025

Published in the United States of America by Oxford University Press
198 Madison Avenue, New York, NY 10016, United States of America.

British Library Cataloguing in Publication Data
Data available

Library of Congress Control Number: 2025943534

ISBN 978–0–19–897249–5

DOI: 10.1093/law/9780198972495.001.0001

Printed and bound by
CPI Group (UK) Ltd., Croydon, CR0 4YY

MIX
Paper | Supporting
responsible forestry
FSC® C013604

The manufacturer's authorised representative in the EU for product safety is
Oxford University Press España S.A. of Parque Empresarial San Fernando de Henares,
Avenida de Castilla, 2 – 28830 Madrid (www.oup.es/en or product.safety@oup.com).
OUP España S.A. also acts as importer into Spain of products made by the manufacturer.

Preface

I am pleased that I have been asked by Oxford University Press to produce a second edition of my *Leadership for Sergeants and Inspectors* book published in 2015. As with the first edition, the new book has academic foundations and it is backed by thirty years of policing experience, and many years of management training conducted both within and outside of the police service with a variety of organisations.

As with the first edition, I have endeavoured to write things down in clear and easy to understand terms. The book is devoid of jargon, although theory often has its own unavoidable technical language. Its concise and brief nature should assist with the quick absorption of facts.

My goal has always been to offer sergeants and inspectors as much practical advice as I can. To that end, the book is again divided into two distinct parts. Part One includes theory and practice. Part Two includes comprehensive, supporting checklists, with summaries, suggesting to sergeants and inspectors what they might do in a wide variety of different circumstances.

The checklists (toolkit) should be particularly helpful to sergeants and inspectors who have unfamiliar events suddenly thrust upon them. Additionally, although not mentioned in my first book, the checklists can be used as the basis for creating and delivering training and coaching sessions. Finally, the toolkit offers a self-development aspect for, by using it, sergeants and inspectors can put theory into practice and learn valuable lessons through operational usage.

The second edition still retains much of the valuable content of my original book with updating adjustments, and several new supportive, important and quite radical additions. On a wider basis, the second edition considers the change in context for policing since the first edition was published. To put it mildly, policing has experienced some huge and uncomfortable shocks. The changes taken in the inter-book years highlight the importance of first-class leadership and the role of leaders as the managers of change.

Devastatingly, in March 2021, during the Covid period, a serving but off-duty Metropolitan Police Service constable, Wayne Couzens, stopped, handcuffed, kidnapped, raped and strangled Sarah Everard, before burning her body. This must have been one of the worst murders in the annals of crime. It rocked not only the nation, but also all honest and conscientious police officers. It was particularly devastating for public perceptions of police and roused fears for the general safety of women.

A second damaging incident concerned two police officers, Deniz Jaffer and Jamie Lewis, who were imprisoned for photographing the murdered bodies of Bibaa Henry and Nicole Smallman. The women had been stabbed in Fryent

Country Park, Wembley, in July 2021, by Danyl Hussein. The officers placed pictures taken of the dead women on 'WhatsApp' describing them as 'dead birds'. This was a horrifying and outrageous act, lacking in humanity, empathy, professionalism and a concern for the dead women's families.

Public opinion ratings can go up and down, often rising when selfless and brave police officers are severely injured or killed acting for the public good. However, at this point in time public esteem for the police service is at a low point. This is not entirely down to the behaviour of individual police officers but also related to high levels of public expectancy and the increased complexity of police work. Police seem always to lack adequate personnel for their increasingly multi-functional role and forces are prone to under-funding. However, even in these straightened times, sergeants and inspectors can play their part in ensuring that officers under their command behave sensitively, firmly and professionally as a means to gain and retain public confidence.

The first edition, under the heading 'How we police in England and Wales', made clear that gaining public support, and behaving professionally and ethically, are key ingredients of successful policing. This element has been retained in the new book. However, it has now been greatly reinforced by the College of Policing and its increased insistence on ethical behaviour.

Given current circumstances, I have created a new chapter entitled 'Valuing, protecting and enhancing public esteem'. I must confess that I found this to be a thought-provoking and difficult task. I did not want to adopt a moralistic and lecturing approach. What I wanted to do was highlight the damage caused by miscreant officers who taint the reputation of good and decent colleagues whilst recognising the conscientious and dutiful professionalism shown by the majority of police officers. In accordance with an over-riding aim of my book, I have tried to suggest practical ways of dealing with poor behaviour which often occurs at high as well as low levels. I hope that I have succeeded.

As already indicated, since the first edition the College of Policing has adopted a pre-eminence in policing that cannot be ignored. As a consequence, I have included some of its critically important work on ethical behaviour and leadership in the new book under the title 'The College of Policing—ethics, leadership standards, competence and values, and decision making'. The entry complements the 'Valuing, protecting and enhancing public esteem' entry. Because the College of Policing's pronouncements on standards are necessarily technical, insistent and directive its narrative is noticeably different from my own. Therefore, I have tried to knit the College's work into my style of presentation without damaging content.

The Covid-19 virus (2019) hit not only the police service but also the entire population of the United Kingdom and peoples across the world. Everyone found the virus and ways of dealing with it difficult to manage. Police officers discovered themselves in uncharted territory when trying to enforce (not always transparently clear) regulations governing the restricted movement of members of the public. Long Covid is still an issue for many people and for some it may be a lifelong concern. Its symptoms can appear and be misinterpreted in the workplace.

A new chapter entitled 'Stress management and long Covid-19 considerations' recognises the stresses and strains visited upon busy and often hard-pressed officers and staff—including sergeants and inspectors. It also discusses the biological causes of stress and its effect upon people and efficiency and effectiveness. Stress can come into the workplace from a number of sources including the home environment, but one of the major causes of stress is an inappropriate management style. This matter was and is still covered implicitly in both the first and second edition books. However, I have laid a fresh emphasis on the matter in the new stress chapter, noting how corrosive a bad management style can be in terms of morale, motivation and workplace efficiency.

Another new chapter, entitled 'Dealing with unethical behaviours and workplace ineffectiveness sometimes without obvious causes', is intended to be particularly helpful to sergeants and inspectors who are likely to come across poor behaviours and workplace inefficiency in various forms. Sometimes the causes of inefficiency are not obvious and require the use of sophisticated interpersonal skills to disclose and deal with problems.

A further new chapter bears the title 'Coaching skills'. Coaching has an enormous part to play in officer development. As with all training, it is used to impart knowledge and skills and can be used to encourage desired attitudes. It does not stand alone and should form part of an integrated training programme. It should hold few fears for sergeants and inspectors who will almost certainly automatically coach officers informally on a daily basis so as to improve their policing skills. The chapter includes an example coaching scenario based on encouraging assertive behaviour where there are behavioural issues that need addressing. This ties in nicely with the sections entitled 'Valuing, protecting and enhancing public esteem' and 'The College of Policing—ethics, leadership standards and decision making'.

The former first edition chapter 'Treating people equally and valuing diversity' has now been divided into two separate chapters with equality and diversity being treated separately although they do have similarities. The diversity element now includes neurodiversity, and how neurodivergent people can harmoniously and creatively work alongside their neurotypical colleagues to the benefit of individuals, team work and public service. It also includes an entry on working with multicultural teams where different experiences and outlooks can be harnessed to the benefit of team dynamics and team outputs.

Substantial alterations have also been made to the first edition 'Misconduct and discipline' chapter so as to take account of changes in disciplinary legislation and guidance.

The toolkit has been greatly enhanced as a result of the inclusion of the new chapters. The original twenty-three tools have now increased to thirty-two—a substantial increase to practical assistance.

To conclude, I truly hope that sergeants and inspectors enjoy reading the second edition and that they will find it helpful in carrying out their challenging responsibilities especially when under pressure.

Bryan Boon
June 2025

Preface to First Edition

I have long wanted to write a book on leadership for police officers and in particular the key operational ranks of sergeant and inspector. Leadership is important because it offers purpose and direction in a complex and continuously changing world. Good leadership embraces a whole range of often difficult to acquire skills. These encompass, for example, team work, planning, problem solving and the ability to motivate others to give of their very best not only for themselves and the police service but most importantly of all for the public they serve.

I have tried to write the book in clear and easy to read terms, devoid of jargon although theory often has an unavoidable language of its own. Its concise and brief nature should help quick absorption and easy access to helpful checklists ('toolkit').

The book has academic foundations but it also contains useful practical comment. This is based on my 30 years' experience as a police officer and many years in management training both within and outside the police service. Should the reader require further information, the sources used are listed at the end of each chapter. However, the reader may wish to enhance learning by undertaking independent research of their own.

The leadership book comprises two distinct parts. Part One covers theory and practice and Part Two includes the comprehensive supporting checklists mentioned earlier, detailing what a sergeant or inspector might do in particular situations. The book does contain subject summaries but these do not figure at the end of each chapter in Part One. Instead, they have been located to head the checklists in Part Two. This is in order to enhance the benefit of the toolkit approach by offering a brief introduction prior to the use of a particular tool.

The book has a self-development aspect in its own right and by using the toolkit the reader will be able to learn through experience. Additionally, the book has a chapter on self-development and also it emphasises the need to develop leadership skills in others.

I hope that the sergeant and inspector reader will find the book enjoyable, practical and helpful with the carrying out of their often difficult public duties.

Bryan Boon
October 2014

Acknowledgements

Writing the first edition of Leadership for Sergeants and Inspectors was a difficult if fulfilling task, and when I was asked to produce a second edition I thought that my experience would stand me in good stead—and it did. However, in some ways I found the job of modernising the first edition quite difficult. Firstly, the context for policing has changed considerably. The emphasis on ethical policing, championed by the College of Policing, is predominant in a bid to improve professionalism and regain public support which has been in decline. Secondly, I did not find it easy inserting new material into a settled and proven structure. I had to make it enter seamlessly into existing narrative in a logical order so as not to inhibit the book's rhythmic flow.

In helping to keep me on track and encouraging me in my efforts I have to thank Fiona Briden, Senior Acquisitions Editor, Crime, Police and Criminology Academic and Professional Law, Oxford University Press (OUP) and Lindsay Glick, Project Editor, Professional Law and Medicine Content Development—Books (OUP). Without their invaluable help my second edition book would not have got off the ground.

Where the first edition book is concerned, I was remiss in not thanking all those people at OUP who brilliantly designed and produced the book and made its content both attractive and eminently usable. Belatedly, I thank them now and also all those similarly engaged on producing the second edition.

I also wish to thank the OUP appointed reviewers who, with independent oversight, looked at my early drafts. I truly learned and gained a great deal from their highly valuable contributions. I do not know who my reviewers were, but I am indebted to them.

As with my first edition book I once again offer thanks to my wife Rosalie for her support. Being a writer is quite a selfish activity. I have spent many hours on the computer researching, writing and endlessly revising material to the exclusion of neglected responsibilities and other matters important to us both.

Contents

Part Two Leadership—competence checklists (toolkit)

Special Features

This book contains a number of special features intended to assist the reader. These are explained below.

Key points

Information requiring particular emphasis is summarised in key point boxes throughout the text.

Tables

Some information or concepts have been tabulated for ease of illustration and presentation.

Scenarios and examples

To provide illustrative examples of certain key points and issues from real-life incidents, events and investigations.

Further reading

These features direct readers towards sources cited or used in the text, and to additional material that will amplify and elaborate the content of the book.

Checklists

To provide a list of key issues and considerations practitioners will find useful when planning, managing and interpreting the application of their leadership skills. The lists can also be used as the basis for preparing training and coaching sessions and supporting handouts.

PART ONE

Leadership—theory and practice

1

Policing in England and Wales and the purpose of this book

1.1 Police duties and responsibilities

When Sir Robert Peel introduced his Metropolis Police Improvement Bill to Parliament in April 1829 he was concerned about levels of crime which added to existing fears about the potential for public disorder. The Bill was enacted by Parliament and crime prevention was seen as a top priority for the new police. The Metropolitan Police Act 1829 and its practical consequences became the template for policing throughout England and Wales. (See also Emsley 1996.)

Although the social context has changed enormously since 1829, crime prevention, the detection and arrest of offenders and the maintenance of public order remain at the heart of policing. However, our society now is much more complex, and it is multicultural and multifaceted. Additionally, it has experienced and is still experiencing tremendous communication and technological changes. Therefore, today's policing priorities include managing:

- public expectations and complex relationships with the public at large and the various different communities that make up society;
- legitimate democratic expressions of public concern by way of marches and gatherings as well as unlawful and sometimes violent assemblies;
- alcohol-induced disorders and offences;
- destructive drug dealing and drug dependency;
- domestic disputes and violence towards spouses and partners;
- terrorism, fraud and violent crime.

To these can be added:

- managing and getting the best out of increasingly scarce resources—both human and material;
- creating meaningful relationships with other services and cooperating closely with them so as to maximise the help and protection offered to members of the public (e.g. liaising with social services, local authorities, community groups, schools and ambulance and fire services).

1.2 How we police in England and Wales

How police officers, singly and collectively, operate is absolutely critical to how successful they are in carrying out their duties and responsibilities. They must be able to keep people safe and secure whilst at the same time maintaining public support. The need for officers to behave ethically cannot be overstated.

In England and Wales we have a system of 'policing by consent'. The numbers of police and available resources have always been and always will be insufficient to deal with a massive breakdown in law and order. We rely upon the majority of citizens to obey the law and keep the peace. We also need the willing cooperation of the public to prevent crime and arrest offenders. The requirement for cooperation and respect for individuals underpins the behaviours police should adopt. If the overall consensus breaks down, the police will fail too.

Adopting the right behaviours is made simple for police officers if they reverse their relationships with the public. In other words: 'If I were a member of the public how would I like to be treated by the police?' Hopefully, answers would include: professionally, efficiently and effectively, courteously, patiently, fairly, honestly, with good humour and without any form of bias, prejudice or discrimination. Tolerance and reasoned discretion in the exercise of authority may be added to this list. It is not always necessary to resort to the courts where there are real mitigating circumstances and a warning will suffice.

Correct behaviours are likely to defuse inflamed and contentious situations and secure public cooperation and active assistance. Poor behaviours cause hostility and bad publicity and a detrimental view of the police service as a whole. In the public arena, the ripple effect of really bad policing can be immense.

KEY POINT—POLICING RELIES ON MAINTAINING A GENERAL CONSENSUS

Policing relies on a general consensus which is likely to fail if police officers do not behave humanely, ethically and professionally. This, in turn, will severely damage or lead to a breakdown in the policing system as a whole.

1.3 How this book on leadership can help police sergeants and inspectors

Of course, all police officers should behave in a professional and ethical manner. However, on occasions some police officers are not professional and their poor behaviours let down conscientious, hard-working officers. Unprofessional behaviour can arise for a number of reasons including: poor training, poor direction and control, a lack of motivation and the absence of corrective feedback but also unsuitability for the role of constable. First-class leadership is required to give a sense of purpose and direction and impetus. Good leadership is inspirational and encouraging, with problems tackled and not avoided, and in the case of policing it is intent on public service and satisfaction.

Leadership is required at all levels of the police service including at the rank of constable—a job which includes offering leadership in many public-contact situations on an almost daily basis. However, sergeants and inspectors have key roles in this regard. They are leaders and supervisors at the main point of contact with the public and are intimately involved with the practicalities of operational policing. As leaders they must set an example and ensure compliance with correct standards of professional and ethical behaviour by those under their command. To that end, this book offers practical help on leadership to uniformed and plain clothes police officers of the sergeant and inspector ranks. This is its clear mission alongside a desire to focus on offering the best possible service to the public. However, the book may also be of assistance to others in the police wishing to add to or refresh their existing skills.

1.3.1 **Defining what is meant by the term 'leadership'**

The term 'leadership' is in fact quite difficult to define because it has very strong overlaps with 'management'. And it must be admitted that a true definition is open to debate. But despite needing similar skills, leaders and managers have quite different functions and this book explores those differences.

Leadership has visionary aspects allied to a strong sense of purpose. At its core are skills relating to: planning, change management, team work, motivating followers and performance measurement. However, there are also other important skills, especially good communication skills, which are vital to success.

1.3.2 **How the book works**

The book falls into two distinct parts. Part One offers a mixture of theory and practice and helpful tips. Part Two contains a series of brief, skills-based checklists (or prompts). The checklists act as a 'toolkit' for the busy police officer trying, with perhaps little available time, to deal with events efficiently and effectively.

The two parts can be used independently of each other: however, to get the best out of the book the two elements should be read together. This is because Part One is the storehouse giving rise to the toolkit. As in a real toolbox, the checklists (or tools) are together for ease of access and immediate use.

1.3.3 **The rationale behind the book**

This book is not designed to act as an alternative to authorised police training manuals or textbooks or other official instructions. Instead, it is intended to supplement and add to those valuable means of teaching. It takes quite a while to gain a substantial bank of operational experience and this book hopes to assist that developmental process. As well as existing sergeants and inspectors, it should prove especially useful for newly promoted sergeants and inspectors and, in particular, officers confronting new and challenging situations.

References and further reading

Emsley, C. (1996), *The English Police: A Political and Social History* (2nd edn, New York: Longman).

Home Office Statutory Guidance on Professional Standards, Performance and Integrity in Policing, Schedule 2, Conduct Regulations 2020.

2

Exploring the concept of leadership

2.1 What is leadership and why is it important?

Leaders are visionary, forward-looking, change agents, who plan in order to inspire a strong sense of purpose in followers. Critical to success is the motivating of followers who are required to 'buy into the vision' and complete its supporting objectives. Motivating people is not always an easy task and it is particularly difficult when things go wrong or fail.

Qualities of leadership are not just the preserve of appointed or self-appointed leaders. They can exist in anyone at any level of an organisation.

At times, a leader must act as a 'champion' in adversity for those being unfairly treated or placed under undue pressure. 'Threats' to team members may come from within the team itself, for example through bullying behaviour or racial or sex discrimination. Equally, it may come from external forces hostile to police.

It is necessary that a leader should be highly visible to inspire confidence in his or her followers. A leader should stand back to have a clear and comprehensive overview of events. However, on occasions a leader is required to lead from the front. In the police service, rank carries certain personal responsibilities and authorities that cannot be delegated. In public order situations, sergeants and inspectors are expected to lead by example. Also, inspectors and sergeants routinely attend serious incidents that occur during their tours of duty to offer on-the-spot leadership, advice and support.

Leaders are required to imaginatively manage scarce human and other resources. A police leader is unlikely ever to have all the resources that he or she would like to possess.

To maximise their efficiency and effectiveness police leaders, including sergeants and inspectors, have to network not only with colleagues but also with external agencies. These will include, for example, other emergency services, social services, educational establishments and community groups.

KEY POINT—BEING A VISIBLE LEADER IS ESSENTIAL

There is little doubt that to be successful a leader has to gain the support of followers by being visible, approachable, open, honest, fair and competent.

In particular, good leadership provides:

- a clear sense of purpose and direction through well-thought-out and well-executed plans;
- efficient and effective use of scarce resources;
- motivated followers and team harmony;
- team efficiency through optimum use of available skills and attributes;
- objectives completed on time;
- the best possible service to members of the public.

KEY POINT—THE CONSEQUENCES OF POOR LEADERSHIP

Poor leadership leads to negative outcomes including disenchanted followers, wasted resources and public disapproval.

2.2 What is the difference between leadership and management?

Different people have different interpretations about the precise nature of leadership. This means that the definition of leadership is always open to debate. Part of the problem of definition arises from a genuine overlap of skills and the fact that managers are usually expected to exercise leadership skills in their role as managers. This presents no problem provided a manager remembers his or her real function—managing. Equally, a leader should be clear about the distinction between the two roles.

However, there does appear to be some form of agreement on the core nature of leadership. In essence, it is the leader's job to lead in the current circumstances but also to look ahead to what is required in the immediate and long-term future. This involves sophisticated planning and objective-setting skills and also an ability to manage change with its power to disrupt if not managed effectively. To attain their vision for the future, a leader has to persuade followers to willingly execute his or her plans. This requires first-class communication and motivating skills. When driving through initiatives it is up to the leader to remove all obstacles to progress and completion.

A manager's role is to carry through the practical consequences of the leader's plans. Leadership is strategic whereas management is tactical. Leaders always have an eye to the future and thus are change agents. Managers are concerned with production in the present—the here and now. Leaders and managers use similar skills to carry out different functions.

It is essential that leaders and managers recognise these differences and that both seek to work in perfect harmony; one is unlikely to do well without the other. But it is absolutely vital that a leader is clear about what he or she has to do otherwise a lack of definition will lead to a lack of purpose.

Perhaps the clearest definition for defining leadership and management derives sense from Adair (1988) who points out that the word 'lead' derives from the Anglo-Saxon language and correlates with a road or sea path. In other words, it infers a sense of direction, of travel and of destination. The word 'managing' has its origins in Latin and relates to the hand or, by interpretation, manual activity or, it can be supposed, day-to-day skill application.

2.3 Does it matter that sometimes the leadership and management roles often seem to function together through the same person?

It is desirable that the leadership and management functions are separate as this offers greater role clarity. However, in reality managers are quite often expected to adopt a dual role. Additionally, where people work alone they will of necessity have to take on both functions. However, it remains essential that there is a clear understanding of what each of the two functions entails and the appropriate skill sets required.

2.4 Can anyone be a leader? Can I be a leader on my own?

Anyone can apply leadership skills but this will be with a lesser or greater degree of success. This is a natural consequence of life—some people are better at doing certain things than others. Personal qualities are important, but behaviours can change and skills can be improved with practice.

The nature of police work demands that police officers from the rank of constable upwards exercise leadership in all manner of situations. The lone constable on the beat or on patrol never knows what is around the corner requiring immediate action or resolution. Sometimes lives depend upon a prompt response. Incidents might involve, for example, a traffic accident, a fire, a fight, public disorder or even a murder.

2.5 Can leadership be taught or is it a natural attribute?

First-class leadership relies on motivating behaviours and excellent interpersonal skills. A leader who is ill-tempered and unapproachable and fails to listen, consult with others and accept feedback is unlikely to succeed. Team members respond best to those leaders they respect and who value them for what they can bring to the proper fulfilment of plans.

It seems that who we are and how we develop affects our personality and the ways in which we interact with others. Obviously, we can change through feedback and experience and it is possible to encourage desired behaviours in others. However, pinning down exactly which common characteristics leaders should have is very hard to establish as researchers have discovered.

Appropriate personality and behaviours are important but leadership also relies heavily on using practical skills. These include, for example, planning and motivating followers. All leadership skills can be taught, practised and improved upon.

Most of us could sit down and list those traits and qualities that we think are desirable in a good leader. However, whilst there might be common ground there might also be a considerable divergence of opinion. Further, much research has been carried out on the importance of traits (characteristic features) and qualities but these studies have not come up with any definitive conclusions.

Rogers (2008) in his book on police leadership skills draws attention to the works of Stogdill (1948) and Mann (1959) who noted that many works on traits did draw a distinction between the characteristics of leaders and non-leaders. However, Rogers notes to the contrary that Wright (1996) had found that others had discovered no differences between leaders and followers insofar as these characteristics were concerned. Also, and perhaps surprisingly, some people with the characteristics were less likely to become leaders.

Secretan (1994) says that a leader needs the foundations of intelligence and positive attitudes allied to the qualities of courage, shrewdness and common sense. It is upon these attributes that the leader builds the necessary skill base through experience. Butler and McManus (1998) agree that intelligence may be slightly more evident in leaders than followers.

Armstrong (1990) adds that although it may be difficult to assign a particular set of traits or qualities to leadership there is 'good evidence' that leaders do tend to have a little more intelligence than those they lead. And, 'they tend to be better adjusted, more dominant, more extroverted, less conservative and to have a better understanding of people than the rank and file'. Armstrong suggests that these characteristics are only sometimes apparent when an individual takes up a leadership role.

2.6 What should leaders do?

It is suggested that successful leaders should:

- take full cognisance of the situation they find themselves in as they cannot operate in a vacuum. For example, police officers need to be aware of what their colleagues are doing but also of changes in society, political and public expectations of them as well as material and financial constraints;
- plan taking into account the overall aims, risk-management issues and the availability of resources (commonly in short supply). It is also necessary to fix objectives, agree work structures and roles, monitor progress and deal with problems;
- develop good communications within the team and with peers and colleagues but also with people at all levels within and outside the organisation. The importance of introducing the best possible communication system

cannot be overemphasised. Good communications should lead to a healthy and successful organisation;

- manage well the changes resulting from the implementation of plans. This is especially significant where alterations to working practices are concerned. Failure to manage change effectively will almost certainly damage the changes envisaged;
- motivate people, especially those who are reluctant to follow or participate, to achieve and exceed expectations;
- make the best use of the skills and abilities of each individual team member so as to complete tasks but also to satisfy individual needs and aspirations;
- remove obstacles to progress by using problem-solving skills where appropriate;
- share success (and failure) with team members;
- measure outcomes by creating appropriate performance measures.

2.7 **When is leadership absolutely essential?**

Good leadership is always important because it offers a sense of purpose, direction and achievement. However, *it is absolutely necessary when a team has lost its way and does not know what to do*. Also, a leader should intervene when a team is under attack by misinformed protagonists.

2.8 **Are there different types of leaders?**

Types of leader vary greatly but there are certain accepted categories of leader (Cole 1996) and these are as follows:

- the *charismatic leader* leads by force of personality. He or she gives off an aura that compels people to follow. However, not everyone is charismatic. Additionally, there is no guarantee that a charismatic leader is a good leader—this depends on actual performance and outcomes;
- the *traditional leader* has little relevance to the police service or any other organisation. This is because leadership is based upon inherited roles. A monarch taking on a hereditary position epitomises the traditional leader. It could be said too that a family that passes a business down from one member of the family to another in succession has an affinity with the traditional leader. Inheritance is no guarantee of competence which will vary from ruler to ruler or person to person;
- the *situational leader* is a person who has the right qualifications and abilities to suit a particular set of circumstances. However, when the situation changes the situational leader may be made redundant or become largely ineffective;

- the *appointed leader* is common in the police service and elsewhere. He or she gains his or her authority based upon selection to fit a particular position in the police service. Appointed leaders should be chosen on their merits and judged on their performance and results;
- the *functional (or action-centred) leader* changes his or her approach to meet competing priorities and prevailing demands. Action-centred leadership as proposed by Adair (1983) relates to task, group and individual needs. However, as these elements are linked any neglect of one constant will affect the other two negatively. For example, although the functional leader may of necessity concentrate on the task for productive purposes he or she must remain aware that at some stage all three constants need to be placed back in equilibrium.

2.9 Is leadership style important and is there one style or several?

Leadership style is very important because it underpins the practical process of carrying through objectives to a successful conclusion. It is strongly linked with the power to communicate effectively at all levels. It is also integral to motivating people through good and bad times to achieve their tasks and objectives. How a leader behaves is critical to how followers behave in response.

On a personal level, leaders bring their own acquired attributes and ways of doing things to leadership matters. This makes leadership unique to each individual concerned. However, the desire to improve and a willingness to learn from experience should greatly enhance leadership ability. Learning about the effect of certain behaviours and considering the personal and joint needs of followers is very important.

Types of leader vary greatly but so do styles of leadership. The following styles are worth considering (see also Armstrong 1990 and 2009).

KEY POINT—CHANGING CIRCUMSTANCES

The sophisticated leader will adapt his or her approach to suit ever-changing circumstances and demands.

- The *charismatic leader* leads by strength of personality. However, not everyone is charismatic and traits and qualities cannot be taught although behaviours can be developed. Additionally, there is no guarantee that a charismatic leader is a good leader for this depends on actual performance and outcomes.
- The *non-charismatic leader* may find it hard to make an impression when matched against his or her charismatic counterpart. The non-charismatic

leader gains respect and followers through exhibiting purposeful competence. A lack of competence detracts from the perception of how any leader is seen.

- The *autocratic leader* simply tells people what to do and followers are required to act without question. This style can be stifling and may on occasions be seen as bullying. It runs on an assumption that the leader is always right. In practice, it means that followers never or rarely get a chance to voice their opinions on how things should be done. This means that creativity and new ways of doing things may be lost. Additionally, the style may demotivate people and cause conflict with strong-minded individuals.

  However, on occasions in the police service an autocratic approach may be justified: for example, when police officers have to act very quickly in an emergency in operational situations such as riots and where there is no time to debate issues. An autocratic intervention in these circumstances should be selected from a raft of leadership styles and not a permanent fixed position. Finally, autocratic leadership means that vital communication lines from leader to individuals and back are very short. The autocrat might see this defect as a valuable time-saving device.
- The *democratic leader* seeks to involve others in the decision-making process. He or she, to a lesser or greater degree, will involve followers in discussing activities, problems and events. He or she may then accept, reject or amend team proposals but is not ultimately bound by team recommendations. This style has the advantage of being inclusive (and therefore motivational) and it taps inventiveness and new ways of proceeding. The democratic style involves spending a great deal of valuable time in managing team communications. Therefore, meetings should have clear objectives and be efficiently run to maximise and justify the amount of time invested.

  A weak democratic leader may lose control to vociferous and strong team members.
- *Laissez-faire leadership* is often misunderstood. The style has great value if used properly. Essentially, the laissez-faire leader trusts people to get on with their jobs with as few interventions as possible being made.

  Of course, this style may be the resort of the lazy leader and as such it leaves events 'hostage to fortune' and thus is dangerous. In reality, freedom to act in an almost unfettered way can only be allowed when people have clear objectives, are properly trained, have proven reliability and can be trusted to act alone or with others.

  Trusting people to work under light supervision carries risks. Where trust is honoured by the recipient, the rewards can be very high in terms of personal motivation and task achievement. When a person can no longer be trusted, the trust should be withdrawn and a different style of leadership adopted with closer supervision involved.

  To reduce the risks of a laissez-faire style, the sergeant and inspector leader must ensure that he or she never loses oversight of what is happening. He or she must be prepared to make appropriate and timely interventions where necessary.

- *Transactional and transformational* leadership are the brainchild of Burns (1978). Burns proposes that the behaviour of transformational leaders has the ability to transform workplaces by appealing to an individual's ability to look beyond self-interest, task allocation and task fulfilment for even greater achievement. Thus the transformational leader seeks to motivate followers not just for their own benefit but also for the benefit of others and the organisation.

  Transformational leadership requires a sophisticated approach as it relies heavily on motivating people to exceed traditional workplace expectations. However, rewards for individuals may be high in that they will be encouraged to exhibit, develop and extend their abilities and aspirations. This leadership approach is greatly supported by the concepts of valuing equality and diversity (see Chapters 7 and 8). Most importantly, perhaps the greatest beneficiary of the transformational style is the public that the police serve.

  According to Burns, transactional leadership is much more narrowly defined in that it only involves managing, maintaining and completing allocated workloads. In simple terms, workplace transactions involve agreeing what should be done, how it should be done and what rewards will follow successful completion of tasks.

  This interpretation appears to downgrade transactional leadership when measured against transformational leadership. However, regardless of the enormous benefits that can accrue from transformational leadership large elements of work are transactional and mechanical. For example, most organisations necessarily set people objectives, review their progress, appraise their performance and offer 'rewards' according to results.

  It is up to the leader to decide which style to adopt and when to use it. Some people who require close direction may respond better to the transactional style. Others who seek to extend their capabilities may respond more favourably to the transformational approach.

2.10 **How do leaders exercise their authority?**

Leaders (sergeants and inspectors and police officers in general) need to be able to assert their authority in order to carry out tasks, give directions and maintain discipline where necessary. The exercise of authority is a serious business and it must be exercised appropriately, properly and with sensitivity.

Where the public are concerned, an abuse of power can be absolutely disastrous. The resultant 'ripple effect' can damage police reputation and operational matters long after the abuse of power has taken place. This is because people who think that they have been unfairly treated may withdraw their support from the police and encourage others to do the same. Sometimes it is another officer in another situation who may suffer because of the failure of an offended member of the public to offer timely assistance.

At all times, authority or power must be exercised judiciously. The leader must remain fully aware of what he or she is authorised to do and what the limits of his or her power are. An abuse of power is totally unacceptable.

KEY POINT—ABUSE OF AUTHORITY

Where a leader abuses his or her authority with police colleagues and team members it can cause resentment, alienation and a failure to complete tasks.

2.10.1 **Sources of power**

Sources of power—French and Raven (1960) and Raven (1965 and 2008)—comprise the following.

- *Coercive power* relies on the ability to bring about sanctions when people wilfully disobey instructions or orders or are otherwise deficient when carrying out their duties and responsibilities. Coercive power must never be abused. However, on occasions leaders are obliged to exercise discipline. That said, misconduct proceedings should be a last resort and before they take place every effort should have been made to correct faults (see also Chapter 16).
- *Reward power* involves the leader legitimately offering benefits for good or exceptional work. The giving of benefits must be truly merited and the power should be exercised sincerely, without favour and with sound judgement. Leadership and managerial rewards might include the giving of praise (this offers recognition of a job well done, helps to raise self-esteem and motivation levels and encourages like behaviour in similar circumstances). Performance appraisal reviews also offer opportunities to show recognition and appreciation of a job well done.
- *Legitimate power* is what many leaders use to support their authority. Legitimate power comes from appointment to a particular position in an organisation. A police officer gains legitimate power on attaining the office of constable. A police sergeant or inspector gains his or her authority on promotion. Promotion in the police service is based upon proven suitability for carrying out responsibilities (competence).
- *Expert power* relies on possessing a particular knowledge or expertise that is not generally available to others. The knowledge or expertise may be necessarily confined to specialists in a particular field of work. However, expertise in a team, for example, is often the result of specific training for a particular task, therefore it is more job than person related. Expert power leaves open the ability to do or not do something in the hands of its possessor. Whilst

generally this may not be the case, this can mean that an expert may withhold expertise to perhaps gain other advantages or subvert the intentions of the leader.

Leading people with specialist knowledge working in specialist fields requires the leader to understand how those skills serve mutual tasks and objectives. Results should be achieved through good communication used to gain cooperation and commitment.

Sometimes individuals within a team of generalists have specialist skills which serve day-to-day activities. This might include, for example, exercising particular computer or technical skills. However, the team leader should remain aware that he or she has a responsibility to maximise the use that can be made of individual team members. This is made possible by providing new skills or enhancing existing abilities. Therefore, team experts should be encouraged or even directed to impart their competence to others. This widens the available skill base. It may also ease the pressure on perhaps overworked experts.

- *Referent power* (also charismatic) is where the charismatic leader gains his or her power from force of personality. Therefore, he or she does not have to rely heavily on formal authority. This is because followers trust (sometimes mistakenly) their leader and willingly comply with directions.
- *Informational power* involves providing information to an individual that results in them thinking and behaving differently. Bald information on its own may not bring about change, therefore it may have to be supported by arguments making the case for accepting it. Where information is taken on board and believed and importantly is acted upon, then 'socially independent change' is said to have occurred.

Of course, sergeant and inspector leaders have to regularly supply information to, for example, encourage people to entertain necessary changes to working practices or when offering feedback to individuals. It is important that information is delivered honestly and is based upon facts and evidence and not supposition.

Information provided may not be accurate because of the deliverer's genuine misconception of what the truth actually entails. However, information may also be deliberately distorted to bring about changes to suit the deliverer's perhaps less than honest ends—an undesirable behaviour likely to result in bad outcomes.

Equally, power can be exercised by withholding information for perhaps the wrong reasons. All this re-emphasises how difficult the communication process is and how skilled and perceptive sergeants and inspectors must be to check and verify the validity of messages both dispatched and received.

It is essential that a leader should be aware of the sources of authority, what authority he or she actually possesses and how it might best be exercised. Improper use of authority can have negative consequences in terms of tasks to be completed and individual people.

2.10.2 Male and female leaders

Rosener (1990) notes that research suggests that although male and female leaders both adopt transactional and transformational leadership styles, women are more transformational than men. However, it would appear that male and female leaders perceive no difference in the way that subordinates regard and follow them. Research also shows that male and female leaders use power sources in different combinations.

The research into male and female leaders is interesting and thought provoking and the reader may wish to explore this issue further (Owen 2000; Cole 1996). However, the point of discussing the matter here is to suggest that regardless of a leader's sex, sergeants and inspectors should seek to learn from the best (and the worst) that individuals have to offer with a view to improving personal performance.

2.11 What sort of environment should leaders seek to create?

The police leader needs to create an environment where team members can be happy and flourish and work well to the best of their ability.

KEY POINT—TEAM MEMBERS' ETHICAL BEHAVIOUR

In carrying out their duties and responsibilities, team members should:

- never lose sight of the quality service that they must provide for the public who should be treated with respect, fairly, courteously and professionally at all times;
- value and support each other and regard each other with respect and act at all times with honesty, openness and integrity.

Additionally, the sergeant and inspector leader should:

- set a good example, act as a 'role model', behave professionally and exhibit competence;
- be approachable, sensitive to what is happening around him or her and considerate and fair in his or her dealings with others;
- act without prejudice or discrimination and value the differences that each team member brings to the workplace;
- strive to be a good communicator able to communicate with and influence followers, peers, seniors, external agencies and the public;
- invite followers to make contributions to workplace tasks and objectives and practices—ideas and suggestions should be solicited and valued;

- encourage mutual respect between team members and not permit intolerable or improper behaviour between individuals or groups;
- encourage feedback for him- or herself and avoid defensive responses;
- facilitate open and honest communication throughout the team;
- ensure that team members share in success but also share in failure where this is appropriate.

2.12 How do I know if I am a successful leader and how do I ensure that I continue to improve in a leadership role? What do I do if I am a poor leader?

A leader needs to establish how effective he or she is in carrying out his or her responsibilities. Critical self-analysis will help and this may be aided by looking closely both at successes and failures to establish the reasons why things turned out as they did. This process can be greatly aided by being unafraid to ask for feedback from juniors, peers, seniors and even members of the public where appropriate. Additionally, performance appraisal reviews are likely to help with establishing levels of efficiency and effectiveness and provide any corrective measures.

Success can also be measured by establishing whether or not tasks have been completed and objectives achieved. Value added might include increased efficiency and effectiveness, for example completion of tasks more quickly, with fewer resource costs and with a decreased error rate. The 'icing on the cake' would be positive comment and praise from persons external to the police service. These might include, for example, other agencies and members of the public.

A true and honest assessment of performance will help with self-development and continuous growth in the leadership role. This is because the assessment will reveal gaps and areas where improvement is desirable. If self-assessment and the views of others suggest that an individual is a poor leader then effort needs to be made to improve the situation. Improvement may necessitate asking a 'mentor' (usually a more senior person) to offer regular guidance and suggestions. Additionally, competence and skills can be improved by training which takes many forms (e.g. on the job coaching, reading books and formal training courses). An individual can seek training on his or her own. However, it would be wise to consult a training expert or perhaps a mentor to find out exactly what is required.

Regrettably, where a leader is identified as inadequate then he or she may not be in the right post or job. This may result in seeking a new position internally or external to the police service. This should not be regarded as a weakness or a failure. Each individual has a skill set which may or may not suit certain tasks or jobs in one place but be more than adequate in another.

References and further reading

Adair, J. (1983), *Effective Leadership* (London: Pan Books; with the kind permission of Pan Macmillan).

Adair, J. (1988), *Director Magazine* (London: Director Publications).

Armstrong, M. (1990), *How to Be an Even Better Manager* (3rd edn, London: Kogan Page).

Armstrong, M. (2009), *Handbook of Human Resource Management Practice* (11th edn, London: Kogan Page).

Burns, J. M. (1978), *Leadership* (New York: Harper & Row).

Butler, G. and McManus, F. (1998), *Psychology: A Very Short Introduction* (Oxford: Oxford University Press).

Cole, G. A. (1996), *Management Theory and Practice* (5th edn, London: Letts Educational; with permission of Cengage Learning EMA Ltd).

French, J. R. P. and Raven, B. H. (1960), 'The Bases of Social Power' in D. Cartwright and A. Zander (eds), *Group Dynamics* (New York: Harper & Row).

Mann, R. D. (1959), 'A Review of the Relationship Between Personality and Performance in Small Groups', *Psychological Bulletin* 66(4): 241–70.

Owen, H. (2000), *In Search of Leaders* (Chichester: John Wiley & Sons Ltd).

Raven, B. H. (1965), 'Social Influence and Power' in I. D. Steiner and M. Fishbein (eds), *Current Studies in Social Psychology* (New York: Holt, Rinehart & Winston).

Raven, B. H. (2008), 'Toward Understanding Social Power: A Personal Odyssey' in R. Levine, A. Rodrigues and L. Zelezny (eds), *Journeys in Social Psychology: Looking Back to Inspire the Future* (New York: Psychology Press). Also available at <http://changingminds.org/explanations/power/french_and_raven.htm>.

Rogers, C. (2008), *Leadership Skills in Policing* (Oxford: Oxford University Press).

Rosener, J. (1990), *Ways Women Lead* (Irvine, CA: Graduate School of Management, University of California).

Secretan, L. (1994), *Managerial Moxie: The 8 Proven Steps to Empowering Employees and Supercharging Your Company* (Roseville, CA: Prima Lifestyle).

Stogdill, R. M. (1948), 'Personal Factors Associated With Leadership: A Survey of the Literature', *Journal of Psychology* 25: 35–71.

Wright, P. (1996), *Managerial Leadership* (London: Routledge).

3

Leadership and team work

3.1 What is a team and why is team work important?

Although constables and other individuals acting alone can and often are required to exhibit leadership skills, they usually form parts of teams under the control of sergeants and inspectors. Teams offer an efficient way of utilising and maximising individual skills and talents so as to offer the best possible service to the public. Creating and leading a first-class team requires a sophisticated and sensitive coordination of events and activities and really top-class communication skills. Teams can be very successful indeed but they do vary and the absence of a good leader may cause untold problems for team morale and public satisfaction.

Team members vary in number depending on the nature of work to be done. In an efficient and effective team, all the participants cooperate and work together to fulfil a common purpose. The composition of many teams is likely to be of a multicultural nature and include both neurotypical and neurodivergent people. This should be celebrated because it brings together many different perspectives and diverse talents which can be harnessed to maximise both efficiency and effectiveness. (See also Chapter 8, 'Valuing diversity'.)

It is up to the leader to ensure that team members know what they are trying to achieve and to motivate them to complete objectives. The leader should ensure that team members have clear roles and that obstructions to progress are removed.

Developing team abilities is an important job for the leader who should use individual talent to full advantage. Utilising and combining skills to suit and match particular tasks can increase the worth of the effort applied to tasks and reduce difficulties and costs.

Leaders are sometimes able to choose their team members; but often they are given or inherit people who have been selected for them. In any event, whether chosen or inherited the behaviours and performance of team members can be variable and these are matters for the leader to understand and deal with. The leader must strive for team 'synergy' (working together in cooperative harmony) but not all teams function well and some are dysfunctional either in part of fully. Tackling dysfunctional behaviour is of great importance.

KEY POINT—BENEFITS OF GOOD TEAM WORK

Good leadership and good team work help the police service to make the best use of individual and group talent and limited resources. In top teams, leaders encourage individual development to the benefit of the individuals concerned, team growth and the service to members of the public.

3.2 **What are the features of an effective team?**

Effective teams (see also McGregor 1960; Armstrong 1990) have many features but these should include:

- visionary, forward-looking, inspiring leadership and clear objectives for the team and individuals;
- clearly defined roles where team members understand what they and each member of the team have to do separately and together;
- individual team members who are trained and developed to perform their tasks and enhance their own potential;
- leadership which ensures that individual skills and abilities are matched to suit the tasks in hand;
- a communications system which encourages team members to relate to persons they come into contact with in an honest, open, forthright, tactful and respectful way;
- team members who deal with any inter-team conflict in a constructive manner that leads to an absence of ill-feeling and achieves positive outcomes;
- team members who listen to feedback, wherever it comes from, as a means to learn from what they have done well and not done so well;
- team norms which are based on diversity concepts (everyone, no matter what their background, has something to contribute) and valuing each other as individuals and colleagues;
- team members who are praised and rewarded for good results but share success and failure with the leader; *and in the case of police teams*
- team members who, in all that they do, never lose sight of the need for ethical behaviour at all times in order to properly serve the public interest.

3.3 **Can teams be dysfunctional and cause problems and if so what causes dysfunctional behaviour?**

Teams can be dysfunctional for a variety of reasons (see also Armstrong 2009). Being dysfunctional may result in inter-team conflict, a loss in efficiency and effectiveness, failure to complete objectives and possibly disbandment. Dysfunctional police teams can cause reputational damage and incur a loss of public support.

Reasons for dysfunctional behaviour may include the following:

- the leader is seen as weak, disinterested or incompetent. If a leader fails to set an example and show that they know what they are doing and fails to inspire team members then the members will lose their sense of direction. Then they may either do little or nothing or, alternatively, do what they think is right in the circumstances;

- the leader is strong but aggressive and intolerant and this may encourage negative attitudes and withdrawal of cooperation within the team. Aggressive behaviour tends to generate destructive aggressive responses or passive acceptance;
- team members do not understand what they have to do, the tasks and objectives they have to complete and the standards that govern their actions and behaviours;
- a strong team member (or members) may issue a 'challenge' to the leader's authority especially if the leader is regarded as being weak. The challenger may offer notional acceptance of the leader's position but take every opportunity to undermine his or her position;
- disparate and competing groups may develop in a team under the leadership of strong personalities. This may result in open conflict resulting in disharmony, a loss of synergy and poor performance.

3.4 If a team is behaving badly what can a leader do to put things right?

Getting a team to perform to required standards of behaviour and efficiency sums up much of what a sergeant and inspector leader has to do in order to complete tasks and achieve objectives. Sound leadership requires that obstacles to efficiency and effectiveness, no matter what their cause, are promptly removed.

Poor leadership could be one of the reasons that dysfunctional behaviour has taken root and a bad leader may be unable to resolve difficulties. In such circumstances, but only as a last resort, it may be necessary to remove him or her in favour of a more able leader.

A competent leader sensitive to what is happening around him or her quickly identifies the causes of problems or conflicts and deals with them promptly. In this respect, it is important to remind team members of their duties and responsibilities. Further, the leader should make clear to individuals that agreed standards of performance and behaviour must be maintained. Also, team members need to be told that disrespectful and inappropriate behaviour (including undermining the leader) will not be tolerated (it is axiomatic that there is a duty to follow as well as to lead) and that breaches of standards may result in misconduct proceedings.

When problems have been tackled through, for example, individual one-to-one meetings including where necessary individual workplace counselling sessions and through open and frank team meetings based upon mutual respect and honest feedback, the leader should monitor progress to ensure a return to accepted behaviours and performance. It should be noted that the leader is entitled to counsel people in the workplace as a means of removing obstacles to progress. This may be done by a sophisticated use of interpersonal skills—covered in considerable depth in this book (in particular in Chapters 17 to 21). However, the leader is *not entitled* to enter into areas beyond his or her capabilities (i.e. work-based issues) and where appropriate team members should be referred to specialists including human resource personnel, doctors and professional counsellors.

Versatility in adopting various leadership styles is very important. For example, following team antagonism and disharmony and when rules and standards are being insisted upon, the leader is likely to adopt an autocratic or transactional style. However, this can rapidly change to a democratic or transformational style once difficulties have been resolved and can eventually progress to a laissez-faire style when balance is restored in the team (see Chapter 2, 'Exploring the concept of leadership').

3.5 **How does a leader create an effective team and what does a high-performing team look like?**

A leader builds an effective team by planning and inspiring and motivating others to reach agreed aims and objectives. Additionally, a good leader values each team member as an individual and seeks to maximise their talent not only for the sake of each team member but also for the sake of the team and the joint need to complete tasks and achieve public satisfaction.

To get the best out of people, the team leader must be sensitive to what is happening in and around the team. The leader should remain acutely aware of the needs, ambitions and aspirations of individual team members. Further, the leader should be aware of the welfare needs of individuals both within and outside the workplace, making timely interventions where necessary. It should be remembered that sergeant and inspector leaders have considerable executive power and latitude to help individuals with, for example, hours of duty and workloads.

On the basis that all team members have something different to offer, the leader should carefully match individual skills to individual tasks. This recognises that one person might be better at doing something than another whose talents may come to the fore in different circumstances. However, the leader should also endeavour to develop people beyond their preferences both for their benefit and also for the benefit of increased team efficiency and effectiveness.

Deployment in this way maximises the best use of scarce resources. However, individual and team competence may be further enhanced by the transfer of skills through coaching sessions. Additionally, organised training sessions linked to a thoughtful programme of continuous self-development are desirable.

Further, matching people to specific tasks permits the leader to allow individuals to take on leadership responsibilities where their skills are beneficial in achieving results. This encourages a growth of leadership competence in others and acknowledges that leadership activities within a team are not just confined to the 'appointed' leader who, regardless of the circumstances, always retains accountability.

KEY POINT—A LEADER'S ACCOUNTABILITY

Although 'appointed' leaders may delegate responsibility, they cannot delegate accountability for individual or team actions. Accountability remains with the leader at all times.

3.5.1 **Types of work**

Interestingly, Margerison and McCann (1992) identified 'nine key work functions' (Types of Work) which are common to all teams, regardless of their work content (see Figure 3.1). The Types of Work, with the Team Management Roles most likely to prefer them, are listed below.

(1) *Advising* (Reporter-Advisers)—gathering and reporting information.
(2) *Innovating* (Creator-Innovators)—creating and experimenting with ideas upon existing products and services.
(3) *Promoting* (Explorer-Promoters)—exploring and presenting opportunities.
(4) *Developing* (Assessor-Developers)—assessing and testing the applicability of new approaches.
(5) *Organising* (Thruster-Organisers)—establishing and implementing ways of making things work.
(6) *Producing* (Concluder-Producers)—concluding and delivering outputs.
(7) *Inspecting* (Controller-Inspectors)—controlling and auditing work systems.
(8) *Maintaining* (Upholder-Maintainers)—upholding and safeguarding standards and processes.
(9) *Linking*—coordinating and integrating the work of others. Linking is not a function like the eight described above; it is a set of skills and as such can be a feature of any team member's contribution to the team effort.

The nine key work functions assist with planning and enable a leader to draw upon individual preferences and strengths to match particular situations. People may also be able to perform other tasks which complement their overall preferences.

Usefully, Margerison and McCann offer the leader the means to plan team activities by using the Types of Work to prioritise resources. However, it is the

Figure 3.1 Margerison and McCann's Types of Work Model (1992)

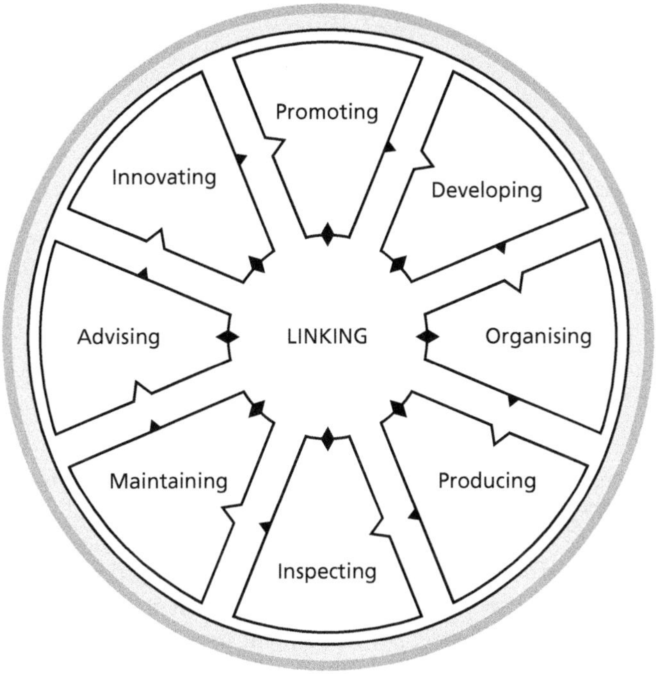

Reproduced by kind permission of TMS Development International Ltd

leader's role to select team members who are well matched for each function. This might be based on their personal preferences or using knowledge of their existing/aspiring experience and skills. This is often apparent where team members are familiar but can be difficult when they are not.

In situations when it is not possible to choose new team members, or bring in other resources to 'plug gaps', a clear understanding of work preferences will help a leader to decide how best to proceed using the team members who are already available. For example, a team member with a strong preference for Inspecting may also enjoy Producing but is likely to be uncomfortable spending a large amount of time in the function of promotion. If this is the case, they will appreciate the 'stretched' nature of their work to be highlighted so that other team members can provide support when necessary. Alternatively, the leader might choose to look for existing team members whose preferences might overlap with Inspecting and might be able to stretch more easily into that Type of Work for longer periods.

3.5.2 **Action-centred leadership**

Adair (1983) developed an Action Centred Leadership Model, which consists of three equal sized interlocking circles. The circles represent each of the main

Figure 3.2 Adair's three circles model (1983)

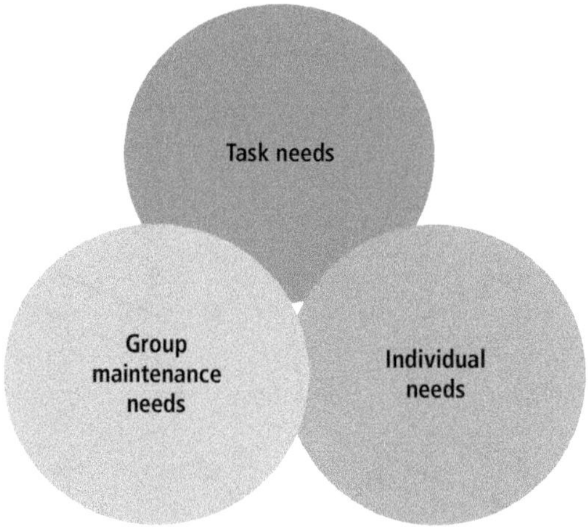

workplace components—the task, the individual and the team (group). See Figure 3.2.

The model illustrates three workplace features—task, group and individual needs. Leaders need to maintain a balance between the three to reach desired efficiency levels. Neglect of one element or over-concentration on another will have a negative effect on all three features resulting in workplace ineffectiveness.

For workplace harmony and synergy the circles need to be kept in equilibrium (i.e. the same size). Action in one work area will have an effect on the other two areas. For example, too much concentration on the task will have negative results on the individual and the team. Too much attention being invested in individuals will prove negative to the team and the task. Over-attention to the team will result in the individual and the task suffering.

To keep the circles equal requires an awareness of the situation in the workplace; this is because the three elements are dynamic and change with circumstances. For example, a major event will cause the task circle to rapidly expand but when the event is over it should be encouraged to return to its normal state. Additionally, maintaining the equilibrium requires sophisticated leadership interventions. The interventions needed will vary greatly depending upon the prevailing situation. However, the following suggestions give some idea of what is required (sometimes one intervention can affect all three circles, e.g. the provision of training).

- *Task*—re-examining the adequacy of plans and the availability of resources including equipment and people. Looking at working practices and training needs.
- *Team*—making better use of team talents, holding meaningful team meetings, providing feedback and offering training as well as considering recruiting new members where there are worrying skill shortages.

- *Individual*—appraising and enhancing performance through, for example, coaching and formal training sessions, acknowledging and praising good work and dealing with inter-team conflict.

KEY POINT—TASK DOMINANCE CARRIES RISKS

In most organisations, including the police service, the task tends to dominate because of the importance of carrying out daily duties to achieve results. Task needs tend to be immediate whereas individual and team needs can be put aside for later consideration. This is understandable but dangerous to team cohesion and synergy and, indeed, the task itself.

A good example for police on how the model works entails public disorder or perhaps even a riot. The ways the circles might react are illustrated below.

- *Pre-disorder*—circles in equilibrium (all the same size) because appropriate corrections and adjustments are being made regularly.
- *Disorder*—task circle grows larger and the team circle also increases but is not quite so big. The individual circle is smaller when compared with the other circles. This is because the demands of the task are huge and effective team rather than individual effort is vital to success in quelling large-scale disorder. (This analysis does not devalue the individual in any way.)
- *Post-disorder*—the task and team circles shrink because the disorder has been quelled but the individual circle grows because of the need to deal with police injuries and trauma which may require counselling.
- *Normal policing resumed*—all three circles back in equilibrium.

The joy of the three circles model is that the leader can easily envisage the three elements (task, team and individual) in the workplace. It is usually obvious when the task predominates or when the team is faltering or when individuals are not performing properly.

3.6 How do teams develop over time and how can a leader influence development to ensure positive outcomes?

Teams do change and develop over time. Therefore, it is essential that leaders recognise the changes and are prepared to manage them well.

Tuckman (1965) suggested that there are four stages of team development and these are as follows:

(1) *Forming*—this takes place when team members get together for the first time. This may be a period of uncertainty and apprehension: for example, there may be apprehension about the job to be done, the conditions under

which tasks are completed and fellow team members. Also, it is a time when acceptable behaviours and boundaries are tested.

There may be potential for conflict during this phase. The leader must properly brief team members as to the importance of the tasks to be carried out and remove obstacles to team progress both on an individual and a team basis. This is a time when the leader should listen to problems and invite team members to help to generate solutions.

(2) *Storming*—a time when team members react badly to the whole nature of the task and what is required of them. It is a time when the leader may be placed under extreme pressure.

This is a time too when the good leader comes to the fore for the storm must be abated. Communication is key and problems must be resolved in the manner described in point (1). However, it is also a time when standards of behaviour, discipline and performance are insisted upon.

Regrettably, when poor leadership prevails teams remain stuck in the storm thereby endangering the existence of the team itself.

(3) *Norming*—a time when team members have accepted required standards of behaviour and performance. Also, they feel comfortable about what they are required to do and how to do it. Team cooperation and synergy develop and the team gains a sense of its own identity.

(4) *Performing*—a time when having put aside past difficulties team members direct their energy towards the efficient and effective completion of tasks and objectives.

A further stage was subsequently added by Tuckman and Jensen (1977; see also Cole 1996).

(5) *Adjourning*—group dispersal. Some people are happy to leave a particular team of people and move on to do different things. Others may cling to the past and past experiences and take them into their new situation—not always successfully.

Importantly, it is possible for the perceptive team leader to look at a team and decide which stage of development it is at and then make appropriate interventions where necessary.

Where there are problems, the leader needs to remove them. This is where consulting, listening and communicating well is of great importance. The leader must always insist on appropriate standards of behaviour and performance. Where team members are performing as expected they should receive praise and encouragement.

When making assessments of team performance a leader would do well to remember that:

- teams may adopt different stages at different times to suit the prevailing circumstances. For example, a 'performing' team may suddenly start 'storming'

because of inter-team squabbles. Equally, a new team member may be 'forming' while another team member is 'storming' and others 'performing';
- losing valued team members and acquiring new members can upset the team's equilibrium. For example, initially newcomers may be viewed with suspicion or compared unfavourably with departing team members; this could also apply to a new leader. New leaders can cause major disruption if they seek to bring about significant changes. Therefore, entry into a team has to be carefully considered and managed.

3.7 How do team members communicate?

Communicating well is one of a team leader's top priorities and most difficult jobs. Sophisticated communication skills require a considerable amount of knowledge, practice, experience and great expertise.

3.7.1 Communication problems

Being able to communicate to everyone's satisfaction is nigh on impossible because of the different ways in which people receive and interpret messages. This means that it is essential that the leader should strive to ensure that messages are well composed, received, understood and acted upon. (See also Chapter 17, which highlights communication difficulties.)

3.7.2 Formal communications

Team meetings are very important, but it needs to be recognised that they are not the whole answer to team communications. Team leaders have to communicate at many levels: for example, with:

- seniors, peers, juniors and other teams;
- support staff acting in all manner of administrative and supply roles;
- representative organisations of all kinds including local authorities, schools, other outside agencies, and to this can be added Members of Parliament;
- members of the public both individually and collectively—for example, when attending neighbourhood watch and housing association meetings.

3.7.3 Team meetings

Aims, goals and objectives filter down to the workplace from the highest point of an organisation. These have to be conveyed by the leader to team members in the form of business plans. Everyone in the organisation has to know what part he or she has to play in achieving business success and, in the case of the police service, public satisfaction.

Team leaders have to communicate objectives, information and instructions to team members. They also have to give and receive feedback, and as well as acting upon worthwhile team proposals they should, where appropriate, convey ideas, views and suggestions upwards to senior management.

Team meetings should be run on a regular basis and minutes or notes should be kept and circulated. This is so that team members see them as important and an integral part of the team communication network. Regular meetings allow team members to plan ahead in terms of attendance and content.

Reasons, additional to those already suggested, for running meetings include:

- reviewing progress and performance, giving and receiving feedback, problem solving and seeking ways to do things even better so as to improve public service;
- allowing team members to express all manner of opinions and voice frustrations which should not be ignored but treated seriously and addressed.

All team members should be encouraged to play an active part in preparing for and contributing to discussions which should run to a pre-agreed agenda. Sergeant and inspector leaders should ensure that everyone has an opportunity to speak while inviting reluctant individuals to participate and valuing all inputs from everyone even when they appear to be uncomfortable to accept.

Chapter 26 discusses meeting skills in some depth, and the contents of this chapter may be usefully adapted to cover team meetings.

3.7.4 **Informal communications**

It is important to consider though that team members also communicate with each other on another level—an informal social level. It is possible to argue that they see this social level as being more relevant to their daily lives than business plans. The social level may include, for example, discussions about where people are spending their holidays, when they are getting married, how a new baby is doing or what someone is going to do with their lottery winnings. Additionally, conversations might also include remarks, favourable or otherwise, about the organisation, the team leader or team colleagues.

The team leader needs to access both the formal and informal communication networks. Broadly, where the formal network is concerned this is so as to be able to manage police tasks and objectives both efficiently and effectively. However, it is much more difficult to manage the informal network because of its complicated and less structured existence. To be involved in a team's informal communications, a leader must gain the trust of individual team members. This is because team members are unlikely to talk to a leader who does not understand their daily personal and social needs. They are more likely to respect a leader who listens carefully, does not act precipitately and recognises the need for confidentiality when it arises.

A leader needs to know what is going on informally because:

- rumours, half-truths and misleading comments can undermine formal communications and workplace interests;
- individual and team frictions can cause individual harm and damage morale, efficiency and public service;
- otherwise hidden welfare issues need to be surfaced and properly dealt with;
- a fully open communication system can help to build trust and aid team cohesion.

However, the team leader must never become overfamiliar with team members. Whilst being amiable and supportive, a sergeant or inspector leader must always maintain a distance between him- or herself and team members. This is in order to retain independence of action and the ability to act without being compromised.

3.8 Carrying out a team audit

Part Two of this book offers a series of competence checklists (toolkit) including a team audit checklist, which is designed to help a new (or existing) leader to scrutinise the quality and scope of the work of team members. Equally, the checklist may be used as a blueprint for success by a leader setting up a new team.

References and further reading

Adair, J. (1983), *Effective Leadership* (London: Pan Books; with the kind permission of Pan Macmillan).

Armstrong, M. (1990), *How to Be an Even Better Manager* (3rd edn, London: Kogan Page).

Armstrong, M. (2009), *Handbook of Human Resource Management Practice* (11th edn, London: Kogan Page).

Cole, G. A. (1996), *Management Theory and Practice* (5th edn, London: Letts Educational; used with permission of Cengage Learning EMEA Ltd).

Margerison, C. and McCann, C. (1992), © TMS Development International Ltd: Content reproduced by kind permission of TMS Development International Ltd (1992) <www.tmsdi.com>.

McGregor, D. (1960), *The Human Enterprise* (New York: McGraw-Hill).

Tuckman, B. (1965), 'Development Sequences in Small Groups', *Psychological Bulletin* 63: 384–99.

Tuckman, B. and Jensen, N. (1977), 'Stages of Small Group Development Revisited', *Group and Organisational Studies* 2: 419–27.

4

Valuing, protecting and enhancing public esteem

4.1 The police and public partnership

The long-standing partnership between the people and the police has been put under pressure at times, but the vitally important cooperation between both sides has somehow endured. However, public cooperation cannot be taken for granted. If the concept of policing by consent is to survive both sides need to work hard to maintain a harmonious balance. Police officers can help to gain public trust by being trustworthy, honest, respected, professional and ethical in their dealings with all people. Bad attitudes and behaviours can be particularly damaging to the work of police forces.

It is self-evident that public perceptions of the police will change over time in line with social, political and technological change and other prevailing circumstances. However, despite the rapidity and complexity of change, officers should strive for a 100% satisfaction rate, even though this is nigh-on impossible. Policing a complex, multi-cultural society, where every move, for good or bad, is subject to close scrutiny by the Press and is reflected on social media, makes the task difficult but it should not be seen as insurmountable.

Recognising that valuing, protecting and enhancing public esteem is not an easy proposition, this chapter explores in some detail what is meant by having 'bad attitudes and behaviours'. It will also suggest ways of dealing with those who are likely to cause harm through the ways in which they approach their duties. The chapter is forthright, but it is not intended to be deeply psychological or 'finger-wagging'. It does include recent cases revealing bad behaviours, but it is fully appreciated that most officers act with sensitivity, professionally and with the public good in mind. Additionally, it is almost certain that officers who carry out their duties conscientiously are more than happy to see officers who sully their reputation, and that of the police service, kicked out of the police force.

4.2 Reputational damage

This section recognises that everyone in the police service has a duty to safeguard its reputation, but it is clear that operational sergeants and inspectors have key leadership roles to play in this serious matter.

Professional incompetence is likely to cause reputational damage, and even when behaving professionally, officers are likely to be severely challenged by the sometimes atrocious behaviours of members of the public. However, perhaps most harm will be done by police officers' own negative attitudes and poor behaviours. Human nature being what it is, once a person has been badly slighted they are almost certain to take a dim and perhaps intractable view of the police officer causing the slight. Not only that, they may well spread news of their poor treatment to others of their acquaintance. In terms of policing this may have serious consequences when calling upon the public for support when urgently needed. Also, of course, officers with bad attitudes may not just confine their behaviours to the public arena but also bring them to bear in the workplace to the discomfort of colleagues.

4.3 Disturbing cases—the murders of Sarah Everard and of Bibaa Henry and Nicole Smallman

It is worth putting forward two extreme examples of the worst kind of behaviour attributed to police.

4.3.1 Sarah Everard

On 3 March 2021 Sarah Everard, aged 33, was kidnapped in South London by Wayne Couzens, an off-duty Metropolitan Police constable, in a preplanned operation. He handcuffed her, put her in his motor car, and took her to Dover where he raped and strangled her with his belt and burnt her body before discarding it in a pond. Couzens was arrested and he was subsequently sentenced to a lifetime in prison.

Sarah Everard Vigil

At the time of the murder Covid restrictions were in force. It seems fair to observe that the complexities of managing the virus caused a certain amount of confusion, not least amongst the government and police forces but other bodies as well.

Reclaim These Streets, a social justice movement operating under the banner: We use legislation, community action and education to ensure no woman needs to be asked to 'Text Me When You Get Home again' decided to organise a vigil on 13 March 2021 at Clapham Common, London, where Sarah Everard was last seen. However, after a High Court judgment, where it was decided that the vigil was a matter for discussions between police and the organisers, the movement decided that a vigil would not take place for fear of prosecutions. Nevertheless, people still gathered at the vigil site. After a peaceful and respectful beginning, disorder broke out and nine persons were arrested (later seven were de-arrested) and Fixed Penalty Notices were issued. Photographs and videos of police officers arresting women were used by the Press and social media—largely to the detriment of police.

It appears that Couzens' behaviour had a devastating effect on members of the public, police officers included, but on women in particular. How could they now involve themselves with a police officer when there could be another killer like Couzens? The damage to the perceptions of police was colossal. The murder also raised concerns about the safety of women in general.

An inquiry into the policing of the event was carried out by Her Majesty's Inspector of Constabulary and Fire Service Rescue Services. Considering whether or not police actions were proportionate, the Inspector noted that police officers had remained calm and professional when being subjected to extreme and abhorrent abuse, made sincere attempts to communicate with the crowds, were patient and professional and that they worked in sometimes challenging circumstances, to maintain public safety and keep the peace.

The Inspector was surprised that more Fixed Penalty Notices were not issued, and more arrests made. Subsequently, 12 public complaints were made, and police received 463 messages of praise and 181 messages of criticism.

4.3.2 **Bibaa Henry and Nicole Smallman**

A second case concerned two Metropolitan Police officers, Deniz Jaffer and Jamie Lewis, who were sentenced to two years and nine months imprisonment, for photographing the dead bodies of Bibaa Henry and Nicole Smallman. The women had been stabbed to death in Fryent Country Park, Wembley, by Danyl Hussein. The officers placed pictures taken of the dead women's bodies on 'WhatsApp' describing them as 'dead birds'. As well as being an affront to dignity, Jaffer and Lewis risked damaging the prosecution's case against Hussein because of assertions that the crime scene was tampered with. Hussein was sentenced to a minimum of 35 years in prison.

It is hard to understand Jaffer and Lewis's total lack of professionalism and empathy for the two dead women and their families. What kind of mind or attitudes encourage this type of outrageous behaviour so thoroughly indecent and unethical?

An inquiry by the Independent Office for Police Conduct recommended that the Metropolitan Police Service:

- review whether supervisors and senior management at Jaffer and Lewis's former police station are taking personal responsibility to identify and eliminate patterns of inappropriate behaviour;
- promote a safe and open culture which makes clear to officers and staff that they are duty-bound to challenge and report behaviour that does not align with the Code of Ethics; and
- take steps to ensure all officers within that same police station conform to the expectations of their behaviour under the Code of Ethics, whilst on and off duty, and are aware that failure to do so could severely damage the public's confidence in policing.

The case of Jaffier and Lewis highlights to sergeant and inspector leaders the need to foster good behaviour, but also that there is a requirement to develop a team culture whereby people who are breaking the rules, or are behaving badly, are exposed by fellow team colleagues. This is not an easy task as often team members' loyalty to each other can be very strong and, officers need to be reminded that decency and professional and ethical behaviour override mistaken loyalties.

NB: The Code of Ethics will be discussed in section 4.4 relating to the work of the College of Policing.

4.3.3 Chief Constable Nick Adderley

It is worth mentioning that it is not just constables who have a responsibility to behave appropriately and help to embed ethical values but also officers occupying the highest levels of the police service. The following case involving a former chief constable emphasises this assertion:

In June 2024, having been found guilty of allegations of gross misconduct, Nick Adderley, the Chief Constable of Northamptonshire Police, was dismissed from the police service without notice. The disciplinary panel noted that 'Mr Adderley's conduct had fallen well below the professional standards of any police officer, never mind a chief constable'.

Among the evidence presented to the disciplinary panel it was noted that Mr Adderley:

- in his application in 2018 to become Chief Constable of Northamptonshire, made several false claims concerning his service in the Royal Navy;
- had been photographed wearing an apparent South Atlantic Medal giving the false impression he had served in the Falklands, when he knew that to be untrue;
- failed to correct inaccurate media reporting of his record with the Royal Navy, a narrative in part based on Northamptonshire Police news releases; and
- gave false information in a phone conversation with a senior member of staff at the Office for the Police, Fire and Crime Commissioner of Northamptonshire concerning his naval service.

4.4 The Angiolini Inquiry

The Angiolini Inquiry, appointed to inquire into the Couzens affair, makes clear that Couzens' background meant that he should never have been accepted as a police officer and the Inquiry's subsequent report (2024) offers important comment and recommendations where ethical behaviour is concerned. Many suggestions have already been taken up by the College of Policing.

The Inquiry report is lengthy and detailed and well worth reading. It is only possible in this section to note some salient points.

Noted below are some observations taken from the report:

(a) 'Sarah's parents believe that it was because Couzens was a police officer and presented himself to her as a plain clothes officer that Sarah died.'

(b) 'Couzens is a predatory sex offender and murderer and should never have been a police officer, but opportunities to deny him that privilege were missed.'
(c) There has been a 'prolonged but public discourse ... expressing the horror and shock, that an off-duty police officer could abuse their powers and carry out the worst crimes ... wider debates have raged about public trust and confidence in the police and women's safety in public places'.
(d) The Couzens 'case has left a stain on the reputation of the police service and damaged the social contract on which British policing is based, namely policing by consent. As Lord Justice Fulford remarked when sentencing Couzens: "In this country it is expected that the police will act in the public interest; indeed, the authority of the police is to a truly significant extent dependent on the public's consent, and the power of officers to detain, arrest and otherwise control important aspects of our lives is only effective because of the critical trust that we repose in the constabulary, that they will act lawfully and in the best interests of society. If that is undermined, one of the enduring safeguards of law and order in this country is inevitably jeopardised."'

The remarks made at (a) to (d) speak for themselves and are deeply worrying for all the good police officers and civilian staff who serve the public cause with integrity. It will take a long time and a lot of hard work to regain the full trust of many people and, in particular, women.

4.4.1 The Angiolini Inquiry recommendations

Lady Angiolini made 16 recommendations, with some actions to be undertaken with immediate effect and others with tight deadlines for completion. Variously tasked with completing recommendations are the College of Policing, the National Police Chiefs' Council, the Home Office, the Ministry of Justice, force vetting and recruitment units and 'all forces'.

The recommendations listed below have been edited to include only important salient points, but they are available at source for the reader to study at will.

Recommendations 1 to 11 cover indecent exposure and masturbatory practice, recruitment and in-person interviews and home visits, recruitment and vetting policy, processes and practices, concerns with professional rigour in decision making, vetting code of practice and transfers and information sharing. All the recommendations are important in putting forward a unified plan of action. However, Recommendations 12 to 16 are hugely significant in terms of practical day-to-day policing and supervision by sergeant and inspector leaders; they have therefore been reproduced in full.

- Recommendation 12: Right to privacy—

  With immediate effect, police forces should convey to all existing and prospective officers and staff that they must be held to a higher standard of behaviour and accountability than members of the public, and that therefore their right to privacy can be fettered in certain circumstances ... This is to ensure that members of the police are fully aware and accountable for the unique powers entrusted to them and the standards of professional behaviour they swear to uphold ...
- Recommendation 13: Aftercare—
  (1) Mandatory, randomised re-vetting should be introduced, as an additional layer to standardised vetting periods, for police officers and staff, akin to randomised drug-testing.
  (2) In addition to police officers and staff being required to declare any material changes in their circumstances within a managed system, such as a human resources system, supervisors, or anyone with concerns relating to behaviour, welfare or performance, should report them to [the] Professional Standards Departments at any point.
  (3) Professional Standards Departments should systematically exchange relevant and necessary information with vetting and counter-corruption units to consider information disclosed by any individual, and any action necessary.
- Recommendation 14: Positive culture and elimination of misconduct or criminality often excused as 'banter'—

  With immediate effect, every police force should commit publicly to being an antisexist, anti-misogynistic, anti-racist organisation in order to address, understand and eradicate sexism, racism and misogyny, contributing to a wider positive culture to remove all forms of discrimination from the profession. This includes properly addressing—and taking steps to root out—so-called 'banter' that often veils or excuses malign or toxic behaviour in police ranks.
- Recommendation 15: Reporting by police officers and staff of harassment, sexual offences and inappropriate behaviour committed by fellow officers—

  With immediate effect, all police forces should take action to understand and confront the barriers that police officers and staff face when reporting sexual offences committed by a person that they work with or in the workplace. This is in order to encourage victims, who are also police officers or police staff, to come forward and submit complaints, as well as to identify and remove those who are not fit for service.
- Recommendation 16: Recruitment and retention of women in police forces—

  By September 2024, [date now past] The College of Policing and the National Police Chiefs' Council should review and examine the conditions of female officers and staff in order to encourage more women to join the police and progress in policing careers. To ensure success, this should include a review of:

a. working conditions that do not address the realities of modern working lives, including families where both parents are officers and share caring responsibilities;
b. processes, training and refreshers for officers returning from parental leave; and
c. kit, equipment and facilities designed largely by and for men.

The government has accepted all the recommendations made by the Angiolini Inquiry (Part 1). The scope of the report and the urgency and speed with which recommendations are to be processed show the intense concern there is about police propriety, and the negative effects that the behaviours of some officers have on the concept of the police working in harmony and partnership with members of the public.

4.5 Social media

Social media has a light and a dark side. It gives pleasure to many and hurt to others, and it is very hard to control except mainly by good sense and decency. Its worst side is instanced by the case of two murdered women, Bibaa Henry and Nicole Smallman, whose dead bodies were photographed by two police officers, Deniz Jaffer and Jamie Lewis, who then circulated the pictures taken on 'WhatsApp' (see section 4.3.2 on Bibaa Henry and Nicole Smallman). It is difficult for sergeants and inspectors, or anyone else, to detect officers putting damaging information on social media platforms.

In this case six officers, who knew what had taken place, were investigated for failing to either challenge or report Jaffer and Lewis's behaviour. This is a reminder that exposure is important, and sergeants and inspectors have a major part to play in rooting out all kinds of wrongdoing. They can do this by creating an environment whereby no one in a team will countenance or accept behaviours that damage the police service and relations with members of the public.

4.5.1 Advantages and disadvantages of social media

Ragharan (2024), notes the advantages and disadvantages of social media. Advantages include maintaining close family ties and friendships, getting quick access to news and events locally and worldwide, promoting professional and business services, being able to search for music and entertainment details, sharing information on a large-scale events and, importantly, being able to visit sites that increase participation in learning initiatives and provide tuition and study materials.

Disadvantages include:

(1) Distraction and loss of productivity resulting from obsessive social platform usage at work.
(2) Spread of misinformation through circulation of fake news and unverified data.
(3) Compromising privacy and data vulnerabilities through oversharing personal information and data thefts which compromise user privacy and expose them to fraud.
(4) Enabling of bullying and harassment—trolling, public humiliation and harassment of individuals made easy by anonymous accounts
(5) Promotion of obsessive self-presentation.

NB: Disadvantage number 5 seems to apply to some degree to Jaffer and Lewis.

4.5.2 **Social media and other technologies**

Given the long-standing presence of social media it would probably be patronising to lecture officers on its dangers. However, it is legitimate to draw attention to inappropriate use where the police service is concerned. As leaders they are in a position and have an obligation to discuss the use of social media with the teams that they lead. At the same time it would be advantageous to discuss the visual applications relative to police body-worn video cameras, mobile telephones, street and shop security cameras and car dashboard cameras. All carry benefits but demand high standards of professionalism from police officers.

4.5.3 **The College of Policing and social media**

The College of Policing has issued guidance on the use of social media and instant messaging, recognising that it has both benefits and dangers. Guidance is framed thus:

> Recognising the potential risks of using social media we will ensure that:
>
> - we think about how others may perceive our social media activities, whether at work or at home;
> - we use social media responsibly, safely, positively and appropriately, knowing the value it can create for community engagement;
> - we do not post any discriminatory abuse, oppressive, harassing, bullying, victimising or offensive material, or post material that is otherwise incompatible with the ethical policing principles, whether on-duty or off-duty;
> - we do not post any material that could undermine the reputation of policing or might run the risk of damaging the trust and confidence of our profession;
> - our membership of any social media group does not undermine the reputation of the profession;

- we recognise that information posted online or in private chats can be shared publicly;
- we do not disclose information that places ourselves, colleagues or operational tactics at risk;
- we recognise that using social media, even when it is out of work and in our private lives, may still breach regulations or the terms of our employment if it discredits the police service as a whole or undermines confidence in it.

On the face of it this appears to be a forbidding list of directions for unquestioning compliance. However, given the power and often destructive nature of social media, guidance on its dark side is absolutely necessary. This is because a lot of people place almost anything on social media without too much thought for consequences. For police officers however, those who fail to recognise the importance of their office, use their common sense and exhibit a sense of decency, the dangers of taking policing matters into the public arena can be catastrophic, and hugely damaging to how police are seen by members of the public.

4.6 The Press

A free Press, which is the cornerstone of a successful democracy, has many benefits, some of which include:

- informing people about events locally, nationally and globally, thus helping to develop reasoned and informed views on all manner of topics, which in turn helps decision making;
- uncovering improper behaviours and abuses of power, for example, in political governance nationally and locally, in government agencies, in the public services for instance the police service and the military, in business and commerce etc.;
- cooperating with police to publicise and seek helpful information regarding the commission of horrendous crimes;
- police working in tandem with the local press for the benefit of local people.

4.6.1 The Independent Press Standards Organisation

Press reporters can be doggedly determined in uncovering stories which are brought to notice with emotive front-page headlines. Often stories are enlarged upon over several days or longer. This is the Press doing their job, but blunt reports can be excruciatingly painful and damaging to the police service, hence the need for honest, professional and ethical policing.

However, the Press like other organisations has to combat its own unethical behaviours. The Independent Press Standards Organisation (IPSO) is the independent regulator for the UK print and digital news industry. It is funded by a levy on the news media and magazine industries and has a majority of lay members to ensure its independence. IPSO upholds high editorial standards to protect the public and freedom of expression.

Publishers have agreed to follow the Editors' Code of Practice It is a system of voluntary self-regulation to which publishers have made a binding contractual commitment. It balances both the rights of the individual and the public's right to know. Editors must resolve complaints swiftly and cooperate with IPSO when it is required to adjudicate on matters. Adverse adjudications must be published in a full and prominent position in the publication concerned.

Acting in the public interest includes:

- detecting or exposing crime, or the threat of crime, or serious impropriety;
- protecting the public from being misled by an action or statement of an individual or organisation;
- disclosing a person or organisation's failure or likely failure to comply with any obligation to which they are subject;
- disclosing a miscarriage of justice;
- raising or contributing to a matter of public debate, including serious cases of impropriety, unethical conduct or incompetence concerning the public;
- disclosing concealment, or likely concealment, of any of the above.

4.6.2 The College of Policing on media relations

The College of Policing notes that—

> A successful working relationship between the police service and the media is vital. Working with the media to communicate to the public can help solve crimes, bring offenders to justice and keep communities safe. It can also give the public insight into what the police are doing and why they are doing it.

The Code of Ethics sets clear guidance on specific issues that are relevant to engaging with the media.

4.7 Trust and confidence in the police

Post, a publication for Parliament (2023), notes that trust in the police involves a belief in the reliability of police to behave fairly and effectively during their interactions. Trust also covers specific officers and the police service as an institution. People are more likely to trust the police if they are seen to act with fairness, effectiveness and integrity. Confidence in the police is the degree to which trust is systematically shown to be warranted.

4.8 **Public perceptions of policing**

Hanway and Hambly (2023) have produced an article for the Home Office titled 'Public Perceptions of Policing: A Review of Research and Literature'. They note that:

(1) Public perceptions of policing are affected by levels of police visibility, perceived declines in availability and a readiness to attend incidents and also by shifts in perceptions of fair treatment of different groups of people.
(2) The relationships between police and communities are affected by levels of police visibility. Those people knowing an officer by name or sight are likely to relate their confidence positively, as do people who believe that they can influence policing decisions in their locality.
(3) Negative contacts between police and members of the public are more influential than positive ones. However, positive contact can increase trust and confidence and a willingness to cooperate with police officers.
(4) Variables, including sex, age, immigration status and ethnicity, can influence public attitudes towards the police and some research shows that trust in the British police is often higher for immigrants than non-immigrants (they may initially arrive with positive views of the police which they use as a base for their judgements).
(5) Confidence in police remains high. However, there has been a decline over recent years and a Crime Survey for England and Wales notes 'overall confidence in the local police' as 63% (2006), 72% (2011), 75% the following year and rising to 79% (2016), dropping back to 74% (2020).
(6) The Office for National Statistics states that confidence was most notably reduced in respondents of black ethnicity between years ending March 2018 and 2020, when confidence fell from 76% to 64%.
(7) Public confidence is likely to have been impacted by the murder of Sarah Everard by Wayne Couzens in 2021. This is borne out by a survey of 1,700 British adults, where 47% of women and 40% of men reported having a declining trust in police after the murder.

NB: It is worth pondering the slump in confidence in the police before and after Sarah Everard's murder in 2021.

A report held in the House of Lords Library notes that surveys conducted by the polling organisation YouGov indicate that over the year 2020, an average of 70% of respondents thought the police were doing a good job, whereas 21% thought that they were doing a bad job. By April 2023 the figures were 47% and 44% respectively. Additionally, the proportion of people who had not very much confidence or no confidence in police to deal with crime averaged 38% in 2020, but by April 2023 the figure had risen to 53%.

The report also alludes to the damage done to police reputation by highly publicised cases of police misconduct and criminality such as the case of ex-P.C. David Carrick (part of the Angiolini Inquiry). In February 2023, Carrick pleaded guilty to 49 offences including rape and other sex-related crimes, coercive and controlling behaviour and false imprisonment. He was sentenced to life imprisonment and will spend at least 30 years locked up.

There will be many different sets of statistics dealing with confidence and trust in the police. However, the messages here appear clear that police visibility and friendly public contact, ethical behaviour, gaining and retaining trust, professionalism, treating all people equally and rooting out miscreant police officers at all levels are important. It is also crystal clear that police still have a long way to go to regain the fulsome trust of women concerned about their personal safety.

4.9 Misbehaviour in general

There have always been corrupt and criminally minded police officers who cause untold harm to the police image. However, damaging and inappropriate behaviour is not always of great magnitude. For instance, most if not all police officers will have come across colleagues who are incompetent, disinterested and lazy or just useless. Particularly damaging to police reputation are officers who act with impetuosity and aggression, taking any criticism or resistance to their involvement in policing events as a personal slight.

Police officers do an incredibly difficult and complex job in a somewhat intolerant, complaint-prone society. They are under constant pressure to act, often in very difficult and trying circumstances, calmly and professionally, no matter what the provocation. The highest standards of behaviour are expected of them, even when off duty.

4.10 Whistleblowing

It is clearly important that police officers and civilian staff need to report malpractices and criminality without delay. However, making a report is unlikely to be easy. People are likely to wrestle with anxieties associated with how they will be viewed by colleagues and the possible negative consequences for them.

Whistleblowing is covered by the Employment Rights Act 1996 (as amended by the Public Interest Disclosure Act 1998). However, although the principles for dealing with whistleblowing are likely to remain intact, changes appear inevitable.

4.10.1 **Whistleblowing definition**

A government definition puts whistleblowing in the following terms:

- You are a whistleblower if as a worker you report certain types of wrongdoing usually relating to work but not always.
- The wrongdoing disclosed must be in the public interest.
- You are protected by law, and you should not be treated unfairly or lose your job because you 'blow the whistle'.
- You can raise a concern at any time about an incident that happened in the past, is happening in the present or is likely to happen in the future.

Your legal protection relates to (i) criminal offences, (ii) someone's health and safety is in danger, (iii) there is a risk of or actual damage to the environment, (iv) a miscarriage of justice, (v) the company is breaking the law, (vi) someone is covering up wrongdoing.

4.10.2 **Whistleblowing features**

Whistleblowing—some significant features:

(1) The term worker includes police officers.
(2) Confidentiality clauses are not valid if someone becomes a whistleblower.
(3) Personal grievances including bullying, harassment, discrimination are not covered by whistleblowing law, unless there is a public interest.
(4) A whistleblower may raise cases anonymously with their employer or with a 'prescribed person' of which there are many, including, for example, the Information Commissioner, and the Independent Office for Police Conduct which has set up a Report Line.
(5) A whistleblower may request confidentiality, and this must be taken seriously.
(6) If a whistleblower notifies the media then in most cases they are likely to lose their legal rights.
(7) A whistleblower has no say in how a matter is dealt with.
(8) If a whistleblower is dissatisfied and considers that their complaint has not been taken seriously or the alleged wrongdoing persists then they should raise the matter with, for example, a more senior member of staff or 'a prescribed person or body'.
(9) An employer involved in malpractice may be subject to severe penalties, including imprisonment and unlimited fines.

4.10.3 **Detrimental treatment of a whistleblower**

(a) Employees are protected under the legislation if they have a reasonable belief in the validity of the alleged wrongdoing (even if proved ultimately to be wrong).

(b) An employer can be found to be liable if one employee causes detriment to another employee because of their whistleblowing; those who victimise whistleblowers are personally liable, and employers are then vicariously liable for these actions as well; an employer will have a defence if it can be shown that all reasonable steps to prevent the detrimental conduct or any conduct of that description were taken.
(c) Whistleblowing allegations if they are revealed can often lead to a breakdown in workplace relationships between different employees and action to resolve issues between employees must not amount to detrimental treatment of the whistleblower.
(d) Two main barriers whistleblowers face are a fear of reprisal as a result of making a disclosure and that no action will be taken if they do make the decision to 'blow the whistle'.

4.10.4 **Whistleblowing policies**

- Employers should create policies for dealing with whistleblowing. If they do so they are less likely to be taken to an employment tribunal.
- If an employee is dismissed for making a qualifying disclosure it is automatically an unfair dismissal subject to certain conditions; however, if there is a policy in place and the worker or employee ignores it and, for no good reason, blows the whistle externally (for example to the Press) then the employer may be able to query the worker's motive.
- A policy indicates that good practice is being followed, and an open and honest culture of honesty is good for internal morale.

4.10.5 **Employment Tribunal action**

Chief officers are vicariously liable for the actions of the people who work for them. An officer subjected to a detriment or dismissal because they made a protected disclosure can seek redress from an Employment Tribunal. The officer must contact the Advisory Conciliation and Arbitration Service (ACAS) within three months less one day of the date of the alleged unlawful act.

A Tribunal can award compensation which could include injury to feelings. Awards are based on lost earnings and are not subject to the usual limits on unfair dismissal compensation. Tribunals have the power to deduct up to 25% from damages where they find that the disclosure was in 'bad faith'.

4.10.6 **Action to be taken by sergeants and inspectors**

If a whistleblower approaches a sergeant or inspector with information they should remain aware that this may be an extremely difficult thing for the person concerned to do. *Right from the outset the matter should be treated as confidential* with no one else being involved unless some immediate and necessary action needs to be taken, for example when a crime is about to take place. The matter should be dealt with in compliance with local instructions and will likely be referred to a more senior officer in the first instance. Thereafter, the sergeant or inspector concerned must take directions from whomsoever is assigned to deal with the matter. However, they should remain alert to the fact that sometimes pressure may be applied by a third party to get a whistleblower to withdraw any allegation.

KEY POINT—THE ANGIOLINI INQUIRY

The highly critical Angiolini Inquiry and its recommendations represent a revolutionary shift in the way in which policing takes place and in the manner in which police relate to the general public. Major changes at a strategic and tactical level have to be made, and embedded, if police efficiency and effectiveness, driven by ethical behaviour, are to be improved and maintained. It will take a lot of goodwill, time and effort at all levels if the police service and operational sergeants and inspectors, along with the officers they command, have important roles to play in this regard and are absolutely key to success.

4.11 What can sergeants and inspectors do to manage bad behaviours?

All police officers, whatever rank they hold, have a duty and responsibility to adopt attitudes and behaviours commensurate with the actions of an ethical and professional police service.

The police service is unlikely to be successful if it is distrusted by members of the public whose cooperation and support it needs if it is to flourish.

Sergeants and inspectors have vital parts to play setting an example and in encouraging officers to display the respectful attitudes and behaviours expected of them. This fits in with the role of a leader and the creation of effective teams. Often constables, sergeants and inspectors are fully aware of those officers whose worrying attitudes and behaviours appear to be affecting a team's morale. It is of the greatest importance, therefore, that officers feel empowered and supported when they wish to draw attention to misbehaviours, and that they are not victimised or ostracised for doing so.

Specific actions sergeant and inspector leaders may wish to take:

- Set themselves up as behavioural role models for the officers they lead and for others with whom they work.

- Recognise that both good and bad attitudes and behaviours can be altered by the myriad of influences that come to bear upon them. It is possible for misbehaving officers to negatively influence others and good officers to influence colleagues to behave as they do.
- Acquaint officers under their command with the desired ethical standards which affect the public and police alike. The standards are to be seen as non-negotiable. It should be clear that non-compliance may lead to disciplinary proceedings.
- Knit behavioural standards seamlessly into a team's culture whereby it is quite natural to talk openly about them. Make crystal clear that sexism, racism, misogyny and so-called 'banter' can be a screen for malign or toxic behaviour.
- Remind officers that standards still apply whether on or off duty. Point out that discussion of confidential policing matters on social media is not acceptable and can be hugely harmful to the police image.
- Confront bad attitudes and behaviours head on but do not forget to recognise the good behaviours of most officers. Being negative all the time without redressing the balance is not helpful.
- Make reviews of attitudes and behaviours a natural component of team work. Encourage discussions about behaviours in a sensitive and non-threatening way. Officers wishing to participate in private, confidential discussions about concerns should be permitted to do so.
- Note that conscientious officers ('natural leaders') will take inefficient and misbehaving colleagues to task themselves without reference to their supervisors. However, it should be made abundantly clear that it is a duty to reveal corrupt officers and not safeguard them out of team loyalty.
- Recognise that sometimes officers form into unhealthy, dominant and cynical groupings and may discriminate against colleagues or make their lives difficult. Such groups are likely to challenge the leader and set their own damaging norms. These groups must be investigated and broken up.
- Bear in mind that briefing and debriefing sessions are ideal for discussing attitudes and behaviours. Briefings can emphasise what is expected professionally and ethically from officers, and subtle and sensitive debriefings can ascertain whether or not expected standards were achieved.
- Accept that sergeants and inspectors should not exclude themselves from receiving feedback from those they command. They should also offer feedback to their seniors where this is helpful.
- Take action if persistent complaints against an individual officer by members of the public require attention.
- Be encouraged by the fact that most police officers are of the highest calibre. Good officers resent those who damage the reputation of the police force. Their cooperation should be harnessed in isolating and removing those unfit for police service.

References and further reading

ACAS (2024), *Early Conciliation* (Norwich: TSO).

BBC News (2021), 'Sarah Everard Murder: Wayne Couzens Given Whole-life Sentence' *BBC News* <www.bbc.co.uk/news/uk-england-london-58747614> accessed 15 April 2025.

Brown, R. and Hobbs, A. (2023), *Trust in the Police: POSTnote 693* (London: Parliament Office of Science and Technology).

Chartered Institute of Personnel and Development (2024), *Whistleblowing: UK Employment Law* (London: CIPD).

College of Policing (2022), 'Media Relations' APP (*Authorised Professional Practice*) <www.college.police.uk/app/engagement-and-communication/media-relations> accessed 21 May 2025.

College of Policing (2024), 'Guidance for Ethical and Professional Behaviour in Policing', <www.college.police.uk/ethics/code-of-ethics/guidance> accessed 21 May 2025.

Crown Prosecution Service (2023), 'Update—David Carrick: Police Constable Jailed for a Relentless Campaign of Sexually and Mentally Abusing Women'.

Dearden, L. (2022), 'Reclaim These Streets: Inside the Sarah Everard Campaign Group Police Tried to Silence' *The Independent* <www.independent.co.uk/home-news/sarah-everard-reclaim-these-streets=b2033778.html> accessed 15 April 2025.

Dodd, V. (2021), 'Two Met Police Officers Jailed Over Photos of Murdered Sisters' *The Guardian* (6 December 2021).

End Violence Against Women (2021), 'Almost Half of Women Have Less Trust in Police Following Sarah Everard Murder' <www.endviolenceagainstwomen.org.uk/almost-half-of-women-have-less-trust-in-police-following-sarah-everard-murder> accessed 15 April 2025.

Gov.UK (2021), *Whistle Blowing for Employees* <www.gov.uk/whistleblowing/sites/default/files/2021-11/whistleblowing.pdf> accessed 24 July 2025.

Gov.UK (2023), Department for Trade and Business, *Review of the Whistleblowing Framework: Terms of Reference* <www.gov.uk/ government/publications/review-of-the-whistleblowing-framework/review-of-the-whistleblowing-framework-terms-of-reference> accessed 24 July 2025.

Gov.UK (2023), Home Office, *Public Perceptions of Policing: A Review of Research and Literature.*

Gov.UK (2024), *Government Accepts All Recommendations by Angiolini Inquiry.*

Gov.UK (2024), *The Angiolini Inquiry*, Part 1 Report (HC530).

Her Majesty's Inspector of Constabularies and Fire and Rescue Services (2021), *The Sarah Everard Vigil—An Inspection of the Metropolitan Police Service's Policing of a Vigil Held in Commemoration of Sarah Everard on Clapham Common on Saturday 21.3.2021.*

Independent Office for Police Conduct (2022), *Met. Accepts I.O.P.C. Recommendations After Investigation into Photos Taken at Murdered Sisters Crime Scene.*

Independent Office for Police Conduct (2023), *Report Line—Frequently Asked Questions.*

Independent Office for Police Conduct (2024), *Northamptonshire Chief Constable Dismissed for Gross Misconduct.*

Independent Press Standards Organisation (2025), *Editors' Code of Practice.*

Institute for Government (2022), *Timeline of UK Government Coronavirus Lockdowns and Restrictions.*

Morton, B. (2021), 'Sarah Everard: How Wayne Couzens Planned Her Murder' *BBC News* <www.bbc.co.uk/news/articles/cl4y0453nv5o> accessed 15 April 2025.

Police Federation (2017), *Whistleblowing—Advice on Raising an Issue of Concern.*

Ragharan, R. (2024), 'Top 20 Advantages and Disadvantages of Social Media' *Web and Crafts* <https://webandcrafts.com/blog/social-media-advantages-and-disadvantages> accessed 15 April 2025.

Sheila McKechnie Foundation (2023), 'Reclaim These Streets' <https://smk.org.uk/awards_nominations/reclaim-these-streets/> accessed 15 April 2025.

Tudor, S. (2023), *Police Standards and Culture: Restoring Public Trust* (London: House of Lords Library).

Useful websites

<https://cipd.co.uk> (The Chartered Institute of Personnel Development)

<www.college.police.uk> (College of Policing)

<www.cps.gov.uk> (Crown Prosecution Service)

<https://hmicfrs.justiceinspectorates.gov.uk> (Her Majesty's Inspector of Constabularies and Fire and Rescue Services)

<www.instituteforgovernment.org.uk> (Institute for Government)

<www.ipso.co.uk> (Independent Press Standards Organisation)

<www.policeconduct.gov.uk> (Independent Office for Police Conduct)

<www.polfed.org> (Police Federation)

5

The College of Policing—ethics, leadership standards, competence and values, and decision making

5.1 The College of Policing—ethics, leadership standards, competence and values, and decision making

The College of Policing is a professional body serving everyone in policing. Police and support staff work across England and Wales from four locations sited at County Durham, Coventry, Harrogate and London. It has operational independence and was formed in December 2012.

The College's stated aim is to:

- connect everyone working in the police and law enforcement to understand their challenges;
- use evidence-based knowledge in everything it develops;
- help police officers and staff, researchers, academics and learning providers, the international policing community and the public;
- give a voice to professional policing on standards, skills and capabilities;
- support professional development;
- set standardsand guidance;
- share knowledge and good practice.

The College has a significant part to play in the direction that the police service is travelling and the professional standards it adopts. Additionally, the continuous development of professional policing is an ongoing feature of its work.

5.2 The ethical foundations of policing

It is important for police officers to remember and keep in focus some underlying principles upon which policing is founded and behaviours expected of the New Police.

Home Office guidelines on policing by consent draw attention to the philosophy behind Sir Robert Peel's principles for policing. However, it is likely that the principles were produced by Colonel Rowan and Sir Richard Mayne, the first joint Commissioners for the Metropolitan Police. The principles were provided to all new police officers by way of force General Instructions.

The principles note that the police were formed to prevent crime and disorder as an alternative to military interventions. The principles include the need to honour the historic tradition that the police are the public and that the public are the police, the police being only members of the public who are paid to give full-time attention to duties which are incumbent on every citizen in the interests of community welfare and existence.

Importantly, it is stressed that *police support depends upon public approval which can only be secured by their actions and behaviour in gaining public respect and this needs the willing cooperation of the public* in the law enforcement process. However, this *cooperation is likely to diminish proportionately according to the amount of force and compulsion that police use in achieving their objectives*.

The principles state that the *police should* always *act impartially* when enforcing the law and without regard to individual status. They should also act *in a friendly fashion with courtesy, good humour* and be prepared to offer individual sacrifice in the protecting and preserving of life [this is a huge burden for officers to carry]. *Physical force should only be applied when persuasion has failed* and then only to the minimum level to carry out an objective.

The principles conclude that the test of police efficiency is the absence of crime and disorder and not the visible evidence of police action in dealing with them.

5.3 **Procedural justice**

Thibaut and Walker first explored the concept of procedural justice in their book entitled *Procedural Justice: A Psychological Analysis* (1975), and the subject has been developed by several authors over the ensuing years.

In writing for the College of Policing, Detective Chief Inspector Tansill and Chief Inspector Firman, respectively, discuss procedural justice and its applicability to stop and search and custody procedures. The articles are particularly relevant to the work of sergeant and inspector ranks and are worthy of their attention. However, procedural justice has a broad application both within and outside of the police service, for it is based on treating people decently and in a participative manner. Additionally, when police officers act with fairness and are respectful they are more likely to gain trust, legitimacy and cooperation.

Jonathan-Zamir and others (2015), placed procedural justice into four main categories Voice, Dignity, Trustworthiness and Neutrality.

- *Voice*—encouraging people to be heard and allowing them to participate in discussions where they can explain their side of the story and involving them in decision making even if they cannot determine the outcome.
- *Dignity and respect*—people should be treated courteously and are likely to react negatively when officers display dismissive or demeaning behaviour. This would include shouting, interrupting and making critical or condescending comments. On the other hand, treating people with dignity and respect conveys a sense of value and self-worth.
- *Trustworthy motives*—people want to believe that the police are sincere and focused on their needs and concerns. Trustworthy motives concern how police justify the use of their authority and power. For example, officers should explain why they are taking a particular action and what it is hoped to achieve in order to create participation and even, on occasions, compliance.

- *Neutrality*—people want to know that police officers are open and honest in their dealings with them and that they act impartially without consideration of any personal characteristics.

Although the codification of procedural justice is helpful, it amounts to a summation of what decent police officers have tried to achieve over many years.

5.4 The importance of behaving morally and ethically

The field of study for ethics and morality is quite complicated and it is not proposed to go into any detail here, but the information that follows should be helpful to the reader.

The two concepts, ethics and morality, appear to be interrelated and although different they have common features. Morality may be seen as behaviour that expresses consideration and respect for others (treating others as one would like to be treated) and adhering to accepted behavioural norms formed by social convention and often codified by, for example, religious practices, and expressed and governed by rules, codes and laws which govern behaviour. Morality is inculcated by strong personal beliefs. Perhaps more sagely the economist and philosopher Adam Smith (1759) said: 'When ethically perplexed, the question we should always ask is "Would a disinterested observer, in full possession of the relevant facts, approve or disapprove of our actions"'? Ethics help to establish guidance on the desired behaviours and what is not acceptable in this respect. The College of Policing offers such guidance to police personnel.

Difficulties occur in policing (and elsewhere) with amorality where police staff are indifferent to what is right or wrong. Obviously, this represents a problem for sergeant and inspector leaders who can only be vigilant in spotting for signs of (perhaps consistent) inappropriate behaviours. They should also encourage the officers they lead to identify those who deviate from accepted norms in a troublesome and worrying way.

5.5 Setting standards to govern behaviour

Without delving too deeply, police officers can easily anticipate public expectations of them because they too are part of society. Empathy is a key ingredient of policing. It is always helpful for police officers to consider how they or members of their families should be treated by police colleagues. Acting professionally, impartially, without prejudice or preconceived ideas and without aggression, rudeness or ridicule is essential. Patience when exploring issues and allowing people to put forward their own side of events is also important

(See Chapter 1, 'Policing in England and Wales and the purpose of this book', section 1.2).

5.5.1 The Final Report of Royal Commission on the Police 1962

The Final Report of the Royal Commission on the Police 1962 listed eight main policing functions. The last listed function is shown below:

- Eighthly, they have by long tradition a duty to befriend anyone who needs their help, and they may at any time be called upon to cope with minor or major emergencies.

The report was written at a time when beat walking by constables was the mainstay of policing. The Royal Commission noted that 83% of people surveyed professed great respect for police, 16% had mixed feelings and 1% stated that they had little or no respect for police. It should be noted that people were largely supportive of police who were not then exposed to the current complexities of law enforcement and the critical, multi-media scrutiny of today. Trying to match these statistics will always be challenging. However, the police service must always strive to do so if public support is to be maintained at the highest possible levels.

The report also reinforces the notion that police and community are as one but also that friendliness and offering small assistances encourages positive views of the police and lays the foundation for support and cooperation. This concept is not new, and it suggests that whenever police officers come into contact with members of the public, whether on foot, in a vehicle or elsewhere, they should take the time, where possible, to build up and establish friendly relationships.

5.6 The College of Policing—Code of Ethics

Listing qualities and operating standards can be an endless and somewhat confusing exercise. However, they can be tailored to suit an organization's particular needs. In this way they act as an important guide in explaining to police personnel what is expected of them in terms of their conduct. The College of Policing has taken on the task of issuing a Code of Ethics for police officers and everyone in the policing sphere. The 2024 Code of Ethics is inclusive and supports everyone in policing. All officers and personnel are bound to take account of the Code which is binding.

The Code has two parts (shown below) both of which are non-statutory but do have the same status as other guidance produced by the College:

(1) Ethical Policing Principles, and
(2) Guidance for Ethical and Professional Behaviour in Policing.

The Code of Ethics is supported by the Code of Practice for Ethical Policing. This is a statutory Code of Practice which provides chief officers with direction on promoting and supporting ethical and professional behaviour within their forces.

It is essential that police sergeants and inspectors and indeed all officers should read the material created by the College in order to capture its full meaning. Realistically, this book can only capture some salient points offering an overview of material.

5.6.1 **Ethical Policing Principles**

It is stated that:

- The ethical policing principles are a series of guiding statements that should be used to help people in policing do the right things, in the right way, for the right reasons.
- Each of us [all police personnel] is responsible for upholding the integrity of our profession. We support each other, but never to the detriment of the public. We treat each other with respect and behave in ways that demonstrate and reinforce the standards of our society, and the standards expected of us.

5.6.2 **Using the principles**

It is stated that:

> We will use the ethical policing principles to help us make and reflect on our professional decisions. As policing professionals, we commit to the following:
>
> - *Courage*—making, communicating and being accountable for decisions, and standing against anything that could bring our profession into disrepute.
> - *Respect and empathy*—encouraging, listening to and understanding the views of others, and seeking to recognise and respond to the physical, mental and emotional challenges that we and other people may face.
> - *Public service*—working in the public interest, fostering public trust and confidence, and taking pride in providing an excellent service to the public.

Within the context of Chapter 4, 'Valuing, protecting and enhancing public esteem', the declaration below is of considerable significance:

- we always challenge behaviours, language and attitudes that undermine our profession;
- we challenge all prejudice, discriminatory behaviour and any activity that undermines the impartiality of policing;
- we are courageous in challenging colleagues, irrespective of rank or grade;
- we support an environment where ethical issues can be raised and addressed;
- we may have to engage in difficult conversations with colleagues when we hear or see things that are unprofessional;
- we call out unprofessional behaviour, report incidents of unprofessional conduct, ask for assistance and/or offer support to those involved.

These are worthwhile principles. The courage and challenging aspect harks back to the previous chapter dealing with attitudes, and behaviours and has an affinity with the equality of opportunity section of this book (see Chapter 7, 'Treating people equally'). It also taps into a major theme of the book. How does a leader create an environment whereby team members feel confident to speak out about misdemeanours without fear of recrimination and retribution?

A leader will have to work very hard to create an open environment whereby excellent communications are conducive to individual well-being and team harmony and effectiveness. They are very unlikely to succeed in these objectives without securing the support of team members. Exercising courage and challenging inappropriate behaviours is not at all easy in the face of hostility from the leader or individuals within the team. However, acting courageously can be bolstered by an instilled strong sense of moral purpose and professionalism.

5.7 Guidance for Ethical and Professional Behaviour in Policing

The Guidance for Ethical and Professional Behaviour in Policing should be read in its entirety so to gain its full meaning and only a few major points are noted below:

- Policing professionals are more likely to be judged as behaving ethically when their decisions and actions are lawful and consistent with the Ethical Policing Principles.
- The guidance does not, and cannot, cover every situation that someone working in policing might face, either in the course of their work or when not working. The guidance does not replace the need for common sense and professional judgement.
- The Code of Ethics does not set out the standards against which conduct should be assessed for these are determined by terms of employment and the Police Conduct Regulations (see Chapter 16, 'Misconduct and discipline', section 16.5).

5.7.1 Being a member of the policing profession

The College of Policing notes that there are higher expectations of propriety placed upon police officers than on members of the public. This means that police are likely to attract heightened attention to misuse of office and failures to meet the requirements of the profession. Also, it is stated that the reputation of the police service is promoted by acting lawfully, fairly and respectfully, and with integrity, trust, confidence and legitimacy. The guidance covers a number of subjects for consideration including:

- being open honest and candid;
- fairness and respect;
- respecting the public;
- relationships;
- wellness and well-being;
- social media and instant messaging;
- recognising the opportunity to learn;
- decision making;
- challenging unprofessional behaviour;
- when behaviour does not meet expectations.

5.8 Code of Practice for Ethical Policing

The College of Policing has developed a statutory Code of Practice to complement a non-statutory Code of Ethics. Its purpose is to set out the actions that chief officers should carry out to ensure that they lead an ethical culture, where staff are supported and directed to use the Ethical Policing Principles in decision making and to demonstrate professional behaviour. It also describes what needs to be done to proactively and positively identify and respond to misconduct and corruption when it occurs.

5.9 What can sergeant and inspector leaders do to support the Ethical Policing Principles and the Guidance for Ethical and Professional Behaviour in Policing?

Clearly, the College of Policing has put an immense amount of effort into producing the Code of Ethics, and the Guidance for Ethical and Professional Behaviour in Policing and set them out in a clear accessible form. However, as noted in the Report of the Lord Leveson Inquiry into the Culture, Practices and Ethics of the Press, '*No code of ethics can make an unethical organisation or sector an ethical one. An unethical organisation will simply find ways round or disregard any code it purports to apply to itself when motivated to do so.*' (paragraph 4.12)

The College of Policing is unable to implement its strategy on its own and needs the help of everyone in the police service, regardless of their rank or status, to make both strategic and tactical interventions. Sergeants and inspector leaders are particularly important in this regard because with the people they lead, they are at the operational heart of policing. Implementation will take time and considerable effort. However, there should be immediate and noticeable incremental advancements as change brings about noticeable improvements.

To assist implementation, sergeants and inspectors need to be fully conversant with the Code of Ethics and the Guidance for Ethical and Professional Behaviour in Policing. They need also to ensure that the officers they command are also familiar with the Code and the Guidance and the consequences of non-compliance.

Code and Guidance conformity should be tested from time to time, on a one-to-one basis or as a group, and by way of briefings after significant incidents have occurred. Also, sergeants and inspectors should concentrate on creating a team atmosphere with open but respectful communications that make it easy to discuss *any* matter and *any* cause for concern freely and without fear of recrimination. Eventually, the Code and the Guidance should become a natural part of policing.

5.10 College of Policing—leadership standards

The College of Policing has laid down the standards of leadership expected at all levels in policing (including police officers, staff and volunteers). The standards assist with leadership development, promotion and progression at all levels within the police service. They are based on the Code of Ethics, the Competency and Values Framework (CVF), policing professional profiles, leadership research and national policing priorities.

5.10.1 Leadership levels

Guidance sets out leadership standards at five organisational levels:

(1) Stage one—leadership foundations (constables and staff with equivalent levels of responsibility)
(2) Stage two—first-line leaders (sergeants and staff with similar levels of seniority and responsibility)
(3) Stage three—mid-level leaders (inspectors and chief inspectors, and staff with equivalent levels of seniority and responsibility)
(4) Stage four—senior leaders (superintendents and chief superintendents, and staff with equivalent levels of seniority and responsibility)
(5) Stage five—executive leaders (currently working at, or aspiring to, chief officer level)

Standards set a benchmark for the leadership knowledge and understanding, skills, attitudes, behaviours and performance expected of police officers, staff and volunteers. They set out what good leadership means when those designated are carrying out the accountabilities of their role.

It can be seen that the standards are not exactly the same for everyone. They are set at different levels and they display a wide variety of competencies needed to be both efficient and effective. In essence, the leadership standards drive the messages delivered by the Code of Ethics. It is essential, therefore, that sergeants and inspectors should study closely all the leadership levels but most importantly the levels of those that they supervise as well as those of their immediate superiors.

5.11 Competency and Values Framework

The Competency and Values Framework (CVF) has three values and six competencies (see section 5.6.2—'Using the principles').

Values:

(1) Respect and empathy
(2) Courage
(3) Public service

Competencies:

(1) We are innovative and open-minded.
(2) We are emotionally aware.
(3) We take ownership.
(4) We collaborate.
(5) We support and inspire.
(6) We analyse critically.

As with other work of the College it is necessary for the reader to look at the accompanying guidance in detail. Six significant points are noted below:

(1) Values are beliefs which are important to us as individuals, and which motivate particular behaviours and actions. Policing is a deeply ethical profession.
(2) The framework can be used in performance assessment, for example as part of a professional development review or when selecting applicants for a role. The behaviours should not be used in isolation or as a checklist for there will be many other ways in which an individual might demonstrate the competencies and values.
(3) The framework sets out the behaviours expected of people working in policing. They are associated with effective performance in policing roles. However, all people have different strengths and preferences, in terms of skills, abilities and personal attributes. The framework should be used in ways that allow for differing abilities. This includes those that stem from disabilities or neurodiversity.

(4) Each competency has three levels, which can be used flexibly to allow for a better fit with frontline and non-frontline policing roles, and at different levels of seniority. The values are not split into levels as everyone in policing is expected to display the same values regardless of their role or seniority. The levels are:
   - Level 1: Practitioner
   - Level 2: Supervisor/middle manager
   - Level 3: Senior manager/executive

(5) When setting standards for assessment it is necessary to consider the importance of each competency and value for the particular role with assessments being designed accordingly. When assessing competencies and values allow for candidates to demonstrate strengths in particular areas. Reasonable adjustments should be made for people who have disabilities that have an impact on their ability to demonstrate competencies.

(6) The framework works in conjunction with the Code of Ethics.

5.12 APP (Authorised Professional Practice)

The College of Policing has issued guidance on Authorised Professional Practice (APP) in a number of important areas and the guidance ties in well with the National Decision-making Model (see below). The model is regularly updated to offer the best possible service. Topics covered include for example:

- Armed policing
- Covert policing
- Critical incident management
- Engagement and communication
- Operations
- Professional standards
- Public order safety and
- Risk

5.13 National Decision Model

The National Decision Model (NDM) devised by the College of Policing is suitable for the making of all decisions and is intended for use by everyone engaged in policing. It can be used for spontaneous incidents, planned operations and by individuals or teams engaged with operational and non-operational events. Additionally, the model can be used for debriefing events so as to learn through experience, encourage new ideas and improve practices.

5.13.1 **The National DecisionModel—six key elements**

The NDM has six key elements:

(1) The NDM is founded upon the Code of Ethics and Ethical Policing Principles, and the Guidance for Ethical and Professional Behaviour in Policing.
(2) Gathering information and intelligence (establishing what is happening or has happened and clarifying information and intelligence).
(3) Assessing threat and risk and developing a working strategy (considering harm and potential benefits and the objectives of preventing discrimination, promoting good relations and fostering equal opportunities).
(4) Considering powers and policy (and legislation).
(5) Identifying options and contingencies (with the lowest risk of harm).
(6) Taking action and reviewing what happened.

5.13.2 **Recording decision making**

It is a matter of fact that decision makers will always be held responsible for the choices that they have made and subsequently they may be asked to account for their actions before some form of inquiry. 'In some circumstances the need to document decisions is prescribed by statute, required by organisational strategies, policies or local practices, or left to the decision maker's discretion.'

Pragmatically, it is recognised that it is not possible or practicable to record every decision made in every situation and that not all decisions need recording. To record or not to record the decision-making process is, in most cases, a matter of professional judgement and depends upon the magnitude of the incident or occurrence concerned.

It is noted that even where the 'outcome was not as planned, if the decision was reasonable and proportionate in the circumstances, and made in accordance with the Code of Ethics, the decision maker deserves the support of their supervisor and that of the organisation'. This supportive statement should be welcomed for laid plans, especially complicated ones, rarely go as expected.

5.13.3 **The National Briefing Model**

The College of Policing has produced a National Briefing Model which also includes the debriefing process. Details are shown below. However, it is important that sergeants and inspectors seek access to all the supporting information accompanying the model.

5.13.4 **Briefing styles**

Briefing styles differ, but there are three key objectives to meet in any briefing, that is to:

(1) ensure that the team has assimilated the relevant information contained within the briefing (random knowledge checks to confirm understanding are helpful);

(2) ensure that individual members of staff understand their responsibility for the allocated task;
(3) confirm there are sufficient resources to conduct the required tasks (this includes situations where staff may self-brief, for example at remote stations).

5.13.5 **Briefing and debriefing**

Briefing and debriefing sessions both have five key elements:

(1) Briefing and intelligence
(2) Individual and team tasking
(3) Delivery methods
(4) Debriefing
(5) Results

5.13.6 **Briefing**

Briefings should be:

- secure to prevent unauthorised access or sensitive information being compromised;
- concise but sufficiently detailed to thoroughly inform;
- adequately timed;
- consistent, particularly where large numbers of officers are involved;
- documented as part of an operation audit trail.

5.13.7 **Debriefing**

Structured debriefings are for identifying good practice and areas of improvement. They should begin at the beginning of an operation so that those deployed in the initial phases can provide information for those taking part in later phases of the police response. A record of the debriefing should be retained for audit and disclosure purposes.

Effective debriefing using the National Briefing Model leads to positive results as it ensures a consistent flow of communication between different departments, and from managers to patrol and neighbourhood teams. This means that more staff have a better understanding of their role in the organisation and how they can contribute to performance. It also allows more information to be collected, which in turn assists future command decision making.

5.13.8 **Reviews**

When reviewing actions taken as a result of a briefing consider the following:

(1) Were decisions proportionate, legitimate, necessary and ethical?
(2) Were decisions reasonable in the circumstances facing the decision maker?

(3) Were decisions communicated effectively?
(4) Were decisions and the rationale for them recorded as appropriate?
(5) Were decisions monitored and reassessed where necessary?
(6) What lessons can be learnt from the outcomes and how the decisions were made?

5.13.9 Using The National Briefing Model on a daily basis

Regular use of the briefing and debriefing processes should be incorporated into the daily business of policing for this benefits the organisation as a whole and more outputs from operational teams in respect of, for example, intelligence material, arrests and public reassurance.

KEY POINT—THE WORK OF THE COLLEGE OF POLICING

The directions and advice issued by the College of Policing on ethical behaviour, competency and values, leadership, decision making and briefing mark a sea-change in the ways in which policing is being reshaped. Putting strategy and advice into practice will provide significant challenges for sergeants and inspectors, the people they lead and, indeed, everyone else in the police service. Success should be marked by improved efficiency and effectiveness and high levels of public approval.

5.14 What can sergeant and inspector leaders do to embed ethical leadership standards in the workplace?

It will take a considerable amount of time to embed the ethical leadership principles and standards proposed by the College of Policing. This is because they represent a big and necessary change in the direction of policing. It is important from the outset that sergeants and inspectors commit themselves to applying the principles themselves, and that they are fully aware of what these entail and are intended to achieve. They need to exhibit the required standards of behaviour and encourage them in others, reminding officers that policing is a demanding 24-hour-a-day responsibility. Operationally, as well as exercising leadership sergeants and inspectors should encourage leadership and learning in others and insist on professional and ethical behaviour at all times.

This chapter is supported by four helpful checklists (Numbers 5–8) designed to offer immediate practical help.

References and further reading

Armstrong, M. and Taylor, S. (2023), *Handbook of Human Resource Management Practice* (16th edn, London: Kogan Page).

College of Policing (2020), 'Briefing and Debriefing' *APP (Authorised Professional Practice)* <www.college.police.uk/app/operations/briefing-and-debriefing> accessed 21 May 2025.

College of Policing (2023), 'Code of Practice for Ethical Policing' <www.college.police.uk/ethics/code-of-practice> accessed 21 May 2025.

College of Policing (2024), 'Competency and Values Framework (CVF)' <www.college.police.uk/career-learning/competency-and-values-framework> accessed 21 May 2025.

College of Policing (2024), 'Ethical Policing Principles' <www.college.police.uk/ethics/code-of-ethics/principles> accessed 21 May 2025.

College of Policing (2024), 'Guidance for Ethical and Professional Behaviour in Policing', <www.college.police.uk/ethics/code-of-ethics/guidance> accessed 21 May 2025.

College of Police (2024), 'Leadership Standards' <www.college.police.uk/career-learning/leadership/leadership-standards> accessed 21 May 2025.

College of Policing (2024), 'National DecisionModel', *APP (Authorised Professional Practice)* <www.college.police.uk/app/national-decision-model/nationalmodel> accessed 21 May 2025.

College of Policing (2025), 'About us' <www.college.police.uk/about> accessed 21 May 2025.

College of Policing (2025), *APP (Authorised Professional Practice)* <www.college.police.uk/app> accessed 21 May 2025.

Firman, K. (2023), 'Procedural justice in custody' *Going Equipped* [Spring/Summer 2023] <www.college.police.uk/article/procedural-justice-in-custody> accessed 21 May 2025.

Gov.UK (2012), *Establishment of the College of Policing*.

Insights by Language Tool, 'What's the Difference Between Ethics and Morals?' <https://languagetool.org/insights/post/ethics-and-morals/> accessed 15 April 2025.

Jonathan-Zamir, T. with Mastrofski, S. D. and Moyal, S. (2015), 'Measuring Procedural Justice in Police-Citizen Encounters', *Justice Quarterly* 32(5): 845–71.

Royal Commission on the Police (1962), *Final Report, Presented to Parliament by Command of Her Majesty May 1962* (London: Her Majesty's Stationery Office).

Smith, A. (1759), *The Theory of Moral Sentiments* (Liberty Fund Inc., Indianapolis) quoted in Armstrong, M. and Taylor, S. (2023), *Handbook of Human Resource Management Practice* (16th edn, London: Kogan Page).

Tansill, G. (2024), 'Procedural Justice in Stop and Search' *Going Equipped* [Autumn/Winter 2024] <www.college.police.uk/article/procedural-justice-stop-search> accessed 21 May 2025.

The Leveson Inquiry (2012), *Report into the Culture, Practices and Ethics of the Press.*
Thibaut, J. and Walker, L. (1975), *Procedural Justice: A Psychological Analysis* (Hillsdale, NJ: Lawrence Erlbaum Associates).
UK Home Office (2012), 'Definition of Policing by Consent', <www.gov.uk/government/publications/policing-by-consent/definition-of-policing-by-consent> accessed 21 May 25.

Useful websites

<www.college.police.uk> (College of Policing)

6

Stress management and long Covid-19 considerations

6.1 Stress—introduction

The stress response is a sophisticated chemical response produced by the body to help us manage our lives and the various pressures we face on a daily basis. At work, for example, police officers may feel stressed when dealing with serious life-threatening incidents or violent public disorder. Equally, undue stress may arise from pressure to meet unrealistic deadlines or from having a bullying boss, a racist colleague or an excessive workload. Stress can also have its origins outside of the workplace, for instance when looking after a very sick child at home where the outlook is precarious or having trouble meeting financial commitments. Some people may thrive under certain types of pressure whereas others may not. Continuous and relentless pressure may result in illness and an inability to function normally.

6.2 A definition of stress

Stress is likely to accrue many definitions because of its complexities. However, Armstrong and Taylor (2023) note that '[s]tress is a state of mental or emotional strain or tension resulting from adverse or demanding circumstances. Undue stress can seriously affect mental health. In the workplace it can impact significantly on productivity, performance and happiness.'

6.3 The autonomic, sympathetic and parasympathetic nervous systems

Without going into too much detail it is worth gaining an understanding of the autonomic nervous system which is subdivided into two separate parts—the sympathetic and the parasympathetic nervous systems. As its name suggests, the autonomic system works of its own accord. The sympathetic and the parasympathetic systems operate in different but complementary ways when balancing bodily activity.

The sympathetic system is of importance when individuals are under pressure and feeling stressed by providing the means to cope with it. With police officers, stress may be induced when dealing with serious life-threatening incidents. However, stress can also arise from, for instance, experiencing continuous and unremitting administrative work.

The sympathetic system helps to provide the stimulus needed to deal with the pressure when, for example, pupils dilate, the heart pumps rapidly and adrenaline pours into blood vessels. The parasympathetic, however, has the means to assist recovery by conserving energy and bodily resources and in re-balancing bodily functions.

Maintaining a bodily equilibrium is important to enjoying good health. Continuously drawing upon reserves is unsustainable and can lead to exhaustion and ill-health. Police personnel need to appreciate the sympathetic and parasympathetic duality and seek to keep a healthy balance between the two functions. This is not always easy as some problems can be overwhelming, especially where personal and domestic difficulties are concerned. Not all problems are resolvable on one's own and reliable help should be sought where possible, for example from a medical practitioner. Additionally, sergeant and inspector leaders have key roles in this regard in noticing the symptoms of stress and providing necessary help and support.

6.4 Stress-related illness

Stress illnesses manifest themselves in many different forms both mental and physical. Stress-related conditions include, for example, angina, strokes, heart attacks, heart disease, sudden cardiac death, hypertension, colds, influenza, ulcers, indigestion, nausea, diarrhoea and adult diabetes.

6.5 Common effects of stress

Problems associated with stress include:

- anxiety
- depression
- digestive problems
- headaches
- muscle tension and pain
- heart disease, heart attack, high blood pressure and stroke
- sleep problems
- weight gain
- problems with memory and focus

6.6 Stress—workplace issues

In their work police officers are subjected to many stressful situations in the operational sphere, but stress can strike those in administrative posts as well. However, a great deal of stress is generated from outside of the police service, for example from within the domestic environment. It is axiomatic that stress concerns can transfer from the home into the workplace and vice versa.

The Health and Safety Executive notes six aspects of work that can have an impact on stress:

(1) The demands of people's jobs, such as workload, working patterns and the work environment.

(2) The amount of control individuals have at work, or how much say they have over the way they do their work.
(3) The support employees receive from their line manager and colleagues.
(4) How well relationships are functioning in the workplace, including preventing bullying and harassment, managing conflict and ensuring positive relationships.
(5) How clear people are about their role.
(6) How well change is managed and communicated.

When experiencing stress employees may, for example, lose motivation, commitment and morale, work long hours for little return, and their condition may cause tension between colleagues and when serving members of the public. Stress will almost certainly result in poor decision making, increased errors and reduced productivity as well as absence from work.

Although senior management should carry out stress audits there is no good reason why sergeants and inspectors should not carry out their own audits for there are many issues mentioned above which they can assist with.

6.7 Extent and costs of stress

The Chartered Institute of Personnel and Development research shows:

- 35.2 million working days were lost to work-related ill-health in 2022/23, with stress, anxiety and depression accounting for almost 24 million of these;
- employee sickness absence is at the highest level reported for 15 years and around three-quarters of respondents (76%) report some stress-related absence;
- over two-thirds of contacted respondents report that senior leaders take well-being seriously, however, *lack of line manager skills and confidence is the top challenge for employee well-being, and 'management style' remains among the top causes of stress-related absence.* In addition to this, many people continue to work when unwell, even if they are working from home, while many employees use holiday or sick leave to work.

The costs of stress will vary depending upon the individuals concerned and the strength and persistence of the stressors. However, stress can have devastating long-term physical and mental effects upon people whose self-esteem and confidence are likely to suffer. The costs of stress for the police service can be high too, for stress damages policing capacity and service to the public as a whole. Absences from work detrimentally affect both operational and administrative outputs.

NB: This draws upon information provided by the Health and Safety Executive, Working Days Lost in Great Britain 2022/23.

6.8 What can employers do to fight stress?

Both the Chartered Institute of Personnel and Development and Armstrong and Taylor (2023) together suggest that, amongst other considerations, employers should:

(1) Train line managers to manage people well for they are key to employee well-being and should ensure people's workloads and deadlines are manageable. They should also provide clear objectives and give constructive feedback, as part of a trust-based relationship. They should have the confidence to have sensitive conversations with people and offer support and flexibility if a team member needs adjustments to help manage their health and work.
(2) Build a robust organisational framework to promote good mental well-being and foster a culture where people can talk about mental health and seek help where needed.
(3) Job design—clarify roles, reduce the danger of role ambiguity and conflict and give people more autonomy to manage their responsibilities.
(4) Take care to place people in jobs that are within their capabilities.
(5) Targets and performance standards—set reasonable and achievable targets that may stretch people but do not place impossible burdens on them.
(6) Provide management training— that enables managers to cope with their own stress and alleviate stress in others that they manage.

6.9 Employee resilience

The Chartered Institute of Personnel and Development observes that personal resilience appears to help employees to adapt and cope with and respond positively to workplace stressors. It is widely believed that resilient employees are better able to deal with organisational change and adverse events, and it is posited that as result they will be more committed, satisfied and healthier. It should be noted, however, that some people are naturally more resilient than others, although interventions can be made to help to improve resilience.

In psychology, resilience is described in one of two ways, that is, (1) the ability of an individual to rebound or recover from adversity, and (2) the ability to maintain psychological and physical health despite exposure to a traumatic event.

6.10 Measures of employee resilience

Naswall, Kuntz and Malinen (2015) have developed an employee resilience scale which assesses an individual's capacity to cope, adapt and thrive in response to changing work circumstances. It treats resilience as something that can be developed rather than being a permanent trait. The measures invite sergeants and inspectors to review how well they manage the officers they command, whether or not their management style is appropriate and supportive of colleagues.

(1) I effectively collaborate with others to handle unexpected challenges at work.
(2) I successfully manage a high workload for long periods of time.
(3) I resolve crises competently at work.
(4) I learn from mistakes at work and improve the way I do my job.
(5) I re-evaluate my performance and continuously improve the way I do my work.
(6) I effectively respond to feedback at work, even criticism.
(7) I seek assistance at work when I need specific resources.
(8) I approach managers when I need their support.
(9) I use change at work as an opportunity for growth.

Clearly this scale is very useful for sergeants and inspector leaders to look at their own resilience and invite team members to do the same on the basis of it being a helpful instrument to raise self-awareness and inspire change.

6.11 What can sergeants and inspectors do to help build resilience?

As leaders sergeants and inspectors have a responsibility to create efficient and effective teams capable of serving the public in the best possible way. This means truly valuing the officers that they lead professionally but also recognising that different people have different personalities, abilities and ambitions, and this involves making sophisticated interventions where required. An open communication system whereby supervisors and team members are able to discuss any issue together without recrimination is vital as it will encourage honest feedback, innovation and a sense of meaningful contribution. On an individual basis it will embolden individuals to speak up when things are rough for them, and they need help. Recognising and valuing officer differences, encouragement and praise, regular updating and coaching and training are also essential as motivators.

KEY POINT—STRESS PREVENTION

It is clear that team leaders can take preventative action to manage their own stress and the stress of those they command by understanding the biological response to stress and by helping to control the environment and the conditions under which people work. Most importantly, sergeants and inspectors have significant roles to play in creating a workplace where team members unite to help each other to manage stressors.

6.12 Legislation

Stress-related legislation appears to be quite complicated and bewildering; however, the Chartered Institute of Personnel and Development note the following legislation:

- Health and Safety at Work etc. Act 1974
- Protection from Harassment Act 1997
- Management of Health and Safety at Work Regulations 1999
- Equality Act 2010
- Data Protection Act 2018
- The Worker Protection (Amendment of Equality Act 2010) Act 2023—the Act compels employers to be proactive in preventing sexual harassment. As well as including colleagues at work it also includes harassment from third parties (e.g. members of the public).

NB: The Employment Rights Bill 2025 under consideration by Parliament proposes to strengthen sexual harassment provisions (see Chapter 9, section 9.6, 'Dealing with unethical behaviours and workplace ineffectiveness sometimes without obvious causes').

Broadly—

- Employers have a legal duty to protect the health, safety and welfare of their employees and other people who might be affected by their work activities.
- Employers must do whatever is reasonably practical to achieve this protection.
- Employees have responsibility for their own health, safety and well-being.
- Organisations must carry out risk assessments to identify potential hazards at work. This includes carrying out an assessment of work-related stress.
- High turnover, increased sickness absence and decreased performance can be signs of stress. Employers should take action to prevent such stress.

Further, an employer owes a duty of care to its employees to provide proper staffing, adequate materials, safe premises and a safe system of work. This arises under what is known as the common law of negligence.

6.13 What can sergeant and inspector leaders do to manage stress in the workplace?

When managing stress sergeants and inspectors:

- Need to understand the body's biological response to stressful situations. If a person keeps drawing upon their bodily resources, without taking time to replenish them, then they are likely to suffer a severe and damaging bout of stress. Consider explaining the response to team members mentioning that everyone is responsible for taking good mental and physical care of themselves.

- Should consider that although it is usually businesses that take stress audits there is no reason why team audits should not be taken with the cooperation of team members.
- Should invite officers they command to examine their own stress issues and their resilience to stress whilst recognising that workplace stress can start at home and vice versa.
- Should, when suffering from stress, do something to alleviate it straight away and encourage others to do the same. Sitting on stress problems can make them worse. Although other people can assist with helping to put things right, it needs individuals to make the first move.
- Need to adopt a management style that is professional, ethical and sensitive to what is happening around them. Additionally, endeavour to create an atmosphere whereby officers feel able to have open and frank discussions about work pressures and any excessive stress that is bothering them.
- Should recognise that although the police service is always under pressure, excessive hours on duty can cause stress in officers. Also it is important that people are properly trained to do their jobs, that there is clarity of purpose and that individual objectives, workloads and deadlines are not unreasonable, with help being provided where possible. Sometimes people are unsuited to particular tasks but good at others. It is up to sergeants and inspectors to match skills to tasks.
- Should recognise that all people, including themselves, are likely to suffer stress at some time and that team members should be self-supporting—helping each other in practical ways with, for example, managing workloads.

6.14 **Long Covid—introduction**

Doubtless, almost everyone is aware of the devastation wreaked upon individuals, families, businesses and society by the Covid-19 outbreak in 2019. The lingering effects of long Covid have manifested themselves in the UK population. Sergeants and inspectors are likely to come up against some officers suffering long Covid distress. When it is known about they can offer tangible support.

However, some individuals may not even be aware that they are suffering from long Covid. If sergeants and inspectors suspect its presence then they should advise the person concerned to receive immediate medical help. However, sometimes long Covid symptoms can get confused with other unrelated symptoms.

For example, there may be concern about an officer's drop in workplace performance with suspicions that the cause may be due to sloppiness and inattention to detail. In cases where the cause is uncertain, therefore, sergeants and inspectors should explore the circumstances with an open mind and then act accordingly.

6.15 Long Covid—symptoms

The Health and Safety Executive note that:

- In some instances Covid-19 can cause symptoms that last weeks or months after the infection has gone. This is sometimes referred to as long Covid.
- People who had no symptoms or mild symptoms at first can still have long-term problems after Covid-19.
- How long it takes to recover from Covid-19 is different for everybody.
- People may feel better in a few days or weeks after a Covid-19 infection has gone. Most people will make a full recovery within 12 weeks. However, for some people, symptoms can last longer.

Commonly, long Covid symptoms include:

- Extreme tiredness (fatigue)
- Shortness of breath
- Chest pain or tightness
- Problems with memory and thinking
- Sleeping difficulties (insomnia)
- Heart palpitations
- Dizziness
- Pins and needles or numbness
- Joint pain or muscle pain
- Depression and anxiety
- Tinnitus/ear aches
- Feeling sick, diarrhoea, stomach aches, loss of appetite, weight loss
- A high temperature, cough, headaches, sore throat
- Changes to smell or taste
- Rashes.

6.15.1 Long Covid—diagnosis

A person may be diagnosed with long Covid if symptoms:

- Continue three months after infection with Covid-19.
- Are present for at least two months (symptoms can come and go).
- Have an impact on daily life.

6.15.2 Long Covid—treatment

Anyone with concerns regarding ongoing or new symptoms, or if things get worse or do not improve after four weeks, should contact their medical practitioner (GP) who may, for example, run tests, give advice, discuss care and support or make a referral to a service that specialises in the symptoms expressed or a long Covid clinic. However, there is no single treatment for long Covid, which depends upon symptoms.

6.16 Prevalence of ongoing symptoms following Covid-19 infection UK (2023)

The Office for National Statistics has issued statistics on the progress of the Covid-19 infection. These are experimental statistics and estimates are currently under development, meaning that they may change as scientific understanding of long Covid improves. The two abstracts shown below are for oversight purposes only and the reader may wish to undertake their own study of the statistics in full.

- *An estimated 1.9 million people living in private households in the UK* (2.9% of the population) *were experiencing self-reported long-Covid* (symptoms continuing for more than four weeks after the first confirmed or suspected coronavirus infection and unexplained by something else).
- As a proportion of the UK population, the prevalence of self-reported long-Covid was greatest in people aged 35 to 69 years, females, people living in more deprived areas, those working in social care, those aged 16 years and over who were not working and not looking for work, and those with another activity limiting health condition or disability.

An estimated 1.9 million people experiencing long Covid symptoms appears to be a relatively low number across the population as a whole. This statistic refers to reported cases, but some people may have the condition without reporting it or without knowing that long Covid is the cause of their being unwell.

6.17 Treating patients with long Covid

The British Medical Journal when addressing physicians treating patients with long Covid notes that:

- Long Covid is a complex, highly variable, and sometimes relapsing-remitting condition that may have profound impacts on a patient's wellbeing and ability to work. Many people living with long Covid are attempting to return to work, or stay in work, while learning to manage an emerging long-term condition

- The Journal advises physicians of the need to assess a person's current abilities compared against their previous performance and that patients do not need to be 100% fit in order to return to work. It is suggested that going back to work too early after an acute illness can be counter-productive and that a patient should not make a hasty decision about resignation or retirement in the first instance. Finally, it is suggested that 'Fit notes' be issued to facilitate someone's return to work whilst emphasising the need for flexibility to accommodate day-to-day fluctuations.

These supportive principles can be appreciated in the policing environment.

KEY POINT—COPING WITH LONG COVID

Where cases of long Covid are diagnosed and people are allowed to work, sergeants and inspectors need to give the same sort of support offered in the stress section of this chapter. Where something wrong with performance is suspected, but the cause is unknown, sergeants and inspectors should use their interpersonal skills to establish the possibility of long Covid and if this is the case the matter should then be dealt with by a medical practitioner.

6.18 What can sergeant and inspector leaders do to manage long Covid in the workplace?

Sergeant and inspector leaders can cope with long Covid issues in the workplace by:

- Offering support to anyone who has been diagnosed with long Covid but who has been permitted to carry on working perhaps with conditions attached. Reassurance may be necessary alongside monitoring progress. With possible fatigue in mind, help can be provided with work and task allocation, the suitability of work stations, hours worked and offering extra help with projects.
- Remaining aware that some people may not know that they have long Covid or have decided not to declare that they may have it. Symptoms could become confused with other perceived causes such as inefficiency linked to a general poor performance, or those suffering operational stress. Sergeants and inspectors should then use their interpersonal skills to probe for causes in a confidential environment. Should Covid-19 be suspected the officer concerned should be advised to see a medical practitioner.

References and further reading

Armstrong, M. and Taylor, S. (2023), *Armstrong's Handbook of Human Resource Management—A Guide to the Theory and Practice of People Management* (16th edn, London: Kogan Page).

Chartered Institute of Personnel and Development (2021), *Employment Resilience: An Evidence Review* (London: CIPD).

Chartered Institute of Personnel and Development (2024), *Employee Health and Well Being* (London: CIPD).

Chartered Institute of Personnel and Development (2024), *Stress and Wellbeing: UK Employment Law* (London: CIPD).

Crooks, L. and Stein, J. (1988), *Psychology: Science, Behaviour and Life* (New York: Holt, Rinehart and Winston).

Encyclopaedia Brittanica, 'Homeostasis' <www.britannica.com/science/homeostasis> accessed 15 April 2025.

Gov.UK, Department for Business & Trade, 'Employment Rights Bill—Overview' (Fact Sheet) <https://assets.publishing.service.gov.uk/media/67f6711f555773bbf109e21a/employment-rights-bill-overview.pdf> accessed 15 April 2025.

Health and Safety Executive (2022), 'Living with Long-Covid' <www2.hse.ie/conditions/covid19/long-covid/living-with/> accessed 30 May 2025.

Health and Safety Executive, 'Working Days Lost in Great Britain, 2022/3' <www.hse.gov.uk/statistics/dayslost.htm> accessed 21 May 2025.

Health and Safety Executive, 'Work-Related Stress' <https://healthservice.hse.ie/staff/health-and-safety/work-related-stress/> accessed 15 April 2025.

Mayo Clinic Staff, 'Stress Management—Chronic Stress Puts Your Health at Risk' *Mayo Clinic* <www.mayoclinic.org/healthy-lifestyle/stress-management/in-depth/stress/art-20046037> accessed 15 April 2025.

Naswall, K. with Kuntz, J. and Malinen S. (2015), *Employee Resilience Scale (EmpRes): Technical Report.* Resilient Organisations Research Report, 2015/04. ISSN 1178-7279.

O'Connor, R.J., Parkin, A., Mir, G., Mullard, J., Baley, S., Ceolta-Smith, J., and Rayner, C. (2024), Work and Vocational Rehabilitation for People Living With Long-Covid, *British Medical Journal* (BMJ 2024;385:e076508-10th May 2024).

Office for National Statistics (2023), *Prevalence of Ongoing Symptoms Following Coronavirus (Covid-19) Infection in the UK: 30 March 2023.*

Useful websites

<www.cipd.co.uk> (Chartered Institute of Personnel and Development, the professional body for those involved with the management and development of people)

<www.hse.gov.uk> (Health and Safety Executive)

<www.ons.gov.uk> (Office for National Statistics)

7

Treating people equally

7.1 What is meant by the term 'treating people equally' and why is this important to individuals, the team, the public and the police?

A very important part of a leader's role involves being fully aware of the nature of interactions between team members and their colleagues in the police service and police officer relationships with members of the public. Unprofessional behaviour is unacceptable at all times. Particularly abhorrent is prejudicial and discriminatory behaviour arising from inappropriate attitudes which can cause untold damage to police reputation and hostility.

Bad behaviour can be offensive, demeaning and demotivating. Where team members operating singly or together are concerned it may lead to:

- anger, feelings of unfairness, bitterness and resentment, stress, withdrawal, a lack of cooperation and even sickness;
- inter-team conflict, a loss of synergy, poor performance and a failure to complete tasks and objectives on time or at all;
- misconduct procedures.

Where members of the public are concerned, it should be remembered that the police service is a high-profile public body that receives a great deal of media attention on a national as well as local basis. Poor behaviour where the public is involved is likely to lead to:

- a loss of confidence and trust in the police (which may take a long time for the police to recover) as well as the fostering of resentment, uncooperative and even hostile attitudes;
- complaints about inappropriate police behaviours;
- misconduct proceedings and perhaps even legal action;
- imposed reforms to the police organisation.

Police sergeant and inspector leaders being largely operational and in very close contact with the public must set high standards of personal behaviour as an example to others. Additionally, they must remain alert and vigilant to poor police officer behaviour making clear from the outset that it is unacceptable, will not be tolerated and will be dealt with quickly and severely when the occasion demands.

7.2 Institutional racism and public sector equality duty

The murder of Stephen Lawrence in London in 1993 proved to be a milestone in looking at how organisations behave towards the people they serve. The focus for the inquiry conducted by Sir William Macpherson was the actions of the Metropolitan Police Service. Macpherson found that organisations were capable of 'institutional racism' which failed to offer a professional service because of an individual's colour, culture or ethnicity. He suggested that 'institutional racism' could be unwitting but was evident by virtue of an organisation's policies, procedures and working practices. It could also manifest itself through its employees' attitudes and behaviours.

Macpherson's findings mean that police forces have a corporate responsibility to ensure that none of their working practices are discriminatory. This obligation has now been enshrined in the Equality Act 2010 (the 'public sector equality duty'):

> A public authority [includes police forces in England and Wales—Police Act 1996] must, in the exercise of its functions, have due regard to the need to—
> (a) eliminate discrimination, harassment, victimisation and any other conduct that is prohibited by or under this Act;
> (b) advance equality of opportunity between persons who share a relevant protected characteristic [see 7.3.1] and persons who do not share it;
> (c) foster good relations between persons who share a relevant protected characteristic and persons who do not share it.

7.3 Equality law provisions in brief

Equality law is quite complex and this section can only cover some of the main features in a brief but hopefully useful manner. When in doubt (and things must not be allowed to fester), sergeant and inspector leaders should consult senior colleagues or a human resources expert or the Equality and Human Rights Commission for guidance. The Commission set up by the Equality Act 2006 has produced the *Equality Act 2010 Code of Practice* which, although a little complicated, offers great help.

7.3.1 Protected characteristics

The Equality Act 2010 refers to 'protected characteristics', and they are:

- age;
- disability;
- gender reassignment;
- marriage and civil partnership;
- pregnancy and maternity;
- race;
- religion or belief;
- sex;
- sexual orientation.

Some of these characteristics which operational police officers are most likely to meet directly during the course of their duties are worth amplifying.

- Disability is defined as: 'a physical or mental impairment, and the impairment has a substantial and long-term adverse effect on [one's] ability to carry out normal day-to-day activities'.
- Gender reassignment is defined as circumstances where a 'person is proposing to undergo, is undergoing or has undergone a process (or part of a process) for the purpose of reassigning the person's sex by changing physiological or other attributes of sex' and 'A reference to a transsexual person is a reference to a person who has the protected characteristic of gender reassignment'.
- Race includes colour, nationality and ethnic or national origins.
- Religion covers 'any religion and a reference to religion includes a reference to a lack of religion'. Belief includes 'any religious or philosophical belief and a reference to belief includes a reference to lack of belief'.
- 'Sexual orientation means a person's sexual orientation towards—persons of the same sex, persons of the opposite sex, or persons of either sex'.

7.3.2 **Supreme Court Ruling (2025)**

On 16 April 2025, the Supreme Court passed a judgment in a case where *For Women Scotland Ltd* acted as the *Appellant* and *The Scottish Ministers* as the *Respondent.* The judgment based on meaning within the Equality Act 2010 is thoughtful and deserving of reading in detail. The most significant point made by the judges is 'that the words "sex", "woman" and "man" … mean (and were always intended to mean) biological sex, biological woman and biological man' (Section 171). The judges also noted that 'the provision of separate services for persons of each sex will not constitute unlawful sex discrimination in the provision of services … where joint services for both sexes would be less effective and such provision is a proportionate means of achieving a legitimate aim' (Section 212).

The judgment is hugely significant in that some people are non-binary, for example transexual people who still retain protection under the Equality Act. However, for example, transgender females may be denied access to certain areas designated for women only. Equally, they may be denied participation in sports designed just for women. The consequences of the Supreme Court's judgment though, are far wider than this, and businesses and organisations will have to review all their practices and procedures so as to conform with the court's rulings. This will take time, but with sensitivity imagination and cooperation from all concerned it should be possible to make suitable and acceptable accommodations.

7.3.3 **Direct discrimination**

The Act defines direct discrimination thus: 'A person (A) discriminates against another person (B) if because of a protected characteristic, A treats B less favourably than A treats or would treat others.'

7.3.4 **Indirect discrimination**

Similarly, the Act defines indirect discrimination as 'A person (A) discriminates against another (B) if A applies to B a provision, criterion or practice which is discriminatory in relation to a relevant characteristic of B's'.

Discrimination occurs with regard to a relevant characteristic if:

(a) A applies, or would apply, it to persons with whom B does not share the characteristic,
(b) it puts, or would put, persons with whom B shares the characteristic at a particular disadvantage when compared with persons with whom B does not share it,
(c) it puts, or would put, B at that disadvantage, and
(d) A cannot show it to be a proportionate means of achieving a legitimate aim.

7.3.5 **Harassment**

Any form of bullying or harassment is unacceptable. Under the Equality Act 2010:

- A person harasses another if they engage in unwanted conduct related to a relevant protected characteristic, and the conduct has the purpose or effect of violating their dignity, or creates an intimidating, hostile, degrading, humiliating or offensive environment for that person.
- A person harasses another if they engage in unwanted conduct of a sexual nature, and the conduct has the purpose or effect of violating their dignity, or creates an intimidating, hostile, degrading, humiliating or offensive environment for that person.
- A person harasses another if they engage in unwanted conduct of a sexual nature or that is related to gender reassignment or sex, and has the purpose or effect of violating their dignity, or creates an intimidating, hostile, degrading, humiliating or offensive environment for that person.
- Harassment also takes place if as the result of a person's rejection of or submission to the conduct a person treats them less favourably than they would have done if they had not rejected or submitted to the conduct.
- Protected characteristics include age, disability, gender reassignment, marriage and civil partnership, pregnancy and maternity, race, religion or belief, sex and sexual orientation.

The Worker Protection (Amendment of Equality Act 2010) Act 2023, introduced a legal responsibility compelling employers to be proactive in taking reasonable steps to prevent sexual harassment. The Act covers colleagues at work or settings connected to work and also includes harassment from third parties such as customers, service users or members of the public. An employer may be guilty of sexual harassment if they are aware that an employee is being sexually harassed but do nothing to protect the employee.

The Employment Rights Bill currently under consideration is proposing to:

(a) strengthen employers' duty to prevent sexual harassment of their employees by requiring them to take *all* reasonable preventative steps;
(b) introduce an obligation on employers to not permit harassment of their employees by third parties;
(c) specify steps which are to be regarded as *reasonable* for an employer to take in order to prevent sexual harassment;
(d) add sexual harassment to the list of issues that workers can make protected disclosures on.

This section on harassment in particular shows what an important job a sergeant or inspector leader has in enforcing standards of behaviour and creating an environment where everyone (including members of the public) feels valued and respected and is free of bullying and unacceptable behaviour.

7.3.6 **Victimisation**

Victimisation is a very serious offence. The Act describes victimisation in the following manner:

> A person (A) victimises another person (B) if A subjects B to a detriment because—
> (a) B does a protected act, or
> (b) A believes that B has done, or may do, a protected act.
>
> Protected acts include:
>
> (a) bringing proceedings under this Act;
> (b) giving evidence or information in connection with proceedings under this Act;
> (c) doing any other thing for the purposes of or in connection with this Act;
> (d) making an allegation (whether or not express) that A or another person has contravened this Act.

7.3.7 **Positive action**

Positive action is designed to help remove inequalities. The Act states that:

> Positive action is relevant if a person (P) reasonably thinks that—
> (a) persons who share a protected characteristic suffer a disadvantage connected to the characteristic,

(b) persons who share a protected characteristic have needs that are different from the needs of persons who do not share it, or
(c) participation in an activity by persons who share a protected characteristic is disproportionately low.

Then the:

> Act does not prohibit P from taking any action which is a proportionate means of achieving the aim of—
> (a) enabling or encouraging persons who share the protected characteristics to overcome or minimise that disadvantage,
> (b) meeting those needs, or
> (c) enabling or encouraging persons who share the protected characteristics to participate in that activity.

The Act sets out the conditions for positive action with regard to recruitment and promotion (Chapter 2, 'Positive action', s 159).

7.3.8 **Proceedings**

Sergeant and inspector leaders should strive to prevent prejudice and discrimination arising in the workplace and in police contact with members of the public. They can do this by making it clear to officers that discriminatory behaviour is totally unacceptable. If a case of discrimination does occur it must be dealt with quickly and, in appropriate cases, by way of misconduct proceedings. However, outside internal police action, discriminatory conduct may be dealt with by employment tribunals or the civil courts (depending on the context) and claims arising from the 'public sector equality duty' by way of judicial review in the Administrative Court.

KEY POINT—LEADERS AND ETHICAL BEHAVIOUR

The importance of police leaders maintaining the highest possible standards of ethical behaviour when leading teams and in police contact with members of the public cannot be overstated. Respect for each other and for differences between us is absolutely critical to police success and consensus policing.

7.3.9 **Leaders and police officers' personal development**

Police sergeant and inspector leaders are ideally appointed to help to satisfy the personal and professional aspirations of those they lead. They can do this by making available workplace opportunities and facilities to all, by mentoring and coaching, and by involving outside elements where appropriate: for example, human resource departments and training sections. Developing individuals benefits not only them but also the team they belong to, the police service and the public at large.

References and further reading

Equality and Human Rights Commission (2019), Equality Act 2010 Code of Practice (Norwich: TSO).

For Women Scotland Ltd (Appellant) v The Scottish Ministers (Respondent) (2025) Supreme Court Judgment <https://supremecourt.uk/uploads/uksc_2024_0042_judgment_aea6c48cee.pdf> accessed 21 May 2025.

Gov.UK (2024) *The Angiolini Inquiry, Part 1 Report.*

Gov.UK, Department for Business & Trade, 'Employment Rights Bill—Overview' (Fact Sheet) <https://assets.publishing.service.gov.uk/media/67f6711f555773bbf109e21a/employment-rights-bill-overview.pdf> accessed 15 April 2025.

The Stephen Lawrence Inquiry: Report by Sir William Macpherson of Cluny (Cm 4262-I, 1999).

Useful websites

<www.cipd.co.uk> (Chartered Institute of Personnel and Development, the professional body for those involved with the management and development of people)

<www.equalityhumanrights.com> (Equality and Human Rights Commission)

8

Valuing diversity

8.1 What is meant by the expression valuing diversity?

Diversity is linked to equality of opportunity but it is not the same. However, they are both similar in that they jointly recognise the importance of ensuring that people are free to achieve their aspirations without unlawful or unreasonable and unacceptable hindrance.

Of course the Equality Act 2010, although it does have a moral dimension, seeks changes in attitudes by changing behaviours and it is backed by legal sanctions. Diversity too has a moral dimension, and it is ethically right that the police service and police sergeant and inspector leaders should recognise that each individual has a unique worth and that they should be able to express and fulfil their ambitions. Action to help people to fulfil their potential has enormous benefits because it helps to motivate them and utilise their skills and abilities not only for their own benefit but to the benefit of the team, the police service and, importantly, the public.

The Chartered Institute of Personnel and Development (2024) notes that diversity includes the differences in colour, ethnicity, abilities, age, gender, beliefs, interests, socioeconomic (class), marital or partnership status, sexual orientation, geographic, academic/professional backgrounds, opinions, backgrounds, thinking, experiences and many other characteristics. Diversity recognises that everyone is different in a variety of visible and non-visible ways, and that those differences are to be recognised, respected, valued, promoted and celebrated. They may include, but are not limited to, differences protected by equalities law.

One of the themes of this book is that leadership is very much centred upon developing individuals to satisfy their own needs as an ethical means to maintain high levels of team efficiency and effectiveness. Further, a continuous thread winding its way through the narrative is that in the final analysis public satisfaction is the most important aspect of police work and this can be greatly enhanced by individual police officer development.

The police service can assist with the development of diversity by making sound policy decisions with regard to, for example, offering human resource department support where required, engaging in meaningful performance appraisal interactions and by providing targeted and well-thought-through training initiatives. However, sergeant and inspector leaders can play their part too for they are best appointed to establish the needs of those people they lead. Also, they have the executive authority to make many meaningful interventions in the workplace itself. Chapters 2 and 3 on leadership and team work should be helpful in this regard and so should Chapter 15 dealing with motivation and Chapter 27 concerning self-development.

8.2 **Neurodivergence—introduction**

It is probably true to say that in the recent past people who are described today as neurodivergent were seen quizzically as 'different'. As a result, their contributions to workplace objectives in terms of their knowledge, skills and aptitudes were undervalued and underused, this being to the detriment of the individuals concerned and the police service as a whole. Increasingly and belatedly, however, there is a growing realisation that neurodivergent people have much to offer alongside their neurotypical colleagues and that all 'labels' in the workplace should be dropped and the talents of all individuals harnessed for the greater good.

8.3 **Neuroscience**

Kings College London note that neuroscience is the study of the nervous system—from structure to function, development to degeneration, in health and in disease. It includes the nervous system, with primary focus on the brain. Complex, our brains define who we are and what we do. They store memories and allow us to learn from them. Brain cells and their circuits create new thoughts, ideas and movements and reinforce old ones.

8.4 **Neurodivergence**

The Advisory, Conciliation, and Arbitration Service (ACAS) cover the issue of neurodivergence in some depth in an article entitled Neurodiversity at Work-Understanding Neurodiversity (2025). Some of the salient points are covered below with author additions:

- Neurodivergence is still being researched and understood.
- Neurodiversity describes the *natural differences* in how people's brains behave and process information. We all think, learn and act differently and have different strengths and things we find challenging.
- The term neurodivergent is used to describe someone whose brain works differently to what is considered more typical.
- Some neurodivergent people do not see themselves as disabled. However, being neurodivergent will often amount to a disability under the Equality Act 2010.
- Neurodivergent employees might mask their condition at work. This entails hiding parts of a condition to fit in better. Someone might not be aware they are doing it. Masking can cause health problems. (This is a matter for sergeant and inspector leaders to heed when endeavouring to create an environment

whereby neurodivergence is understood and team members support each other no matter whether they are neurodivergent or neurotypical.)
- The Cleveland Clinic notes that

no two neurodivergent people are the same. People can be very different even when they have the same underlying condition.
- ADHD Aware note that people with one neurological condition may also have another condition at the same time. For instance, approximately one in two people with ADHD may also have dyslexia or dyspraxia.

8.5 Neurodivergence—ADHD, autism, dyslexia and dyspraxia

It is beyond the scope or competence of this book to discuss neurodiversity in detail. Some well-known types of neurodivergence are shown. However, it should be noted that they are representative and that there are other conditions to consider.

- *ADHD* (attention deficit hyperactivity disorder). Someone with ADHD might:
  (1) find it difficult to concentrate on tasks;
  (2) struggle with time management and organisation;
  (3) have trouble following instructions;
  (4) have times of hyperfocus—where they are entirely focused on a task;
  (5) be good at thinking creatively;
  (6) have lots of energy.
- *Autism*—autism affects how people communicate and interact with the world. Someone who is autistic might:
  (1) take things literally;
  (2) react differently to senses like sound and smell;
  (3) get anxious about social situations;
  (4) have difficulty interpreting social cues—for example, facial expressions and body language;
  (5) like a consistent routine;
  (6) seem rude without meaning to;
  (7) have a keen interest and expertise in particular topics;
  (8) have good attention to detail;
  (9) be good at problem-solving and thinking creatively;
  (10) have a good memory.
- *Dyslexia*—mostly affects reading and writing skills. It can also affect how someone processes information more generally. Someone who is dyslexic might:
  (1) read or write more slowly and find it difficult to listen and concentrate;
  (2) forget things easily;
  (3) have difficulty with spelling;

(4) be good at problem-solving and thinking creatively;
(5) have strong verbal communication skills;
(6) be good at tasks involving 3D shapes and spaces.

- *Dyspraxia*—affects movement and coordination. Someone who has dyspraxia might:
  (1) have poor balance;
  (2) have difficulty pronouncing some words;
  (3) take longer to do some tasks;
  (4) have strong verbal communication skills;
  (5) be good at thinking creatively.

What is striking with all the conditions mentioned above is the remarkable talents that neurodivergent people possess. Their abilities should be valued and incorporated into team activities by sergeant and inspector leaders to sit alongside the skills of all team members striving for professional excellence. The descriptive outlines listed above give hints as to how sergeants and inspectors can offer realistic support to neurodivergent colleagues.

8.6 Neurodiversity—neurodivergent and neurotypical people

The Cleveland Clinic notes that everyone's brain develops similarly but no two brains function the same. Being neurodivergent means having a brain that works differently from the average or neurotypical person. Neurodivergent is not a medical term, condition or diagnosis.

If the police service works hard to enhance its inclusivity efforts, benefits arising from including neurodivergent people (alongside neurotypical people) could include: (a) improved staff well-being, (b) a reduction in absence levels and employee turnover, (c) attracting employees with a wider range of skills and experience, and (d) a reduction in the risk of disputes and legal claims, for example unlawful discrimination. Ideally, an environment should be created whereby the neurodivergent and neurotypical labels are not even a matter for discussion or debate and all people are valued for who they are.

8.7 A study of neurodiversity in the workplace

The Chartered Institute of Personnel and Development cooperated with Uptimize to produce a Neuroinclusion at ork report. Their findings make plain that (a) organisations that fail to plan for neurodiversity in the workplace, including taking on board work-design issues, are failing to harness the talents and abilities of neurodivergent people who as a result may be demotivated and even leave an organisation, (b) it is essential to create an open and supportive environment where neurodivergence and all related issues can be openly discussed with managers and team members, and (c) not just neurodivergent people but all people should be protected from harassment and discrimination which can affect mental health and performance.

Harassment, bullying and discriminatory practices are totally out of order and are extremely damaging to victims and team cohesion. Sergeants and inspectors have to enforce ethical and professional behavioural standards and come down hard on corrosive individual or group behaviours which may manifest themselves in the public domain as well as at work.

The report notes the reasons for not informing a line manager or the human resources department about neurodivergence. These are:

- Private matter not for sharing (44%)
- Concern about assumptions based on stereotypes (37%)
- Unnecessary to inform manager or HR (36%)
- Too much stigma (34%)
- Concerns about the impact on my career (29%)
- Organisation would not be understanding or offer support (18%)
- Manager would not understand or offer support (16%)
- Concern about prying questions (14%)
- Not had the right opportunity (13%)
- No reason (5%)
- Other (15%)
- Don't know (0).

These statistics are worrying and if replicated in the police service they offer a cause for concern. Neurodivergent people may wish to keep things to themselves, and it is their right to do so. However, these statistics indicate a failure to understand neurodiversity, the value of neurodivergent people and a lack of understanding of neurodivergence at management and team level.

8.8 What can sergeants and inspectors do to help neurodivergent colleagues?

Sergeants and inspectors can do a great deal to help to build well-motivated, efficient and effective teams capable of high-quality contributions to policing. However, caring for people is part of being a decent person genuinely concerned for individual happiness and well-being. It just so happens that this has beneficial workplace spin-offs including team cohesion, efficiency and effectiveness, and returns in respect and loyalty from team members.

By definition, a workforce is neurodiverse as all people are unique but have different attributes and skills. When leading their teams sergeant and inspector leaders may wish to take account of the following:

- Provide flexible working in terms of hours of duty (employers and sergeants and inspectors have some capability in this regard but see below).
- Make reasonable adjustments or adaptations, for example, to job roles, furniture and equipment (something sergeants and inspectors can assist with).
- Create and commit to an action plan (relates to employers and sergeants and inspectors).
- Create an open and supportive neuroinclusive culture whereby people feel comfortable talking about neurodiversity and its benefits.
- Be guided by individuals about their needs and requirements and physical well-being—do not make assumptions and regularly monitor progress.

8.9 Employment Relations (Flexible Working) Act 2023 and the Flexible Working (Amendment) Regulations 2023

The Chartered Institute for Personnel and Development has outlined the key points regarding employees' requests for flexible working under new legislation:

(a) Employees do not have a right to work flexibly but many do have the right to formally request more flexible working arrangements.
(b) Under the Flexible Working Act, individuals holding employee status in Great Britain will have the right to: (i) request flexible working from day one of employment, and (ii) be able to make two requests in a 12-month period.
(c) Employees will no longer need to explain how the proposed working pattern will impact their job or employer.
(d) Employers are required to consult employees before rejecting any flexible working requests and will have to make a decision on any requests within two months.
(e) Employers have a duty to consider requests in a reasonable manner. A refused request may give rise to a claim for breach of the flexible working legislation, or for sex discrimination, or potentially for age discrimination.
(f) Fixed-term and part-time employees are included by the legislation, but self-employed contractors are excluded. Agency workers are also generally excluded except when returning to work following a period of parental leave.

8.10 The College of Policing and neurodiversity

The College of Policing Neurodiversity Working Group has produced a comprehensive Neurodiversity Glossary of Terms which assists in understanding the nature of neurodiversity. The College has also provided information on

Diversity and Inclusion which includes flexible working and other important information.

KEY POINT—VALUING THE ABILITIES AND TALENTS OF NEURODIVERSE PEOPLE

Neurodivergence means having a neurology that differs significantly from typical neurology. A workforce is by definition neurodiverse. Neurodiversity brings a variety of different talents to the workplace in terms of skills, abilities, experience, ideas and suggestions. Different perspectives add to creativity and problem solving. Inclusion draws all team members together with exclusion doing the opposite.

8.11 Multicultural teams

Multicultural teams are now a common feature of the workplace brought about by migration and greater workforce diversity. This means that leaders must understand and appreciate cultural differences to benefit from them and create highly motivated, harmonious teams whose combined talents and potential help them to reach their potential.

The Chartered Institute of Personnel and Development, working with Westminster Business School, note that multicultural teams are groups of people from different nationalities and cultures whose shared goal is to deliver for an organisation. Noticeable in these teams is that members have spent a significant portion of their formative years in different countries and have learned different values and behaviours. Being part of a particular culture provides a source of identity for people.

Cultural diversity in teams possesses the following characteristics:

- People are attracted to working alongside those they find similar to themselves in terms of values, beliefs and attitudes.
- People categorise themselves into groups and categorise others as outsiders or as members of other groups. This leads to favouritism towards those belonging to the group and the stereotyping of others.
- Cultural diversity can be seen as an opportunity rather than a problem as it helps bring more varied contributions to teams, making use of new information and perspectives to be heard, thereby enhancing the team's problem solving and creativity.

8.11.1 Language issues

Speaking a foreign language in multicultural teams creates anxiety, particularly for those who perceive their skill at speaking a particular language to be insufficient. This can isolate them and inhibit their ability to make meaningful contributions to team objectives. Leaders may be able to obtain help with language improvement and confidence. However, they should uphold language discipline and guide people back to the shared language, if necessary. Also, leaders should highlight the achievements of each team member in meetings. This counteracts perceptions of incompetence and encourages people to look beyond their language proficiency and acknowledge their skill elsewhere.

8.11.2 **What can sergeants and inspectors do to lead successful multicultural teams?**

Sergeants and inspectors, regardless of their own ethnicity, have a responsibility to create harmonious and happy teams, where everyone is valued for their unique contribution to the team effort. Creating a common culture enriched by diversity is very important. However, of huge significance is the ability of officers to communicate effectively with each other, and, in the case of police officers, with members of the public. Helping people to improve their language skills requires sensitivity and empathetic understanding. It is likely that those having language difficulties will improve their skills through contact with colleagues, and professional courses of instruction may prove helpful.

Finally, team members should be encouraged to value and support each other. Intolerance and discrimination of any sort have no place in an effective team.

KEY POINT—MULTICULTURAL TEAMS

Well-led and motivated multicultural teams can prove to be a great asset in the successful achievement of team objectives. Individual experiences, abilities and perspectives can bring creativity and enhance problem-solving potential. It is up to sergeants and inspectors to nurture multicultural teams with the full cooperation of team members. All individuals must be valued for what they can do for each other and the police service.

References and further reading

ACAS (2024), Code of Practice on Flexible Working.

ACAS (2025), Neurodiversity at Work—Understanding Neurodiversity.

ADHD Aware, 'Neurodevelopmental Conditions' <https://adhdaware.org.uk/what-is-adhd/neurodiversity-and-other-conditions/> accessed 16 April 2025.

Chartered Institute of Personnel and Development (2024), *Flexible and Hybrid Working: UK Employment Law* (London: CIPD).

Cleveland Clinic (2022), 'Neurodivergent' <https://my.clevelandclinic.org//health/symptoms/23154-neurodivergent> accessed 21 May 2025.

College of Policing (2024), 'Diversity and Inclusion' <www.college.police.uk/support-forces/diversity-and-inclusion> accessed 30 May 2025.

College of Policing (2022), 'Neurodiversity Glossary of Terms' <www.college.police.uk/support-forces/diversity-and-inclusion/neurodiversity-glossary-terms> accessed 21 May 2025.

Gifford J., Green M., and Young J. (2019), Chartered Institute of Personnel and Development and Urwin P., Westminster Business School, University of Westminster, *Diversity Management that Works, An Evidence-Based View* (Research Report).

Gov.UK (2024), Explanatory Memorandum to ACAS Code of Practice for Flexible Working.

Kings College London, 'What is Neuroscience?' <www.kcl.ac.uk/neuroscience/about/what-is-neuroscience> accessed 16 April 2025.

Thompson, E., Uptimize, and Miller, Dr J. (2024), *Chartered Institute of Personnel and Development, Neuroinclusion at Work Report* (Ref. 8545) (London: CIPD).

Young, J. (2021), *Managing Multicultural Teams—Exploring the Opportunities and Challenges* (London: CIPD).

Useful websites

<www.acas.org.uk> (Advisory, Conciliation and Arbitration Service)

<https://adhduk.co.uk/> (ADHD UK)

<www.bdadyslexia.org.uk/> (British Dyslexia Association)

<www.cipd.co.uk> (Chartered Institute of Personnel and Development, the professional body for those involved with the management and development of people)

<www.college.police.uk> (College of Policing)

<www.autism.org.uk/> (National Autistic Society)

<https://dyspraxiafoundation.org.uk/adults> (The Dyspraxia Foundation)

9

Dealing with unethical behaviours and workplace ineffectiveness sometimes without obvious causes

9.1 Introduction

A main function of sergeants and inspectors is to ensure that the teams they lead meet targets, deadlines and objectives in the most efficient and effective way. This is to offer the best possible service to the public. Key to success is the performance of each individual in the teams that they lead. If any team member is not performing well for some reason, then this will damage the team effort as a whole and desired results. It is imperative, therefore, that sergeants and inspectors address underlying problems apparent in a team member's performance.

Often personnel issues requiring attention appear when least expected and with people whose involvement will come as a surprise. Although perhaps new on occasions, many issues brought to notice are likely to have been experienced by sergeants and inspectors in the past. Experience is helpful. However, some problems may be new and perhaps extremely challenging to deal with, especially where crime and ethical matters are involved. This chapter is designed to signpost some of the people issues that may arise in the workplace, and which are likely to fall on sergeants and inspectors to deal with in the first instance at least.

9.2 Setting standards

Sergeant and inspector leaders are responsible for enforcing standards for ethical behaviour and professionalism and should lead by example. Team members must be familiar with the Code of Ethics and be cognisant of what is required of them professionally. They must also be aware of the consequences of misbehaviour in their private lives, the workplace and the public domain.

9.3 Inefficiency

Sergeants and inspectors have a perfect right to speak to officers about issues affecting their efficiency and effectiveness in carrying out their responsibilities. Most concerns in this regard will be resolved satisfactorily by way of discussion, giving advice and perhaps additional instruction or training. In other circumstances, inefficiency may just be a symptom of a deeper more complicated worry that does require close, personal attention.

9.4 Team dynamics and the formation of cliques

Cliques are groups of people who associate almost exclusively with each other whilst excluding colleagues. They set their own norms and operating rules. Exclusivity is divisive and a direct challenge to the leader's role and authority. Additionally, it can result in team conflict and damage to team cohesion, which in turn damages team efficiency and effectiveness. Cliques can dominate a weak leader, but a strong leader should break them up, with perhaps some officers being moved elsewhere.

9.5 **Banter**

Banter or teasing has a playful, convivial and friendly side. However, it is easy to overstep the mark when it goes beyond being friendly and becomes demeaning, humiliating and hurtful, descending into bullying. None of these negative behaviours can be tolerated in the police service.

The Angiolini Inquiry which inquired into the case of Wayne Couzens, a murdering police officer, took exception to bantering. Recommendation 14 of the Inquiry's report demanded the creation of a positive culture with the elimination of misconduct or criminality often excused as banter.

Without damaging team spirit, where good-natured and appropriate humour between team members is a sign of friendly cohesion, sergeants and inspectors should make sure that those they lead are aware that inappropriate banter is totally unacceptable and that it may result in disciplinary action. On a preventative basis, early signs of banter should be acted upon immediately.

9.6 **Harassment and bullying**

Any form of bullying or harassment is unacceptable. Harassment is covered under the Equality Act 2010. The Worker Protection (Amendment of Equality Act 2010) Act 2023 introduced a legal responsibility compelling employers to be proactive in taking reasonable steps to prevent sexual harassment. The Act covers colleagues at work or settings connected to work and includes harassment from third parties such as customers, service users or members of the public.

9.6.1 **Bullying and harassing—consequences**

Bullying and harassing others, no matter who and wherever they are, is abhorrent, and sexual harassment is particularly unpleasant. Victims are likely to suffer all sorts of anxieties, and, as the Angiolini Inquiry infers, such behaviours by police officers may well leak out into the public domain with criminal consequences.

The Code of Ethics is designed to remove unethical behaviours, and senior police officers need to create preventive policies locally. However, once again, sergeants and inspectors are at the forefront of tackling behavioural issues in operational circumstances. Bullying and harassment are not only extremely damaging for individuals, and may lead to very serious consequences for them, but also destructive in terms of team relationships and efficiency and may indicate poor leadership.

Sergeants and inspectors need to make clear to officers under their command that bullying and harassment will not be tolerated and that everyone has an obligation to report incidents that come to notice. They should also create an atmosphere based upon sincerity and trustworthiness where victims feel able to let them know of the discomforts that they are suffering.

Sergeants and inspectors may be able to detect bullying or harassment for themselves. For example, victims may appear unhappy, withdrawn, uncommunicative and not their usual selves. *These symptoms are deserving of discreet enquiry*. Suspicions may not be justified but the enquiry is still a worthwhile example of good leadership.

Officers who come forward to report bullying and harassment are deemed to be whistleblowers. (See also Chapter 4, section 4.10, 'Whistleblowing'.)

9.7 Workplace ineffectiveness—general

Sergeant and inspector leaders should constantly monitor individual performance against personal and team objectives. High morale, good teamwork and enthusiasm are likely to be indicators that all is well, but low morale, especially on an individual basis, may indicate that something is wrong and there may be visible signs of a drop in personal or team outcomes.

There are many causes for a drop in personal performance, and it is up to sergeants and inspectors to try to find out why and put things right. Obviously, a detailed discussion with the under-performer is required. Simply, it may be that an officer does not know what they are doing in certain areas of responsibility. Sergeants and inspectors have the ability to help put things right. For example, they can arrange for additional training or for a competent colleague to mentor and guide the individual concerned. They can also create a development plan for the officer and make regular checks on progress until such time as the desired competence is achieved.

However, it needs to be recognised that some officers are simply in the wrong job and will never reach the high standards required of a police officer, and once they are out of their probationary period it becomes difficult to remove them from the police service. This is why new recruits need careful performance monitoring throughout their probation when it is easier to remove ineffective and problematic personnel.

9.8 Disciplinary issues

Enforcing discipline and ethical and professional policing policies is a key leadership function. Without a regulatory discipline framework everything would be open to individual or group interpretation leading to workplace confusion and chaos. To follow the rules everyone in the police service should know what these are. It is extremely important that sergeants and inspectors set high personal standards of ethical behaviour and self-discipline. If they do not do so then they cannot reasonably expect the officers they lead to do so either.

Exercising discipline is not particularly easy and sometimes needs to draw upon personal fortitude and a strong sense of what is right. Responses to disciplinary action can be accepting but sometimes belligerent and hostile. All cases should be dealt with fairly and impartially and in accordance with recognised procedures.

The nature and consequences of undisciplined behaviour will govern how it is dealt with. People are always likely to make mistakes that are not irredeemable and can be used as a means to learn. A constantly applied heavy hand could demotivate individual officers and team members. However, on occasions disciplinary proceedings are necessary when, for example, officers fail to heed warnings for (a) what would otherwise be minor issues, (b) where officers are rude and aggressive when dealing with members of the public, or (c) where they are persistently late for duty without good reason. (See Chapter 16, 'Misconduct and discipline'.)

9.9 Commission of crime

When a police officer commits a crime or is suspected of committing a crime sergeants and inspectors should act in their primary role as police officers. There can be no toleration of criminal offenders.

9.9.1 Preventative action

To assist them with their responsibilities, sergeants and inspectors should encourage all team members to report cases where they suspect or know that a colleague or colleagues are committing criminal offences. This is an obligation placed upon them as police officers, and it is an onerous one requiring considerable courage, but they are more likely to be forthcoming if they have trust in their supervisors and the support of their team mates. (See also Chapter 4, section 4.10, 'Whistleblowing'.)

It is worth noting that the commission of some seemingly minor disciplinary offence may be a cover for committing crime. For instance, an officer regularly absenting themselves from appointed patrols may well be up to some form of mischief or criminal activity. Additionally, it is not unknown for more than one officer to be engaged in criminal activity. (See Chapter 16, 'Misconduct and discipline'.)

9.10 Workplace inefficiency where the causes are not obvious, and an exploratory interview is necessary

On occasions the causes of an officer's drop in performance may not be obvious. However, there may be symptoms that indicate that not all is well. For example, a normally cheerful and gregarious person may become quiet, reclusive and uncommunicative. When approached by a sergeant or inspector seeking to find out what the problem is an individual may be happy to discuss worries and concerns. Alternatively, they may be extremely reluctant or decline to do so. On another occasion, an officer may ask to speak to a sergeant or inspector about 'a worrying personal matter that cannot wait'. In both instances the sergeant or inspector involved should put aside time to interview the officers and should be not deterred by any initial reluctance to cooperate. As well as acting as concerned colleagues, supervisors have a duty to maintain individual and team motivation, efficiency and effectiveness.

9.10.1 The nature of an exploratory interview with an unknown outcome

Police officers develop interrogative skills as an important part of their work, and these can be used to advantage. When dealing with an individual's problems where the causes are unknown and may have serious consequences for their well-being, a range of sophisticated interpersonal skills need to be deployed. Adaptability is very important, and surprises should be expected. (See Chapters 18–21 dealing with interpersonal skill applications.)

Sergeants and inspectors have a right to interview their officers, but being well respected and trustworthy is very helpful to the interview process. If personal dislike and animosity cannot be put aside and are likely to be destructive to the interview process, then arrangements should be made for some other supervisor to conduct the interview.

Some people may think, for example, that a male officer cannot counsel a female colleague or vice versa. This is not necessarily the case. The most important thing is the context and whether or not the counsellor inspires trust and competence. However, where a person asks for an officer of the same gender, this should be honoured where possible.

During interviews sergeants and inspectors should not only be concerned with the welfare of individuals but also keep in mind the reputation of the police force and the quality of service demanded by members of the public.

9.10.2 Serious health issues

When interviewing, serious health issues may be disclosed. In these circumstances, sergeants and inspectors simply act a means to assist interviewees to gain the help they need from those best able to help them, for example, medical practitioners and counsellors although workplace support may be of some assistance.

9.10.3 **Disclosures of misconduct and crime**

It cannot be ruled out that a person seeking help may be deeply worried and burdened by knowledge of inappropriate behaviours or the criminal activities of a colleague or colleagues collectively. They may themselves even be contributory to a crime. If this proves to be the case, then the exploratory session changes and the prospect of disciplinary or criminal inquiries should be pursued.

9.11 **Conducting an exploratory interview**

When conducting an exploratory interview sergeants and inspectors should proceed on the basis of establishing the causes for under-performance, along with concern for the officer involved, and how to rectify performance issues and any personal matters causing distress.

9.11.1 **Choosing an interview venue**

Arrangements should be made for an interview to take place in a room where *all* interruptions are excluded. External interventions by others can disrupt an interview's flow and cohesion and may arrive at a critical time, perhaps causing an important point to be lost.

9.11.2 **Interviewer's behaviour**

When conducting interviews sergeants and inspectors need to:

- keep an open mind and suspend any judgements that they may hold about the officer being interviewed (professional judgements are necessary where misconduct and criminality are involved);
- stay focused and not let the mind wander, nor talk about themselves and their own experiences as this may show disinterest and insincerity;
- avoid arguments or confrontations as this will destroy the interview process;
- avoid, where personal or ill-health issues are concerned, trying to 'cheer people up' and suggest that 'all will be all right' for this tends to trivialise matters and may be seen as condescending and things do not always reach satisfactory conclusions.

9.11.3 **Creating a beneficial atmosphere and setting the scene**

As a prelude to questioning, a sergeant or inspector needs to put the interviewee at ease and invite them to take a full and meaningful part in discussions. Issues of confidentiality should be discussed with the interviewee where and when appropriate. However, the interviewee should be told that they may subsequently need the help of others to assist with resolving their difficulties. If an interviewee refuses to cooperate the consequences of non-cooperation should be explained, for example they may be required to leave the police service.

9.11.4 **Objectives**

A sergeant or an inspector should tell an interviewee that the objectives of the meeting are (a) to find out why performance levels have fallen, (b) to uncover any debilitating worries that they may have, and (c) to establish how they can help to alleviate the interviewee's concerns and return them to the required levels of efficiency.

9.11.5 **Interview dynamics**

At the outset a sergeant or inspector may elicit an instant, fulsome and detailed response, and then it will be possible to explore possible solutions. Depending upon the outcome of the interview some (but not all) solutions can be negotiated on the basis of mutual agreement. In other instances, solutions may have to be imposed, for example where disciplinary or criminal investigations are necessary.

If, alternatively, an interviewee is clearly reluctant to discuss the reasons behind poor performance it will be necessary to question them at length whilst encouraging them to surface issues. This will require a sophisticated use of the interpersonal skills. For the interviewer this includes empathy, patience, listening carefully, asking follow-on questions, and regularly clarifying, summarising and reviewing progress will be of great significance. It will also be important to take notes as an aid to memory and further action needed. (See Chapters 18–21 which cover offering a range of interpersonal skills.)

9.11.6 **Matters disclosed of a non-disciplinary or criminal nature**

During interviews disciplinary and criminal matters may be revealed and should be dealt with accordingly. However, other issues may include, for instance, the need for assistance with managing workloads more efficiently or coping with stress or long Covid concerns. Questioning may also, for example, reveal the presence of a divisive morale-damaging clique of officers. Sergeants and inspectors can help with all these problems by in most cases making management interventions. However, essentially health problems remain the exclusive province of medical practitioners.

9.11.7 **Generating and implementing solutions**

Hopefully, the examples mentioned earlier in this chapter are helpful in putting forward possible solutions to specific problems. Wherever possible, interviewees should be involved in generating their own solutions which they are more likely to implement than those imposed upon them without discussion or input. However, conditions may be imposed if they involve necessary compliance with behavioural standards, rules or regulations.

9.11.8 **Follow-up action**

No interview should be left open-ended. In most if not all cases a series of activities will be necessary to carry through solutions to a successful outcome. Agreed activities should be recorded and given completion dates. Review dates should also be recorded with adaptations being made where necessary.

KEY POINT—DEALING WITH UNETHICAL BEHAVIOURS AND WORKPLACE INEFFECTIVENESS

Sergeants and inspectors have significant leadership responsibilities that include (a) nurturing individuals and creating and maintaining efficient and effective teams, (b) removing unethical and unprofessional behaviours, alongside their corrosive outcomes, and (c) dealing with workplace inefficiency which can be damaging to individuals concerned, team mates and the completion of objectives. Inefficiency does not necessarily indicate a lack of personal commitment, and health issues may be at play. However, sometimes performance-damaging factors such as bullying or harassment are malign and have to be dealt with expeditiously.

References and further reading

Gov.UK, Department for Business & Trade, 'Employment Rights Bill—Overview' (Fact Sheet) <https://assets.publishing.service.gov.uk/media/67f6711f555773bbf109e21a/employment-rights-bill-overview.pdf> accessed 18 February 2025.

Gov.UK (2024), *The Angiolini Inquiry*, Part 1 Report (HC530).

10

Planning

10.1 Why do leaders need to lay clear plans for others to follow?

Planning is a primary responsibility for leaders and is a vitally important leadership function. Imagine just reacting to things as they occur or failing to look ahead to anticipate what needs to be done in the medium and long term. Think about the consequences for team members. It is likely that they would become confused, disorientated, demotivated, inefficient and ineffective resulting perhaps in anger and perhaps even the withdrawal of their labour because of seemingly pointless activities. Inefficiency and ineffectiveness caused through a waste of effort and resources would almost certainly result in a poor public reaction. This, in its turn, would reflect extremely badly upon the police service which would become subject to political pressure and enforced change. Finally, this state of confusion would destroy a leader's reputation and perhaps halt a police career in its tracks.

If the absence of planning or poor planning is unfortunate, then good planning is important because it offers a sense of direction and purpose with clear outcomes. Further, good planning takes account of the risks involved, resources required, obstacles to be overcome and timescales. Proficient planning necessitates considering the immediate future but also the medium- and long-term future and it is not a one-off process but a continuous one, constantly seeking improvement and increased public satisfaction.

10.2 Planning considerations—strategic and tactical

Strategy involves looking at any particular situation, deciding what has to be done and agreeing how it will be done taking into account all possible factors including the availability of resources such as personnel and materials. To implement strategy, it is necessary to have an overarching vision of what things should look like if the strategy is successful and of the broad goals and objectives.

Strategic plans in the police service are usually set at the highest possible level—a level at which total oversight of police operations is possible.

When police strategic plans have been decided upon they must then be cascaded down through the police structure to the people in the various workplaces who will execute them. This includes sergeant and inspector leaders who usually have a very important part to play in enacting operational plans. Tactics are the means by which strategy is carried out in a practical way. (Taking on force-wide objectives does not preclude sergeants and inspectors from creating their own objectives to suit their own responsibilities, the work of their teams and local conditions.)

10.2.1 **Strategic plans**

Although it is really important that senior police officers should decide upon strategic plans to meet political, social and other considerations and to give the force a cohesive and structured way forward, strategy can be applied at any level of an organisation. For example, local senior officers may wish to set their own strategies not to supplant the force strategy but to add to it to meet purely local demands.

Within the police service, strategy might include, for example, a vision that the force area is free of serious crime, that residents feel safe both within and outside their homes and that the streets are free of hooligans. One might see this vision as the reasons why police exist anyway, but it is important to be absolutely clear about what is required so that each element can be tackled according to its merits and the availability of resources. One could also say that the vision is overambitious, but being unambitious is undesirable because it limits imagination and scope. However, an ambitious vision must fall within the bounds of reason and the ability to achieve its desired ends.

To fulfil the vision it is necessary to set goals which amount to broad objectives. Goals are component parts of the vision and might include, for example, goals to tackle: burglary, drug trafficking and illegal drug taking, human trafficking, domestic violence, street robbery, gang warfare and alcohol abuse in town centres.

Strategic planners must carry out a considerable amount of research before they finally agree their goals. It is important to remember that no business or organisation or police force operates in isolation. There is always an interface with what is happening externally.

Strategic leaders must gather together all the information that they need to be able to make successful plans. This involves looking at, for example:

- what has happened in the past, what is happening now and what is expected in the future, after taking into account current political and public expectations of the police service including matters of reputation and ethical and professional considerations;
- available financial and other resources including equipment, buildings, vehicles and personnel matters including appropriate experience and the welfare of officers and civilian staff;
- any risks, opportunities and constraints;
- the state of the workforce competencies required to carry plans through to a successful conclusion—for instance, it may be necessary to arrange a new training programme to supplement or enhance existing skills;
- other bodies outside of the police service who may be required to participate in plans or be affected by them;

- how plans will be put over and explained to those responsible for implementing them;
- any legal or conduct-based restraints.

10.2.2 **Risks**

All planners, at any level, need to make an assessment of the risks involved. It makes sense to anticipate what might interrupt the satisfactory completion of objectives. Plans rarely run without a hitch and managing and mitigating risks necessitates identifying them clearly at the outset.

Assessing risks is an essential part of the leadership function. This chapter is directed mainly at detailed planning, where opportunities and risks need to be carefully explored and calculated. However, it should be recognised that risks exist at all levels of the police service. For example, sometimes and without much warning street duty officers are faced with immediate and often complex challenges that they have to deal with, for instance, major accidents and incidents where the public are endangered. Clearly, learning and experience help, and often sergeants and inspectors are at the forefront in offering help and assistance where needed. However, it may still be constables who have to make the first critical interventions.

Before setting out on a project it is worth creating a clear understanding of exactly what it is that the project is intended to achieve, for example:

(a) What is the impetus for change?
(b) Why is the status quo unacceptable?
(c) What difficulties have been experienced in the past?
(d) What are the potential problems likely to be experienced when working on the project and what are the resource implications?
(e) What will success look like and what are the anticipated benefits arising from change?

Having decided on clear project aims a detailed risk assessment is necessary. In this regard the following information may be of assistance:

- Examining risks will greatly assist in the construction of realistic aims and objectives.
- Being aware that not all risks can be eliminated is essential. However, after due consideration, it may be possible to accept risks and plan to mitigate their impact if the possible outcome really justifies this. Additionally, life is completely random and chaotic at times and planners will have to rely on those leaders who react quickly and decisively when things appear to go wrong.
- Making decisions on risk acceptability involves measuring the desired outcomes against the disadvantages of taking action. Resource commitment and economic considerations are important and may be expensive but the service the police offer to the public will always be a major consideration.

- Making good use of lessons learned from past experiences is sensible. Additionally, planners should benefit from those people who have experience that will aid plan construction.
- Decisions on how risks should be accepted, prioritised and managed should be made at the appropriate level of responsibility but any one at any level (especially those who will execute plans) can be invited to make contributions to broaden the thinking process.
- Monitoring the progress of plans when implemented is vital and planners should prepare to be adaptable and flexible in making changes.
- It is of great importance that officers at all levels, responsible for executing plans, are fully briefed as to what is required of them. They should also be made aware of potential problem areas. Those in the front line of policing, i.e. sergeants, inspectors and constables, should be encouraged to be flexible when meeting snags. All this means that the briefing and debriefing sessions are of great importance (see also Chapters 22 and 23).

KEY POINT—MANAGING RISKS

The identification of risks should not necessarily halt the planning process unless they are hugely significant, making it foolhardy or unwise to proceed. Most risks can be managed or outmanoeuvred thus preserving first-class initiatives that might otherwise have been abandoned.

10.2.3 **College of Policing—risk**

The College of Policing has offered ten principles to be considered when reviewing risk under Authorised Professional Practice. These complement the information shown in section 10.2.2 above. Only abstracts have been reproduced, and the reader would benefit from finding more about the principles on the College's website.

- The willingness to make decisions in conditions of uncertainty (i.e. risk taking) is a core professional requirement of all members of the police service.
- Maintaining or achieving the safety, security and well-being of individuals and communities is a primary consideration in risk decision making.
- Risk taking involves judgement and balance. Decision makers are required to consider the value and likelihood of the possible benefits of a particular decision against the seriousness and likelihood of the possible harms.
- Harm can never be totally prevented. Risk decisions should, therefore, be judged by the quality of the decision making, not by the outcome. It is in the nature of risk taking that harm, including serious harm, will sometimes occur.
- Making risk decisions, and reviewing others' risk decision making, is difficult. This needs to take into account whether they involved dilemmas or

emergencies, were part of a sequence of decisions or might appropriately have been taken by other agencies.

- The standard expected and required of members of the police service is that their risk decisions should be consistent with those a body of officers of similar rank, specialism or experience would have taken in the same circumstances.
- Whether to record a decision is a risk decision in itself which should be left to professional judgement. The decision whether or not to make a record, and the extent of that record, should be made after considering the likelihood of harm occurring and its seriousness. It is impossible to record all decisions.
- To reduce risk aversion and improve decision making, policing needs a culture that learns from successes as well as failures. Good risk taking should be identified, recognised and shared. More valuable lessons can be learned from examples of successful decisions rather than from the much rarer ones that lead to loss or harm.
- Since good risk taking depends on quality information, the police service will work with partner agencies and others to share relevant information about those who pose risk or those who are vulnerable to the risk of harm. Sharing information about individuals between public authorities is essential to keeping people safe.
- Members of the police service who make decisions consistent with these principles should receive the encouragement, approval and support of their organisation. Where their decisions can be shown to be defensible, decision makers deserve to be actively supported by their organisation.

10.2.4 **Performance measures**

Strategic goals (and objectives—see also section 10.2.6) must have performance measures attached to them. Performance measures help to clarify in definite terms what is expected and required. Also, they guide activities and prevent them from straying into unimportant areas and in the final analysis they are needed to establish whether the desired results have been achieved. Performance measures for a successful initiative to reduce robberies and assaults might, for example, result in more arrests and charges, fewer robberies and assaults and more convictions. As a bonus, police activity may lead to a drop in other crimes in the area in which operations occurred. (For further information on performance measures, see section 10.2.9.)

10.2.5 **Tactical plans**

When the vision has been created and strategic goals set, police leaders have to pass them down the police structure to those police officers and people who have the responsibility for carrying them out in a practical way. Turning strategy into activity involves tactical considerations.

10.2.6 **SMART objectives**

The tactical application of strategic goals at the operational level means drawing up objectives designed to meet actual conditions 'on the ground'. 'SMART' objectives are widely known and used. 'SMART' is a useful mnemonic that helps as an aid to both memory and planning. 'SMART' objectives are the creation of Doran (1981). *Doran's original ideas are flexible and adaptable* (as here) and can be added to as necessary (see also Table 10.1).

Table 10.1 SMART Objectives (Doran 1981)

S	Specific and stretching
M	Measurable
A	Achievable
R	Realistic, relevant and reviewable
T	Time-based or time-bound

Objectives should be written down and explained to those who have the job of completing related tasks. This is in order to create a common understanding of what is to be done. Otherwise, people may implement their own conflicting interpretations resulting in individual and team conflict, as well as frustration, the wasting of resources and the non-completion or late completion of objectives.

The SMART objectives

S *Specific*—objectives must be clear and unambiguous and not open to a number of interpretations.
Stretching—not limiting team talent and innovation and being ambitious to maximise results.

M *Measurable*—measuring performance outcomes to ascertain whether or not an objective has produced the desired result. Measurements should be quantifiable (countable) and qualitative (seeking confirmation from those supposed to benefit from completed tasks and objectives). Cost and time implications should be measured too.

A *Achievable*—setting objectives that can actually be completed. There is no point in creating objectives that are fanciful and likely to fail through lack of forethought.

Leaders must consider resources in particular by asking questions such as:

(a) Do I have enough people to perform tasks?
(b) Are the people I have been assigned capable of completing tasks or do they need training or coaching to improve their competence?

(c) Do the people I have been allocated have the time to complete tasks or are they burdened with other work too? Do I need to remove some individual burdens?
(d) Do I have the time to complete objectives or are other time demands on me from elsewhere likely to derail their completion?

R *Realistic and relevant*—being realistic in terms of the scope of the objective and its relevance to the needs and aspirations of the organisation, its ambitions and the people it serves.
Reviewable—exercising control and keeping progress under regular scrutiny to ensure that proceedings remain on track and any impediments to progress are removed. Engaging problem-solving techniques.

T *Time-based or time-bound*—involves managing time to make a friend of it rather than an enemy. Striving for adherence to tight time limits for objectives and resultant tasks may not only get the job done quicker and save on resources but strict time constraints may also generate enthusiasm and energy.

Importantly, time limits and time milestones (staging points) are a strong form of control. However, when reviewing progress a leader may at times and out of necessity have to adjust time limits but this should never be done lightly.

10.2.7 How to complete SMART objectives—example

The following is an example of a SMART objective based upon a police responsibility—dealing with a spate of robberies. There is no one right way to write an objective in terms of the wording used or the actions to be taken but careful precision is important.

Example objective—drawn up on 1 January (any year):

Eliminate the street robberies currently occurring in Engine Street within the immediate vicinity of Cheap Town Railway Station and the adjoining local authority car parks situated in nearby Steam Square and Coal Street by 28 February (year).

Assuming that the objective is well resourced, achievable and realistic, it is SMART. It is clear and specific in its intent. Also, the objective is challenging because it uses the word 'eliminate'. It could have indicated a percentage reduction but that would have been limiting unless the scale of robberies is very large or the available resources for tackling the crime are small.

The use of verbs assists measurement of both the objective itself and its associated tasks (for tasks see section 10.2.8). Verbs make it possible to ascertain at the conclusion of the operation whether all the tasks have been completed successfully and whether the problem has indeed been eliminated. Additionally, by applying an end date to the proceedings police are able to measure whether the robberies have been eliminated by the desired date—28 February (year). The end date always remains a constant focus and an imperative for action.

10.2.8 **Identifying tasks**

Having decided upon our objective, we now need to identify the tasks (activities) that support it. Tasks should be regarded as mini-'SMART' objectives and they amount to a breaking down of objectives into manageable and logical activities. Crucially, they help to map out a route map and the progress required.

Ideally objectives and tasks should be set out in flow-chart form (see Figure 10.1). This form of visual representation is attractive to the eye and good for creating a common understanding of what needs to be done. Additionally, it reveals the logic behind a considered incremental process.

Figure 10.1 SMART objectives and tasks—example

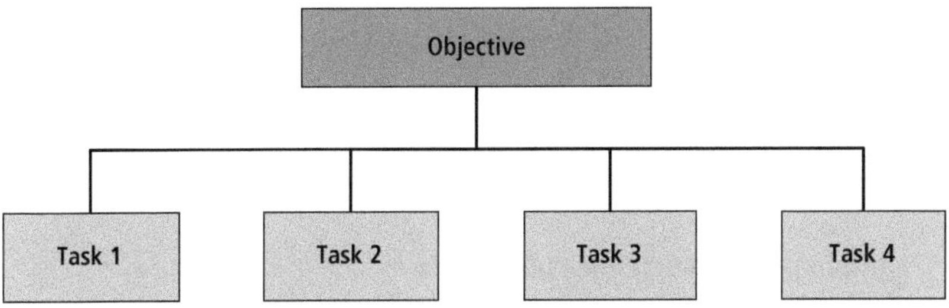

- Task 1—*gather and analyse* crime statistics including frequency, times, dates, locations, victims (sex, age, race, etc), known offenders, other crimes and include any supporting intelligence by 3 January (year).
- Task 2—*consult* with railway police and invite them to participate in the objective by deploying railway police in accordance with mutually agreed arrangements by 4 January (year).
- Task 3—*assess and procure* surveillance and other equipment, including vehicles and personal radios, required for deployed officers by 4 January (year).
- Task 4—*direct* crime prevention experts to examine crime data and visit robbery venues to ascertain any geographical or other features that assist robbers and, where negative features do exist, *plan* to remove or overcome them by 5 January (year).
- Task 5—*designate and equip* a control room to manage deployments and activities by 5 January (year).
- Task 6—*designate* a charge centre/custody suite to manage arrests made by 5 January (year).
- Task 7—*appoint* a press liaison officer by 5 January (year).
- Task 8—*draw up* a comprehensive action plan *detailing* who will do what, how, where and when by 6 January (year).

- Task 9—*implement* action plan, *brief* officers, *allocate* roles and deployments by 7 January (year). Deployment to continue until objective end date unless crime problems are resolved before that time.
- Task 10—*monitor* any crime displaced to other areas and *take any remedial action*—continuous until 28 February (year).
- Task 11—*debrief* events against performance with all personnel concerned in the operation and *evaluate* results and produce a final evaluation report to the direct benefit of similar future operations by 28 February (year).

The allocation of appropriate task end dates is a matter of judgement dependent upon the nature of the objective and other important operational considerations. In this instance, it is important to deal with all the initial planning rapidly so as to tackle worrying street crime quickly. Tasks do not necessarily have to be completed in chronological order; they can be completed simultaneously if available resources permit this course of action.

10.2.9 **Performance measures—examples**

Section 10.2.3 mentioned the importance of creating meaningful performance measures, which among other considerations assist in deciding whether an operation has been successful. Example performance measurements for our contrived objective are shown below.

Example performance measurements

- number of robberies committed or prevented;
- number of robbery victims and any injuries incurred;
- number of persons arrested and charged and the numbers cautioned or released without charge;
- number of other crimes committed or prevented, including the numbers of arrests made, charges brought and cautions administered (it would be reasonable to expect a drop in the number of other crimes committed given a strong police presence);
- number of displaced crimes beyond the area of operations (if any) and any associated arrests;
- number of robbers convicted or acquitted at court;
- costs in terms of equipment and facilities used, personnel deployed in support and operational roles and days expended per officer, all totalled to cover the whole operation;
- positive and negative press reviews;
- expressions of public dissatisfaction (with remedial action) and appreciation.

NB: Of course, once the period of the operation has expired the former situation prior to the objective should not be allowed to redevelop.

10.2.10 **Objectives—a broad range of applications**

Finally, objective setting need not be confined to strategic and crime-fighting plans. It can be used for all manner of police initiatives. These might include, for example, dealing with local public order events, reorganising an administrative function, arranging meetings with the public or even designing a comprehensive self-development plan.

SMART objectives are easy to construct and straightforward in their application. However, there are other options to SMART objectives which can be used on their own or in conjunction with the SMART model. Further, sergeants and inspectors can always add features of their own to models if they wish to do so. (See also Chapter 13, 'Coaching skills', section 13.8.4 regarding the OSCAR and GROW model alternatives.)

References and further reading

Armstrong, M. (2009), *Handbook of Human Resource Management Practice* (11th edn, London: Kogan Page).

College of Policing (2013), 'Risk' <www.college.police.uk/app/risk/risk> accessed 30 May 2025.

Doran, G. (1981), 'There's a SMART Way to Write Management Goals and Objectives', *Management Review* 7(11): 35–6.

Gov.UK (2023), *The Orange Book: Management of Risk—Principles and Concepts*.

Murdock, A. and Scutt, C. (1993), *Personal Effectiveness* (Oxford: Butterworth-Heinemann).

Office of Government Commerce (2002), *Management of Risk: Guidance for Practitioners* (London: HMSO).

Weiss, J. W. and Wysocki, R. K. (1992), *5-Phase Project Management: A Practical Planning & Implementation Guide* (Boston, MA: Addison-Wesley).

11

Delegation

11.1 Why is the delegation of work important?

The ability to delegate successfully is a really important part of a leader's function. A sergeant or inspector leader cannot do everything that needs to be done on his or her own. Additionally, leaders have a responsibility to manage workloads, relieve stress and encourage the development of individual and team competence. This is in order to complete tasks and objectives successfully and ensure the provision of a first-class service to the public.

Ideally delegation should form part of a structured individual and team development programme.

KEY POINT—THE IMPORTANCE OF DELEGATION

A leader who does not delegate is likely to be a poor leader. Failure to delegate stunts individual and team growth, damages overall team morale and impairs levels of efficiency and effectiveness leading to team dissatisfaction and most probably poor public service.

11.2 Reasons why leaders do not delegate

Some leaders appear unable to delegate work to the people they lead. There are, no doubt, many reasons for this, but these are likely to include:

- lack of knowledge about the value of delegation as a leadership tool;
- deficiency in an understanding of delegation techniques;
- fear that officers will let them down by failing to complete tasks satisfactorily;
- concern that officers will do a better job than they can, thereby threatening their prestige and position within a police force;
- failure to make the time to delegate properly to officers.

11.3 Important reasons why leaders should delegate

Leaders need to delegate to get the best out of themselves and their staff. Delegation should not be seen as a threat to the leader's position. Leaders and staff are all part of the same team—all working to ensure police success. Further, failure should not be allowed to inhibit delegation. When things go wrong and, indeed, when they go right, lessons must be learned for the benefit of future delegation and tasks.

Leaders need to delegate for the following specific reasons:

- Invariably, team members share the same overall objectives as their leaders.
- Typically, managers cannot deal with all the work allocated to them on their own.

- Stress pressures can be maintained at appropriate levels when job burdens are shared between leaders and officers.
- Often job specifications place false limitations on the scope of staff abilities—many individuals want and are motivated by increased responsibility.
- Enhanced responsibility helps to encourage individuals by building up their confidence and a willingness to take on even greater responsibility.
- Officers perceive delegation as an act of trust and this encourages independent action and increases personal motivation.
- Leaders may not have the skills or knowledge to be able to deal with a particular matter.
- Delegation is a skills and competence self-development tool.

11.4 **Conditions for delegation**

The following are the conditions under which successful delegation can take place. A leader should:

- be clear about the reasons for acts of delegation and what is to be achieved;
- choose the right people to delegate to as some officers may be totally incapable, even with training, of taking on certain tasks, not because they are foolish but because of their aptitudes and preferences;
- discuss the conditions under which the delegation is to take place before a task is attempted and listen to and address any concerns;
- make clear to officers what powers and scope they have to act—responsibility, authority and freedom to make decisions should be allowed otherwise the leader might just as well do the job him- or herself;
- provide appropriate coaching or training for the individuals concerned;
- offer total support to officers, which includes giving advice, praise, encouragement and ensuring that they do not suffer undue stress;
- monitor the progress of tasks and the individuals performing them;
- ensure that officers learn from and receive credit for jobs well done.

11.5 **A leader's accountability**

When delegating, leaders should delegate responsibility and authority along with the task. However, they *cannot delegate accountability* and are ultimately themselves accountable for things that do go wrong.

KEY POINT—SUCCESSFUL DELEGATION

Where an act of delegation brings forth successful results, the leader and the person achieving the results should enjoy the rewards together. It is not wrong for a leader to enjoy credit for leading people effectively.

12

Problem solving

12.1 What is a problem and why is problem solving important?

Problem solving is important because it is part of our everyday existence. We constantly meet difficulties and problems throughout our social and working lives. Problems stand in the way of activities and progress and need to be removed so as to satisfactorily achieve desired outcomes. However, a distinct focus on problem solving in the police service also amounts to a critically important leadership skill and activity. Removing obstacles, both large and small, on an almost daily basis is essential to team efficiency and the completion of tasks and objectives necessary in order to provide the best possible service to the public.

Problems in the workplace take many forms and can relate, for example, to administrative difficulties requiring perhaps corrective policies and procedures, operational activities and, importantly, individual and collective personnel issues both within and outside the workplace.

KEY POINT—PROBLEM-SOLVING IMPERATIVE

It is absolutely essential that a leader should remove *any* obstacles standing in the way of team efficiency and effectiveness quickly and without any undue delay.

12.2 How does a leader go about solving problems?

Some problems, often of a minor nature, may be solved quickly and easily by recourse to the previous experiences of the leader or team members and a bank of accumulated knowledge and expertise. However, many other problems may be much more difficult to resolve, requiring a systematic and measured approach. To help the sergeant and inspector leader it is suggested that problems may be tackled using a six-stage approach.

- *Stage one* involves the identification of the problem, which is usually self-evident. For example, a computer breaks down and vital information is lost, or an operation to reduce crime in a particular area is failing and crime continues to increase, or team targets and objectives are not being met because inter-team conflict has developed.
- *Stage two* necessitates finding out what has gone wrong and in this respect it is very important to identify and separate the symptoms from the causes. For instance, the fact that team tasks and objectives are not being met and that team harmony and synergy are not what they should be is symptomatic of wider problems. These might include, for example, personal conflict within the team on an individual or group faction basis, a lack of team competence or disproportionate sick absence or even poor leadership. These causes need, of course, to be addressed quickly by the leader.

The investigation into a problem should start with those people intimately involved with what has gone wrong as they are best appointed to put forward suggestions and solutions.

The problem solver should also look at any laid down work standards. Standards set out operating instructions and rules regarding the activities and behaviours required for the satisfactory completion of tasks. Standards are designed, therefore, to maximise resources and guarantee quality by repeating the desired activities and behaviours over and over again.

A police operator receiving a telephone call from a member of the public offers a simple example of a standard in action. The operator might, for instance, be required to answer a call within 30 seconds and to greet the caller by saying who they are and asking how they can help. The call might end with a summary of what the caller has said and what action is to be taken. By tracking agreed standards, a leader or manager can identify any deviation. For example, in this instance there would be a deviation if the call was not answered until two minutes had elapsed. Now there might be very good reason why the answer was delayed but the deviation may reveal some fault in the operator or the system. Similarly, a failure to summarise correctly may have led to incorrect police action arising out of a misunderstanding about what was needed.

- *Stage three* involves generating solutions. This offers an opportunity for the leader not only to restore the status quo but also to enhance existing ways of doing things or bring about a complete change that serves outcomes even better than before. When making changes, the sergeant or inspector leader should be absolutely clear what the objective of change is and what will happen and how things will be when any change is implemented.

When examining a problem logically it is important to gather, for example, facts and information, to look at former and existing practices, documentation and rules and procedures. It is also essential to look at any technological implications. However, there is no reason why inventive thinking cannot be applied to any problem including those that appear to have a clear logic attached to them, for example administrative processes, formal meetings with the public or day-to-day policing initiatives.

Where creativity and inventiveness are concerned, the sergeant and inspector leader has a team of various talents at his or her disposal and such talents should be harnessed to the problem-solving process.

However, a preference for genuine spontaneous creativity and true inventive thinking does not repose in all people. Margerison and McCann's study of managing directors (2018 and 2025) worldwide revealed that of a population of 25,265, only 9% were Creator-Innovators. The same study revealed Creator-Innovators had the highest representation in the Arts and Media Professionals and Psychologists categories.

Of course, one has to treat all statistics with caution as organisations that rely on innovation are more likely to consciously develop a culture of 'Creator-Innovators' than perhaps the police service. However, police sergeant and inspector leaders should try to identify innovators and seek ways of encouraging others to think differently. They can do this whenever an opportunity for creative thinking arises, for example at team and other meetings and at feedback and problem-solving sessions where things that went wrong during a particular task are placed under scrutiny and where there is a desire to do things better. In these circumstances, sergeant and inspector leaders can invite contributions by known innovators and by making clear that challenges to the status quo and radical thinking are an acceptable part of the ideas-generation process. This, in turn, should act as a stimulus to normally less creative team members and help to develop an environment where ideas and spontaneous thinking are seen as the norm.

Nevertheless, regardless of any perceived limitations a sergeant or inspector leader may find it very useful to consider a *brainstorming session* to bring creativity to a problem.

Brainstorming is a widely known concept long established by Osborn (1963). The word brainstorming denotes a useful, high-energy, creative thinking process that team members can participate in. This helps to generate ownership in any outcomes whilst helping to maintain levels of interest and togetherness. Further, brainstorming can be fun; however, if left uncontrolled the process can degenerate into a chaotic, unproductive 'free-for-all'.

Adherence to the following rules will help a sergeant or inspector leader to achieve brainstorming success:

- be absolutely clear about what the objective of the session is, what is to be achieved and what success will entail;
- select a date, time and place when and where team members can give their undivided attention to what is required of them;
- do not (*sergeant or inspector*) take part in the process of generating ideas as this may exercise undue influence over proceedings. Allow those assembled for the session the freedom to produce suggestions in an unhindered and unfettered way;
- consider involving suitably qualified persons from outside the team who can bring unbiased and fresh views to the problem-solving issue;
- appoint a skilled independent *facilitator* to conduct the session. He or she should help the leader to fulfil the session's objective without becoming involved in the detail of discussions or the decision-making process;
- the *facilitator* should tell participants what the objective(s) of the session are and what part they are to play in the generation of ideas. He or she should also set a time limit—for example, 25 minutes to encourage responses—but eliminate unnecessarily long pauses and avoid continuance when the best ideas have already been offered. Further, the facilitator should explain to participants that they are free to make any

suggestions that they wish no matter how unlikely they might initially seem (this aids the creative thinking element of a session and originality), and that no one must subject anyone else to ridicule for a suggestion that they have made (this will help to kill a session off very quickly). Finally, team members will almost certainly find out that they can build upon the suggestions that others make;

- the *facilitator* should not be encumbered by note-taking but lead discussions and manage time. The *sergeant or inspector* leader should engage a non-participating *note-taker(s)* for this purpose. Ideally, notes should be displayed on sequentially numbered, large pieces of paper (perhaps using the flip-chart system) so that all may see the progress being made and allow for even more fresh ideas;
- when a session appears to be faltering, the *facilitator* should stimulate responses by suggesting other avenues of inquiry and seeking the enlargement of ideas already put forward;
- the *facilitator* should close the session at the agreed time unless ideas are still pouring forth (a matter of judgement). However, if a session loses impetus it can be closed down at any stage during the proceedings;
- at the end of the idea-gathering session the *sergeant or inspector* leader should, with the *facilitator's* help, invite team members to place suggestions into categories, eliminate totally inappropriate ideas and identify really worthwhile suggestions in priority order;
- having thanked participants for their contributions, the *sergeant or inspector* leader should later test the validity of good ideas against the session's objective (see also *Stage four*) taking full advantage of the best suggestions and implementing them where possible. However, the leader should bear in mind that brainstorming is not an infallible process and that the search for answers may require further research.

KEY POINT—PRACTICAL APPLICATION

To assist with practical application, see 'Checklist 16—Leader's problem-solving: brainstorming' in Part Two of this book.

- *Stage four* concerns possible solutions which have been reached and which will have to be evaluated and examined for workability, and one way of doing this is to try to find out why they might not work. This strange test may encourage very useful modifications. Additionally, if time permits it may prove useful to run a 'pilot scheme'. However, the danger with 'pilots' is they get the resources and attention to make them work when really under normal circumstances they would be likely to fail.

Workability is linked to implementation and points such as those listed below need to be considered:

- technological implications;

  - personnel commitments;
  - training implications;
  - resource costs—for example, money, equipment, building-space requirements and vehicle needs.
- *Stage five* is the implementation stage and the leader should consider developing a change-management plan as well as an implementation plan, although both can be combined. (See also Chapter 14, 'Leaders as agents of change (change management)'.) Setting objectives is likely to be important too. (See also Chapter 10, 'Planning'.)
- *Stage six* requires monitoring progress after implementation to make sure that it becomes properly embedded. This will necessitate communicating with team members and others concerned with the changes, seeking feedback, offering praise where merited, problem solving and making adjustments where necessary. If solutions do not work out, they should be abandoned and lessons learned before starting all over again.

12.3 How does a leader prevent problems from arising in the first place?

It is not always possible to identify problems before they occur but leaders should try to do so by:

(1) training people to do their jobs to the required standards;
(2) checking procedures and results personally and asking questions of operatives and, where appropriate, members of the public and agencies who co-operate with the police;
(3) being approachable and encouraging people to report problems in their early stages and before they increase in intensity;
(4) running regular team meetings where concerns are aired and dealt with.

References and further reading

McCann, D. J. and Mead, N. H. S. (eds) (2018), *Team Management Systems Research Manual 5th edition: Team Management Profile Questionnaire* (Brisbane: Team Management Systems). © TMS Development International Ltd: Content reproduced by kind permission of TMS Development International Ltd, <www.tmsdi.com>.

Osborn, A. F. (1963), *Applied Imagination: Principles and Procedures of Creative Problem Solving* (3rd edn, New York: Charles Scribner's Sons).

13

Coaching skills

13.1 Introduction

Coaching should not be seen as a new concept by sergeants and inspectors as they, knowingly or unwittingly, regularly coach officers under their command in order to best use and develop their competences and build up self-confidence. Coaching may take the form of, for example, informal chats or asking a more experienced officer to mentor a new or struggling colleague. Coaching also takes place when offering feedback to offer praise but also eliminate errors. These interventions have a high value and should help to form part of an integrated training programme whereby learning takes place on a continuous basis.

13.2 Coaching—a definition

Coaching usually takes place on a one-to-one basis to develop an individual's competence (knowledge, skills and attitudes). It allows the coach to concentrate exclusively on a trainee and their particular needs and is good where the training is of an intensive nature. A trainee may be new to the subject being taught or it may have been decided that they need refresher training to improve existing competence.

Being flexible, it is possible to coach more than one person at a time. For instance, two or three persons can train together, and this may have some benefits. However, it dilutes the attention that can be paid to individuals which may be damaging if the competence being developed is of a complex, hard-to-absorb nature.

NB: It should be noted that the coaching principles covered in this chapter are applicable in principle to the training of larger groups of people (e.g. 12 persons).

13.3 Coaching—benefits

Coaching like all training interventions is designed to embed professional competence and confidence. It has the advantage of being flexible. It can operate on a day-to-day officer development basis. Equally, it can be used in a more structured way when justified, for example when an officer needs particular help or the subject matter is complex. Coaching has a wide remit, and it can be used to develop all manner of skills including, for example, interpersonal skills where these are lacking, arrest techniques, computer and other technological skills as well as operational procedures. However, coaching is dependent on a coach's proven ability to train the subject in hand.

13.4 Coaching competence

A coach must be thoroughly conversant with and competent in the matter being coached. If they are not then they may pass on faulty information or bad habits. Ultimately, the coach will be judged by how well a trainee performs in the workplace although it needs to be recognised that some trainees may never achieve the required level of competence.

13.5 What to do before a coaching session takes place

There is a danger that a sergeant or inspector is so familiar with a coaching subject that they run a session with little or no preparation. This risks a muddled approach, spending too much or too little time on a particular subject, and missing or forgetting to impart some important piece of information. To run an effective coaching session it is necessary to do the following:

(1) Write a brief narrative of the purpose of the coaching session and how training should help the coachee in the workplace.
(2) Fix aims and objectives.
(3) Construct training notes of activities and significant points, in delivery sequence, and estimate how long it will take to deliver inputs. This brings order and coherence and helps to ensure that essential points are not missed.
(4) Create a timetable based upon (3) above.
(5) Draw up a handout using (3) above, to be given to the coachee at the end of training (not before, as it may become an unhelpful distraction).

When appropriate, a sergeant or inspector coach can issue a notification to the officer concerned telling them when and where a coaching session is to take place. The note should include (1), (2) and (4). Other information can be added on a discretionary basis and might include, for instance, encouraging a coachee to make notes during sessions (for reinforcement purposes).

13.6 When and where should a coaching session take place and for how long?

Given operational considerations, sergeants and inspectors should only run formal coaching sessions where there is an important reason for doing so and the abstraction from duty can be justified. When and where a coaching session should take place is a matter for the sergeant or inspector concerned given the accommodation available for use. How long a session takes depends upon the content to be delivered. Sometimes coaching can take a whole day but this may not be realistic in a busy policing environment. Coaching sessions can be delivered in instalments, but ideally gaps between sessions should not be too long.

13.7 Coaching and learning

It is a bonus if sergeants and inspectors are familiar with the personalities of the officers they work with and how they are likely to respond to training, but this is not always the case.

People are far too complex to stereotype, and everyone will have their own views on training and bring their separate personalities to sessions.

Some officers may look forward to acquiring new or enhanced skills and be eager to take part in sessions. They are likely to be content to involve themselves in practical exercises and role play but may be impulsive in trying to force the pace of training. Others may be less sure and have some concerns, especially if they are expected to take part in role play. They may dislike being the centre of attention and prefer to carefully consider the implications of what they are being required to learn and how it might be implemented. This may be regarded as not wanting to participate, but this should not be assumed because the assumption is likely to be wrong. Additionally, depending partly upon the subject matter, some people may assimilate information more quickly than others who are slower on the uptake. This does not mean that they are more able than a slower but perhaps more thoughtful colleague. The time taken to absorb material will vary from person to person.

The success of a coaching session depends significantly upon the attitudes and behaviours of the coach, who must act professionally, never lose sight of the objectives of the training and always be respectful towards the coachee. Bad temper and impatience can destroy a coaching session. Success also depends upon a coachee being able to participate fully by being encouraged to ask questions, offer ideas and even question the relevance of material being taught (this can enrich and aid the development of a course). It should also be recognised that mistakes (which are to be expected) are a means to learn and should be accepted as such. Repetition will help to remove errors. Additionally, all training, insofar as practicable, should be enjoyable as this stimulates a willingness to learn.

Reinforcement in training is necessary as something done just once is unlikely to be embedded. Reinforcement by way of role play can be backed up by student notes, handouts and reviewing progress in the workplace.

At the end of every coaching course the coach should review how things went and whether any improvements are necessary. Honest feedback from the coachee will aid this process. In the final analysis the success of training can be measured by the satisfactory completion of set objectives.

13.8 Specimen coaching scenario

A specimen coaching scenario has been created to help sergeants and inspectors with coaching sessions. It relates to concerns about an officer's behaviour. The officer is generally good-natured and gets on reasonably well with team members. However, they are impulsive and inclined to lose their temper quickly over even minor matters. There is evidence that their behaviour is being visited upon members of the public, risking reputational damage. Taking the individual through an assertive behaviour coaching session would be a good way of addressing the officer's behavioural problems. The scenario supports the concept of ethical behaviour promoted by the College of Policing.

13.8.1 **Questions for the coach**

Before making any preparations for training, coaches need to be fully conversant with what the term 'assertiveness' means and what coaching is intended to achieve.

13.8.2 **Aims**

Fixing aims gives both the coach and coachee a clear indication of what the training is intended to achieve, for example:

- By the end of the coaching session a coachee should be able to behave in an assertive manner that relies on respecting people and achieving desired results without provoking conflict.

NB: See also Chapter 19, 'Positive communications—assertiveness'.

13.8.3 **Objectives**

Objectives are the means to carry out the aims. Chapter 10, section 10.2, 'Planning considerations—strategic and tactical' offers extensive detail on setting SMART objectives (which can also be used for the aims). For quick reference purposes SMART objectives are:

S	Specific and stretching
M	Measurable
A	Achievable
R	Realistic, relevant and reviewable
T	Time-based or time-bound

A coach should list the activities needed to teach a coachee how to behave assertively. It is necessary to create objectives individually and in the order in which they will be delivered. For example:

- By the end of a coaching session the coachee should be able to discuss:
  (1) what is meant by the term 'assertive behaviour' and the benefits of being assertive;

(2) what is meant by the term 'passive behaviour' and the consequences of being passive;
(3) what is meant by the term 'aggressive behaviour' and the likely outcomes of behaving aggressively for individuals and the police service;
(4) the nature and significance of 'rights' and 'responsibilities' when communicating with people;
(5) the beneficial use of the interpersonal skills including voice tone, body language, questioning and clarifying;
(6) the need to consider the views of others especially when compromise is needed; and
(7) behaving in an assertive manner when dealing with anyone including team mates, police colleagues and members of the public.

13.8.4 **Alternatives to SMART objectives**

SMART objectives are easy to construct and straightforward in their application and they can be used successfully in all areas of training (and elsewhere in the workplace) including coaching. However, there are other options to SMART objectives which can be used separately or in conjunction with the SMART model. Additionally, sergeants and inspectors can always add features of their own to models if they wish to do so, for example financial and resource implications.

13.8.5 **The OSCAR model**

The OSCAR model is the result of the work of Whittleworth and Gilbert (2009). The model falls into four separate parts very briefly outlined below:

(1) Outcome (desired destination)—current position, working together and what will success look like?
(2) Situation (starting point now)—creating objectives
(3) Choices and consequences (options)
(4) Actions (the action plan)
(5) Review (monitoring, correcting, completing).

13.8.6 **The GROW model**

The GROW model was developed by Sir John Whitmore and his colleagues. It has similarities with the OSCAR model and operates under four main features:

(1) Goal
(2) Reality
(3) Options
(4) Will—the actions a coachee can commit to undertakings.

13.8.7 **Creating a timetable**

In creating a timetable the coach should take each objective and briefly list its subject matter in the order in which topics will be delivered, along with a calculation of the time each session will last. The coach may wish to include an Introduction to a coaching session noting the importance of applying the Code of Ethics where appropriate.

13.8.8 **Pre-coaching material for coachees**

Before coaching takes place the coachee should be given a written notification showing the date, time and location that the training will take place along with the course's aims, objectives and timetable and any other relevant information.

13.9 **Creating notes, checklists and handouts**

The coach should create notes of activities and important points to be covered in the sequence in which they are to be delivered. This will bring order and coherence to the session, give it a strong sense of purpose and help to ensure that essential points are not missed. Valuably, the notes can form the basis for a checklist or a handout to be given to the coachee at the end of a session.

13.10 **The coaching session**

It is important that the coach helps the person being coached to feel comfortable, relaxed and able to fully participate in the training process without feeling embarrassed or unsettled.

Role play is an essential feature of a coaching session whereby different scenarios can be rehearsed, for example when practising new procedures, arrest techniques, stop and search methodology, report-writing skills, briefing and debriefing techniques, or computer-based skills. Trainer and trainee can swap roles to broaden experience. In most cases coaching will be on a one-to-one basis. However, in the specimen assertiveness scenario it would be possible to coach two persons together which would greatly assist with varied role-playing exercises.

13.10.1 **Using the interpersonal skills**

The coach will need to use their interpersonal skills to full advantage (see also Chapter 18, 'Communications—interpersonal skills'), for example by:

- Asking *Open questions* to avoid one-word answers when more is expected. They can be used to explore important points and test understanding. A coachee should be encouraged to ask open questions when seeking information, for example Why? How? What?

- *Clarifying* that information has been digested and understood by a coachee by regularly asking them to *summarise* their understanding of what has been said. The summary can then be verified or corrected. A coach should also *summarise* from time to time to put information into easily absorbable bundles of information.
- Noting *body language* to see if it accords with what is being said (or unsaid) by a coachee. Body language can indicate agreement, disagreement or puzzlement.
- Taking account of a coachee's *voice tone* which may indicate anger, scepticism, rejection or agreement. A coach should also be conscious of their own *body language* and *voice tone* so as not to show anger or irritation with a trainee which could damage a coaching session.
- Using *silence* at appropriate times to allow a coachee time to absorb information and ask questions. A coachee may become silent when reflecting upon what they have been told. However, long periods of silence may indicate a discontent which needs to be explored.

13.10.2 **Reinforcement**

Reinforcement is an important part of training as it helps to embed learning. Reinforcement can take place through summarising, repetition, handouts, student notes, on-the-job coaching, especially of new skills, and refresher training.

13.10.3 **Monitoring progress**

Newly found skills should be implemented as soon as practicable to instil confidence and avoid lapses in knowledge. Officers practising new procedures are likely to make mistakes which should be regarded as part of the learning process. It would be helpful if a sergeant or inspector could mentor a coachee themselves to check progress and make adjustments where necessary. If this is not possible then a trusted and able mentor could be employed in their stead. When full competence is established the coachee should be given credit for their achievement.

13.10.4 **Measuring success**

It is vital that after any training session checks are made to see if training objectives have been achieved and that a trainee is able to successfully apply new practices in the workplace.

The coaching specimen is built around a fictitious officer who is seen as impulsive and inclined to lose their temper quickly over even minor matters. Also, there is evidence that their behaviour is having a negative effect on colleagues, and that they are abusive towards members of the public, risking reputational damage. This means that after training an improvement in behaviours should be noticeable.

It should prove advantageous if a sergeant or inspector coach spent time watching a coachee perform over several operational instances, offering advice and encouragement where needed. Asking a coachee to comment on their own performance could produce an honest, self-critical response with their own suggestions about what they could do better.

However, with a sergeant or inspector watching a coachee may just be going through the motions and play-acting. Therefore, some corroborative evidence may be needed. For example, an officer's team mates may offer feedback at team meetings or at debriefings when ethical behaviour is a feature of discussions. Also, officers may choose at any time to drop disguised hints about the behaviours of others. All negative feedback should be investigated and standards enforced. Speaking to concerned members of the public and offering reassurance may be appropriate but should not be a substitute for legitimate disciplinary enquiries.

Lastly, it would be worth monitoring any complaints received from members of the public regarding behaviour.

It is a matter of judgement when formal coaching should come to an end.

13.10.5 **Feedback for the coach**

A sergeant or inspector coach should critically examine their own performance. A coachee should be encouraged to provide honest feedback on the coach's training delivery methods and the quality of the coaching session. A coach can ask for clarification of remarks made but avoid defensive responses. Feedback should be used to enhance future sessions for other officers.

KEY POINT—THE VALUE OF COACHING

Formal coaching should be part of an integrated training and development programme. It sits comfortably alongside the informal coaching that takes place on a daily basis. It can be time-consuming and should be carefully targeted at individuals who really need detailed help. Coaching can be directed to where there are operational deficiencies and it is good for skill and attitude development.

References and further reading

Culture at Work, 'The Grow Model Coaching Framework' <www.coachingculturEatwork.com/the-grow-model/> accessed 17 April 2025.

Doran, G. (1981), 'There's a SMART Way to Write Management Goals and Objectives', *Management Review* 7(11): 35–6.

Gilbert, A. and Whittleworth, K.J. (2009), *OSCAR Coaching Model: Simplifying Workplace Coaching Reality* (Monmouth: Worth Consulting).

O'Rourke-Henriette, A. (2024), Making Business Matter, 'Oscar Model: Coaching Skills for Leaders' *Making Business Matter* <www.makingbusinessmatter.co.uk/oscar-model//> accessed 17 April 2025.

Pearce, A. and Patent, Dr V. (2021), 'Everyone Can Learn to Coach! Coaching With the OSCAR Model' (Open University) <www.open.edu/ openlearn/health-sports-psychology/psychology/everyone-can-learn-coach-coaching-the-oscar-model> accessed 17 April 2025.

Whitmore, Sir J. (2019), *Coaching for Performance* (London: Brearley).

Wilson, C. (2020), *Performance Coaching: A Complete Guide to Best Practice Coaching and Training* (3rd edn, London: Kogan Page).

14

Leaders as agents of change (change management)

14.1 Why are leaders seen as change agents and why should they seek to manage change?

Leaders are change agents by virtue of what they are required to do. Their role involves looking at what is happening in the present but with an eye on the future. Leaders' activities are geared to tomorrow rather than today. In an ever-increasingly complex society, police leaders need to meet the demands and challenges of managing changes in social attitudes, public expectations, new laws, advances in technological innovation and new working practices. Leaders must inspire visionary changes so as to be able to compete, improve efficiency and effectiveness and provide an excellent public service.

Sometimes leaders initiate changes that have little significance, and the disruption changes cause may not be worth the effort expended upon them. Some changes are simply not well planned and that is why they fail, but on the negative side sometimes leaders bring about superficial or meaningless changes simply to advance their own reputations.

All change should be necessary, well considered and very well planned indeed.

14.2 What will happen if the need for change is ignored?

Structural change decided at the most senior level is quite common as changes are often required to accommodate the satisfactory completion of police aims, goals and objectives. This may mean, for example, creating new branches or dispensing with now out-of-date functions or adapting existing working practices to suit fresh initiatives. Strategic changes of this nature may involve quite large-scale movements of personnel. *It is worth emphasising that it is absolutely vital that policing structures change in order to meet changes in the ways in which the public are policed.*

Strategic goals and objectives are executed at a tactical, operational level using SMART objectives that exert discipline over the change process (see also Chapter 10, 'Planning').

However, change is not just initiated at a strategic level. It also occurs at any level of the police service even with individuals working on their own carrying out particular functions.

Sergeants and inspectors, especially those leading teams carrying out day-to-day operational policing duties, need to constantly monitor efficiency and effectiveness in order to make changes both large and small to meet modern policing demands.

If any genuine change at any level of a police force is ignored, the consequences may be catastrophic, resulting perhaps in:

- major public dissatisfaction arising from outdated or irrelevant policing practices and a failure to modernise and quicken and improve operational policing methodology;

- police staff dissatisfaction, frustration and demotivation caused by a sense of growing inefficiency and irrelevance, and a failure to modernise to meet ever-changing political and social demands;
- the removal of chief police officers and an enforced reorganisation with a resultant loss of control over progress and a loss of prestige.

14.3 How do people react to change?

The leader should be aware from the very outset that managing change is not easy and it will test leadership skills to the utmost. Persuading people to accept change is particularly hard, but perhaps the most difficult part of change is managing the effect it has on people and the ways in which they respond to what are often seen as life-changing impositions.

It may be helpful for the leader to consider that change has a recognised cycle that needs to be understood so that the leader can manage change dynamics successfully. Usefully, Heller (1998) reveals the stages of change which are listed below: however, it should be remembered that different people are likely to act in different ways, and the cycle is simply a useful, thought-provoking guide. The stages are:

- stability at the point of change;
- inability to act;
- denial;
- anger;
- bargaining;
- depression;
- testing;
- acceptance.

Whilst some people may accept change quite readily, it can have really dramatic and disturbing results on others. Even those who welcome change will find that it has an unsettling element to it.

All stages of change have to be managed so that change takes place as smoothly as possible. Anger and depression are very disturbing features. These emotions as well as the consequences of the other stages will require the leader to exhibit communication skills of the highest order to deal with all the issues and concerns that may arise.

14.3.1 Resistance to change

Drawing upon and adding to observations made by Armstrong (2009), the reasons why people resist change are:

- *the shock of the new*—disturbing the status quo and comfortable, established and familiar routines and practices, working conditions and perhaps even

travel, hours of duty and places of residence. Additionally, people may distrust the reasons for change and assertions that change will benefit them as well as the organisation;
- *economic fears*—worries of perhaps a decline in wages, increased travel costs and concerns about job retention;
- *inconvenience*—suspicions that changes will disrupt life and make things more difficult than they are;
- *uncertainty*—unless addressed this may cause anxiety and all manner of different emotions and if not managed properly it may result in low morale, instability and inefficiency;
- *symbolic fears*—a loss of perceived important benefits such as a loss of status or superior office accommodation;
- *threat to interpersonal relationships*—a lot of people place a high value on working relationships and who they work with including team colleagues;
- *threat to status or skill*—fear of demotion in terms of grade, rank or prestige and the loss of hard-earned skills;
- *competence fears*—worries that individuals will be unable to manage fresh demands for doing things differently and that the need for further skills and competence will be difficult to meet.

Importantly, Woodward (1968) mentions that there is a tendency when dealing with resistance to change to imply that management is always rational when making changes and that employees are irrational in obstructing it. However, individuals are unlikely or unwilling to support changes that yield no benefits for them or even bring disadvantages. Woodward says: 'The interests of the organization and the individual do not always coincide.'

Woodward's observations mean that where the organisation's and the individual's views do not coincide, leaders must make every effort to bridge the gap between the two positions. This may involve making compromises and giving concessions. In reality, if an individual cannot reconcile him- or herself to changes he or she may wish to leave the organisation or find it necessary to do so.

14.3.2 Some positive aspects of change for individuals

However, although many people may fear change and the uncertainty it brings, others either welcome it or are prepared to work with it to benefit from the advantages it may offer. For example, individuals may feel that:

- change is necessary and desirable and that old, stale and conservative ways of doing things should be abandoned in favour of a new and exciting way forward;
- change may bring promotion, extra remuneration and increased status;
- change could offer opportunities to build upon existing skill bases and enhance competence so as to be able to achieve even higher ambitions.

14.3.3 **Attempts to sabotage change**

It is worth bearing in mind that people who cannot see the worth of change may deliberately sabotage plans for its success. A destructive, internal guerrilla war may break out and spread disaffection and resistance. It is commonly known that guerrillas tend to operate in places that are largely inaccessible to the forces they face. In the workplace, that could be the canteen or places that leaders do not normally bother to frequent—a recreation facility, for example. In these circumstances, it is up to the leader to halt the spread of disaffection by frequenting 'inaccessible' places (which should be frequented anyway) and entering into friendly discussions with all concerned. Also, sergeant and inspector leaders should openly acknowledge worries and issues and seek to address them by inviting thoughts and views on impending change.

KEY POINT—RESISTANCE TO CHANGE

Leaders should accept that it is not unnatural for team members to resist change with the uncertainties it brings to an extremely important aspect of their lives—their work and livelihoods. Not all change is well thought out or indeed even necessary. Further, even desirable, well-thought-out and well-planned change can be tarnished by memories of former inappropriate and damaging change where promises were made and not kept. It is, therefore, up to the sergeant and inspector leader to acknowledge and deal with individual concerns and to fulfil commitments made to team members. Should commitments not be kept for genuine reasons, then honest explanations should be offered to those concerned. With change, success depends upon the leader's personal integrity and the full involvement of all those concerned with it.

14.4 **Creating a change plan—what does a leader have to consider to ensure that change is implemented as efficiently and as effectively as possible?**

Plans for change should include how the process itself will be managed. In other words, although the implementation of practical elements is obviously very necessary and important, how will staff reactions and involvement be managed? How will communications flow between those implementing change and those being subjected to change? How will further ideas and improvements be solicited and how will errors be identified and resolved? Finally, how will plans be implemented, monitored and measured?

14.4.1 Thurley's approaches to managing change

Thurley (1979) considers that there are five ways in which change can be brought about.

(1) *Directive*—simply using autocratic, management power to impose change without consultation.

Whilst on occasions people do have to be directed to carry out certain tasks, this way is likely to create real resentment in the workforce and stifle workplace contributions and innovation.

(2) *Bargained*—using a democratic approach and cooperating with the workforce through negotiation, which produces compromise and agreement.

Bargaining in a democratic way will help to secure support for change. Where people are able to make contributions they usually try to make them work because they have ownership in them. However, compromise could damage a leader's vision and tough decisions may have to be made to retain important principles.

(3) *Hearts and minds*—this involves the difficult task of trying to change the values, attitudes and beliefs (which may be entrenched) of the workforce by securing their commitment to a shared vision.

Changing attitudes and beliefs can be very hard. Therefore, the planner who adopts this method needs credible plans that people can 'buy into' and the very best communication skills to convey ideas and objectives. It may be difficult but many plans do require changes in attitudes, which drive behaviours (e.g. changes in police attitudes towards members of the public or sections of the public) and planners will need to take difficulties into account. It seems that 'hearts and minds' may or may not include staff participation.

(4) *Analytical*—bringing change about in a highly structured, purposeful way through diagnosing, analysing and creating objectives and evaluating results.

There is no doubt that this approach is effective but it should not be 'cold-blooded' and would benefit from staff participation.

(5) *Action-based*—this approach relies on creating an understanding that a problem exists. Then there is a seeking of possible solutions, some by 'trial and error'. This, in turn, leads to a clearer, shared awareness of the problem and likely solutions or some idea of how to proceed.

This way is probably fairly typical of what happens on many occasions in the workplace. It is unstructured and may be wasteful of time and resources.

It is possible to combine some of the elements from all of these five ways of managing change although a 'trial and error' way of finding solutions is not particularly desirable.

However, in a sense a leader does have to win 'hearts and minds' when bringing about change given that it is a leader's job to set the 'vision' and inspire followers to share in it. And bargaining and negotiating are important. Additionally, an analytical approach is desirable and at times directions have to be given, especially when change is stalling.

14.4.2 **Lewin's three-stage model**

Lewin (1951) offers advice on managing change using a three-stage model. The stages are 'unfreezing', 'changing' and 'refreezing':

- *unfreezing*—involves altering the current status quo or equilibrium which underpins existing attitudes and behaviours, dealing with the issues and threats that people perceive change brings and motivating people to accept change thereby restoring the natural state of equilibrium;
- *changing*—necessitates developing new ways (responses) of doing things based on new information (research);
- *refreezing*—embedding the change by getting people to introduce the new ways (responses) into the personalities of those involved.

14.4.3 **Lewin's Field Force Analysis model**

Lewin (1951) also offers a useful framework for change in the form of his Field Force Analysis model.

Lewin suggests that there are both 'driving' and 'restraining' forces that may affect the transition from the current to the desired state.

- *Driving forces* are the positive factors that should be clearly identified as beneficial to change plans. Driving forces might include, for example, the existence of a highly motivated, successful, well-trained team eager to take on new challenges. If possible, driving forces should be further strengthened. In this instance, the team could be involved in the entire planning process even taking on some of the issues for resolution themselves. They could also be further trained to take on impending new responsibilities.
- *Restraining forces* are those negative forces that should be listed and addressed as possible harming factors. However, the important thing is that efforts should be made to make negative forces positive. For instance, team members may appear to be demoralised and very apprehensive of change. This is where the good leader steps in and finds out why people are apprehensive and demotivated. Then, after addressing and allaying fears, the leader may decide to use individual skills and talents to aid and support change plans. Also, people can be involved in the problem-solving and decision-making processes. The leader may reinforce this process by offering praise where it is due to show that people are indeed valued for their contributions.

Field Force Analysis reminds the leader that he or she has to consciously move from an existing state to another different state where new behaviours and procedures will have to be firmly established. The model is useful too in reminding leaders that they should harness positive forces in favour of the change while trying to mitigate or eliminate negative restraining forces. Doing away with negative aspects is also part of risk management (see Chapter 10, 'Planning', section 10.2.2).

14.5 What are the helpful and positive change agents?

Change plans can be assisted by recognising useful change agents and some of these are listed below.

- Change requires *commitment from the top* and strong, purposeful, visionary leadership. If leaders lack commitment, why should followers be committed?
- Successful *change needs clarity of purpose* (achieved through commonly understood aims, goals and objectives) and people need to be made fully aware in honest and truthful terms of the state they are changing to and the distinct benefits it will bring.
- *Team harmony and synergy* coupled with proven efficiency and effectiveness will greatly aid change. People with positive views on change are an asset in their own right as they encourage positivity in others. Where harmony and synergy is lacking, a leader must endeavour to create it through involvement and participation.
- Effective change requires *very good communications* and a communication plan, which should be developed by the leader. People need to be reassured about the change processes and have any fears allayed. Importantly, they need to be told what the change plans entail and how they will be implemented. Additionally, they need to be kept up to date with progress by the passing on of relevant information.

  Communication is not the same as information (important though that may be) which tends to be one-way. Change communication involves genuine consultation, listening to other points of view and ideas and taking them into account and, where appropriate, implementing them. Participation helps to secure good suggestions and binds people into the ownership of change. This participation should extend from the start of change plans to their finish. Cooperation is absolutely essential.

  Communication also involves the giving and receiving of feedback. The leader should welcome feedback as a means to judge how plans are progressing and what alterations and improvements, if any, need to be made.

14.6 What does a leader need to do when plans have been put into effect?

When change plans have been implemented, sergeant and inspector leaders should continue to inspire people to complete tasks and objectives and assist them to move from the status quo to the new situation. He or she should deal with any personal or team worries during the transition and also monitor progress, solve problems and make adjustments where necessary. Team members should be encouraged to identify good practice and difficulties and make suggestions for improvement where appropriate. Where team members have helped to implement successful changes, they should be rewarded with praise to show that their efforts have been appreciated.

14.7 What should happen if people will not go along with necessary change?

Where people have difficulty in accepting change because of personal circumstances, every effort should be made to overcome their fears and apprehensions. This may involve relatively simple management interventions such as altering hours of duty or finding people other positions within the organisation.

Some people will not accept change because it does not, for whatever reason, suit them. Sometimes they will leave a changing organisation of their own volition. There is nothing wrong with this. What they have found is that they are no longer suited to their work and they want to move on to gain continuing job satisfaction elsewhere.

Where people resist change and will not support it but wish to remain in the police service they must be treated fairly. As long as they do what they are paid to do efficiently and effectively, an employer can have no complaints. However, where an individual's efficiency levels drop below accepted standards they lay themselves open to corrective action. This is a normal workplace response to people who are ineffective for a variety of reasons. Nonetheless, employers, leaders and managers must always act with propriety and decency, and within the law.

References and further reading

Armstrong, M. (2009), Handbook of Human Resource Management Practice (11th edn, London: Kogan Page).

Heller, R. (1998), Managing Change (London: Dorling Kindersley).

Lewin, K. (1951), Field Theory in Social Science (New York: Harper & Row).

Thurley, K. (1979), Supervision A Reappraisal (Oxford: Heinemann).

Woodward, J. (1968), 'Resistance to Change', Management International Review 8: 137–43.

15

Motivation

15.1 What is motivation and why should leaders be able to motivate those who they lead?

Motivation is an ingrained feature of our lives. To be able to achieve our goals we have to create impulses to act. Sometimes creating an impulse is easy because we enjoy the activity that leads to a satisfactory outcome. However, on occasion we have to do things that we do not particularly want to do; nevertheless, we do still act because the objective is regarded as worthwhile. For instance, we may not like studying hard to pass a promotion examination with its negative family and social downsides. Nonetheless, we may still persevere because the reward of a new job and status is worth the effort. It seems clear, therefore, that people are motivated when they can see that the objective or goal is worthwhile. Where this is not the case, it may prove difficult to get someone willingly to complete a task or objective.

Sergeant and inspector leaders need to be able to maximise the contributions that team members are able to make to objectives. In general, they are likely to have at their disposal people who are motivated to serve the public. If this is not the case, then an individual may be in the wrong team or the wrong job. What a team leader needs to do is find out what motivates individuals and where their strengths lie so that these may be utilised to advantage. The leader needs also to develop a team member's latent abilities and ensure where necessary that any comparative weaknesses are compensated for by other team members with complementary talents. It is important in this regard that the development of individuals should encompass, wherever possible, their own aspirations and ambitions.

Seeking to motivate others is a difficult matter because there are a great many motivators. The task is made more complex by the fact that all people are different and do not always want the same things. Additionally, as motivation is not confined to the workplace this means that demotivating factors may arise from the home or elsewhere.

When people feel motivated and enjoy their work and carrying out the tasks they have to perform this is likely to help team harmony and synergy. This, in turn, should result in the efficient discharge of responsibilities and increased public satisfaction.

15.2 How does a leader try to motivate those that he or she leads?

A leader who wishes to maintain a highly motivated workforce should be aware of motivation theory. This is because it can encourage appropriate interventions. However, theory should not be slavishly followed. It is essential that the sergeant and inspector leader should remain sensitive to the need to be imaginative to satisfy individual aspirations. Therefore, treating theory flexibly is likely to give rise to different and perhaps more appropriate responses to individual needs.

The really essential thing that the leader should know about motivation is that it is an individual, personal condition. For example, something which may motivate one person may not motivate another. Often an individual's motivators may be obvious but in others they need to be established.

In practice, in the workplace the leader should consider meeting with each individual team member to find out what it is that they like doing and why. This consultation is likely to be appreciated in its own right. However, more importantly it is likely to reveal what it is that motivates individuals and what they have to offer in terms of skills and competence. The process is also likely to reveal how competence can be further developed to individual and team advantage.

KEY POINT—MOTIVATION IS A PERSONAL THING

Sergeant and inspector leaders need to remember that all people are not the same and that although there are common motivators this is not always the case. Additionally, leaders have to be aware of imposing their own motivators on others who may well resent this and reject them. It is up to the leader to identify personal motivators for the good of the individual, the team and the public.

15.2.1 **Intrinsic and extrinsic motivation**

There are two types of motivation—intrinsic and extrinsic. (See also Armstrong 2009.)

Intrinsic motivation comes from within oneself—it is self-generated. It includes, for example, searching for work that leads to job satisfaction especially if the work is interesting and challenging. Job satisfaction is enhanced when an individual has freedom to:

- manage his or her own work without constant and unnecessary interference;
- take on responsibility and the authority to make decisions in order to complete tasks without undue reference back to the leader;
- learn from mistakes in a manner which benefits the individual concerned, the team and future tasks;
- look for opportunities and responsibilities that offer prospects for self-development or advancement.

Ambitions that rely on self-motivation have the built-in drive that may well lead to success. People driven by intrinsic factors are likely to have a clear view of what they want and a fair idea of how to achieve their aims and ambitions.

Extrinsic motivation, unlike intrinsic motivation, relies on the application of external factors administered by other parties. Extrinsic motivators might include, for instance, increases in pay, praise, leave, benefits and offers of promotion. Strangely, extrinsic motivators also include criticism and disciplinary interventions. On occasion, people need to be reminded that they are paid for their work and that efficiency is a requirement of their job. However, although enforced compliance can lead to satisfactory work levels it may also cause resentment and workplace disruption. Extrinsic factors may be fleeting in effect because they are not generated from within oneself.

15.2.2 **Instrumentality theory**

Instrumentality theory (Taylor 1911) suggests that people at work are motivated by a 'stick and carrot' approach. This is where individuals are rewarded for good work and penalised for poor work. Used crudely, this approach is not satisfactory. However, the leader should be aware that 'reward' whether monetary or in some other form is a feature of the workplace—and so is the application of misconduct procedures where necessary.

15.2.3 **Reinforcement theory**

We learn much of what we know through experiencing events for ourselves. Further, we are able to learn from both positive and negative situations. Hull's reinforcement theory (1951) suggests that when we are aware of what leads to a particular success we are encouraged to repeat successful actions in similar circumstances. However, when we fail to complete work successfully we should review what went wrong so as not to repeat mistakes in the future.

15.2.4 **Giving praise**

Giving praise for work well done also seems to fall within Hull's notion that 'success encourages success'. Praise offers recipients an acknowledgement of good performance. This recognition is usually well received in people who often wish to be appreciated for the work that they do. However, it is important that leaders explain why the praise is being offered. Individuals usually know what they are being praised for but sometimes they do not, especially if they have been dealing with a long-term task. Therefore, the leader should make clear what it is that a recipient has done to deserve praise. Once an individual knows what it is that he or she is being rewarded for, they are likely to repeat good practice in similar situations. Additionally, praise helps to build up self-esteem and confidence and encourages a 'can do' approach.

All praise is linked to the sincerity and truthfulness of the giver. Praise should not be given unless it is well deserved otherwise it may be devalued in the mind of the receiver. Additionally, if the receiver lacks respect for the giver then he or she is unlikely to value the praise, which may appear worthless.

15.2.5 **Blaming people**

The opposite to 'praise' is 'blame' and blame is an undesirable feature in the workplace. As a team member, imagine receiving nothing but blame in the workplace. It would lead to low morale and be immensely damaging to business efficiency. When mistakes are made a learning process should be commenced through the use of honest feedback.

15.2.6 **Maslow's hierarchy of needs**

Maslow's hierarchy of needs (1954) is perhaps the best-known motivation theory. The theory is attractive because it has a 'common sense' and 'natural' feel about it. However, although Maslow's model is very useful in that it relates to fundamental needs, it should be treated only as a guide and as a means to stimulate thought and then appropriate action.

Maslow sets out five levels of need in ascending form from the lowest (physiological) to the highest (self-actualisation) (see also Figure 15.1):

Figure 15.1 Hierarchy of needs (Maslow 1954)

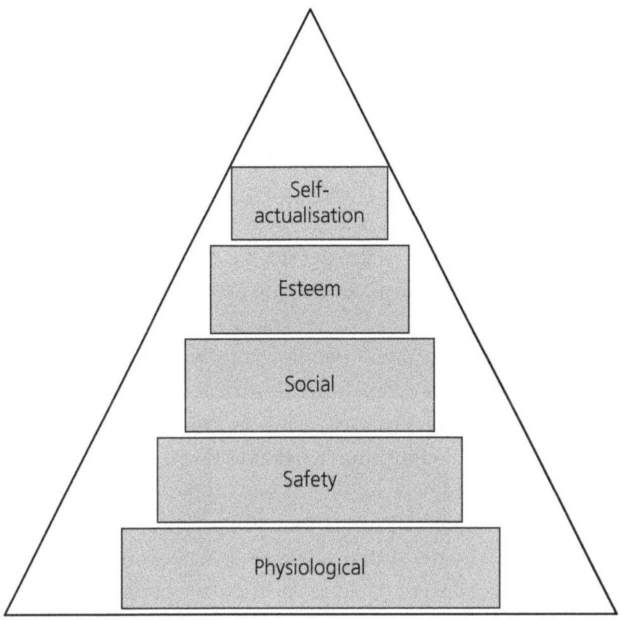

- *physiological needs* (primary)—the need for food, water, warmth, shelter and sleep;
- *safety needs*—the need to feel physically and psychologically safe and socially and financially secure;
- *social needs*—the need to feel loved and valued coupled with a sense of belonging;

- *esteem needs*—the need to be able to be perceived as competent and to achieve success and to be recognised and appreciated by others;
- *self-actualisation* needs (or self-fulfilment)—a complex state but perhaps self-actualisation may be summarised by the need to achieve one's full potential.

Maslow suggested that an individual had to satisfy basic needs before moving upwards through the hierarchy to 'self-actualisation'.

Crooks and Stein (1988) point out that Maslow has been criticised for his hierarchy where one need follows from another and a lower need has to be achieved before a higher need can be satisfied. The implication here is that the hierarchy is too rigid and that it is, if anything, much less orderly. Additionally, critics including Wahba and Bridwell (1976) seem to think that his concept of 'self-actualisation' is too complex to define in operational conditions.

It is worth discussing Maslow's hierarchical structure further. The strict order of ascent may in some cases be true, but the hierarchy does perhaps appear to be too rigid. For example, some people may pay little regard to 'social needs', being much more concerned with 'esteem needs'. Additionally, in times of distress it is conceivable that a person at the 'self-actualisation' stage may experience problems with, say, money difficulties and then drop down to 'safety' and 'physiological needs'. Nevertheless, regardless of the criticism of Maslow it is possible to develop some ideas from his theory that may still prove useful in the workplace.

To satisfy 'physiological needs' (e.g. water and food) and 'safety needs' (e.g. purchasing or renting a home), an individual needs to work so as to be able to earn money to purchase groceries and buy a home. Therefore, money is a primary motivator but to a lesser or greater degree depending upon an individual's perceived requirements. See also Armstrong (2009) for a deeper discussion on this matter.

It would appear also that some people go to work just to satisfy these two basic needs, with the money also funding other motivators that exist beyond the work environment. For instance, an individual may run a guide or scout troop or spend time rock-climbing or become deeply engaged in sport. There is a danger that such people may be seen as 'uncommitted' in the workplace because, for example, they will not work extra hours of duty. But they, in their turn, may see people who perform overtime (especially unpaid) hours as foolish. Here we have a typical clash of motivators since one person goes to work simply to earn money to satisfy basic living requirements and non-work activities and the other gains satisfaction not only from working but also the challenges and rewards to be gained in the work situation. Both circumstances have to be managed by sergeant and inspector leaders because workplace clashes may occur and people have to learn to respect each other's motivators.

Some people with 'social needs' may not, for example, aspire to rank and status ('esteem needs'). These individuals go to work because of their desire to be with others—they enjoy the interaction with and the company of other people. However, while some people appear to regard working with colleagues as a high priority, other individuals may be motivated by status and have little regard for seemingly unnecessary social interaction. The sergeant and inspector leader needs to be aware that removing a team member who enjoys social interaction to a lone role may cause great distress to the person concerned.

15.2.7 **Two-factor theory**

Hertzberg's two-factor theory (1957)—(see also Cole 1996), has similarities with Maslow's work and despite some criticism it appears to be equally well known and regarded. Once again, his observations need not be followed slavishly but should be used to stimulate thought and helpful responses in the workplace.

Hertzberg's research into workplace satisfaction involved some 200 engineers and accountants. He concluded that results could be placed into two distinct categories: those factors that were inclined to lead to job satisfaction (*motivators*) and those that frequently resulted in dissatisfaction (*hygiene factors*). The experiment was repeated in 1968 with manual and clerical workers with similar results.

Motivators linked directly to work content (over which police sergeant and inspector leaders have some control) included:

- achievement;
- recognition;
- work itself;
- responsibility;
- advancement;
- growth.

Hygiene factors (could cause dissatisfaction) related to the work environment rather than work content included:

- company policy and administration;
- supervision;
- work conditions;
- salary;
- relationships with supervisors, peers and subordinates;
- personal life;
- status;
- security.

Opsahl and Dunnette (1966) criticise Hertzberg for his research methods and also because he did not establish the relationship between satisfaction and performance. Neither did he distinguish between 'satisfiers' and improved productivity. However, Hertzberg is useful for drawing a distinction between intrinsic and extrinsic factors and in stimulating the mind to think about motivation in the work environment. That said, it is important to remember that external social or home factors may have a huge bearing on how a person feels and behaves in the workplace.

15.2.8 **Goal theory**

Goal theory (Latham and Locke 1979) put in simple terms suggests that people respond well to set goals especially if they are of a challenging nature. Motivation is likely to be increased where individuals have a say in the setting of goals. Additionally, support in achieving goals and feedback on progress are likely to increase motivation. Feedback enables growth and self-development and paves the way to even higher goals.

15.2.9 **Motivation—leadership intervention**

The sensitive sergeant and inspector leader must remain alert to individual needs and try to respond accordingly, taking into account motivational theory but also the thought processes that the theories generate. The leader is likely to have the authority to make 'managerial' interventions which not only help the individuals concerned but also aid the job to be done. It is important in this regard that people should be consulted about their needs. Leaders need to remain aware that they will be unable to sell their vision of the future to demotivated personnel. This will be detrimental to all concerned, including the public that the police serve.

Police sergeant and inspector leaders need to look at the motivators and hygiene factors carefully because they can have a direct bearing upon many of them by making leadership interventions. For example, a leader can:

- endeavour to make work as varied and interesting as possible for team members;
- involve people in the setting of their workplace objectives, allowing them to comment, point out difficulties and suggest ways of progressing ambitions;
- provide the means for personal growth and advancement for individuals by creating self-development plans, coaching sessions and by offering responsibility through delegation;
- recognise good work by giving praise and encouragement;
- make sure that prejudice and discrimination have no place in the police service;
- try to make improvements to the work environment where necessary;
- ensure that policies and directions are clear and easily understood or, where they are not, make appropriate requests for clarification of content;
- offer sound ethical and professional leadership and provide the best possible communication system to encompass team members and others;

- be aware of individuals' status needs and requirements for personal growth whilst remaining aware of any welfare needs.

15.3 How will a leader know that he or she has a motivated team of followers?

A well-motivated team and well-motivated individuals usually show signs of enthusiasm and commitment to completing tasks successfully. Also, the successful completion of tasks and objectives on time and to budget is a significant sign of highly motivated team members. However, whilst a team can seem to be motivated there may well remain individuals within it who feel demoralised. Motivation can change from day to day depending upon the circumstances impinging on individual lives within and outside work. Poor leadership and a failure to tackle problems may lead to widespread demotivation. Therefore, an effective and sensitive leader must do everything in his or her power to maintain high levels of morale at all times. Gentle inquiry and encouraging honest and regular opinions and feedback should help greatly in this regard.

KEY POINT—FLUCTUATING MOTIVATION LEVELS

Motivation levels are likely to fluctuate according to personal circumstances both within and outside the workplace. This means that the sergeant and inspector leader must remain constantly sensitive to changing conditions within the team. To this end, communication between the leader and individual team members is very important and so is sounding out concerns and problems at team meetings.

References and further reading

Armstrong, M. (2009), *Handbook of Human Resource Management Practice* (11th edn, London: Kogan Page).

Cole, G. A. (1996), *Management Theory & Practice (5th edn, London: Continuum; (used with permission of Cengage Learning* EMEA Ltd)).

Crooks, B. and Stein J. (1988), *Psychology: Science, Behaviour and Life* (New York: Holt, Rinehart & Winston).

Hertzberg, F. (1968), 'One More Time: How Do You Motivate Employees?', *Harvard Business Review* (Jan–Feb): 53–62.

Hertzberg, F. W. with Mausner, B. and Synderman, B. (1957), *The Motivation to Work* (New York: Wiley).

Hull, C. (1951), *Essentials of Behaviour* (New Haven, CT: Yale University Press).

Latham, G. and Locke, R. (1979), 'Goal Setting—A Motivational Technique That Works', *Organizational Dynamics* (Autumn): 68–80.
Maslow, A. (1954), *Motivation and Personality* (New York: Harper & Row).
Opsahl, R. C. and Dunnette, M. D. (1966), 'The Role of Financial Compensation in Individual Motivation', *Psychological Bulletin* 56: 94–118.
Taylor, F. W. (1911), *Principles of Scientific Management* (New York: Harper).
Wahba, M. A. and Bridwell L. G. (1976), *Organizational Behaviour and Human Performance—Maslow Reconsidered: A Review of Research on the Need Hierarchy Theory* (Salt Lake City, UT: Academic Press).

16

Misconduct and discipline

16.1 Introduction

Chapter 15 on motivation shows that discipline is an extrinsic motivator although not a particularly good one because it is imposed.

Disciplined behaviour and operating rules are necessary if an organisation is to fulfil its ambitions and prevent it from becoming an anarchic mess, with people drawing upon different interpretations as to what is needed. Most people will happily follow the rules and need little guidance because they have a self-imposed discipline. Others, however, may lack self-discipline and can cause real problems for an organisation. Having a discipline code guides behaviours and compliance with directives, with non-compliance being strictly dealt with up to the point of dismissal.

In simple terms, the police service sets out the ethical rules and guidance for behaviour and the forms which policing takes, and the law empowers and limits police activities. Most police officers and police personnel join the police force to serve the public honestly and to the best of their abilities. However, some officers may deviate from the norm and get involved in criminality and totally unacceptable misbehaviours. That is why discipline codes carry sanctions designed to enforce compliance, correct behaviours or even dismiss officers from the service. Disciplinary action, as well as being remedial, includes a training element whereby people can learn from mistakes made.

This chapter lightly but seriously explores misconduct and performance matters and it is not meant to amount to an in-depth study of disciplinary issues. Further, the chapter does not discuss complaints against police under Schedule 3 of the Police Reform Act 2023 and the Police (Complaints and Misconduct) Regulations 2024 or a police officer's direct involvement in criminal acts, although many complaints and most, if not all, criminal acts will include misconduct issues. The Independent Office of Police Conduct has issued a Statutory Guidance to the Police Complaints System (2020). Nor does the chapter cover action to be taken when individuals raise grievances about the way they have been treated in the workplace. Usefully, advice on grievances is given in the ACAS Code of Practice on Disciplinary and Grievance Procedures (2015) issued as well as the ACAS Guide to Discipline and Grievances at Work (2020) and Reviewed 2024) which was issued by ACAS to supplement the Code of Practice. Police officers are deemed to be employees only for certain causes of action. However, leaders and managers dealing with grievances would nonetheless be well advised to follow the Code, although most if not all police forces are likely to have their own robust grievance procedures.

16.2 Exercising discipline

For sergeants and inspectors, managing disciplinary matters on any scale is always difficult and requires courage and resolution. All officers, of any rank, need to be fully conversant with what is expected of them by way of public expectations of their ethical behaviours, disciplinary standards and procedures, and what will happen to them if they fail to conform to imposed requirements.

Most people work diligently and conscientiously and cause few problems for their leaders or the police service. However, on occasions some people behave badly towards others, including colleagues or members of the public, or are a disruptive presence in the workplace. Similarly, for example, team members nearly always willingly comply with directions given by sergeants and inspectors without being ordered to carry out a particular act. But others, for a variety of reasons, seek to challenge authority for their own ends. Weak leadership tends to invite such challenges.

Experience is likely to show that where a leader or manager acts fairly he or she will gain the open or tacit support of the entire workforce. Most people perform well and they resent it when others behave improperly or are lazy and incompetent. In the final analysis, it is a leader's job to ensure that people comply with laid-down standards and procedures.

Taking misconduct or disciplinary action against a colleague is the hardest part of any leader's job. However, on occasions disciplinary action is unavoidable because of the offender's behaviour and the effect it has on his or her work, the performance of others or even members of the public. Regardless of difficulty, misconduct matters must be dealt with promptly and professionally.

KEY POINT—CONSEQUENCES OF FAILING TO DEAL WITH MISCONDUCT

A failure by a leader to deal with misconduct issues promptly and professionally can have dire consequences and may result in, for example:

- a continuance of the misconduct and the encouragement of misbehaviour by others who think that they can get away with offending;
- damage to team efficiency and team motivation to succeed with their objectives;
- a loss of respect for the leader which may encourage disdain for them and disobedience;
- damage to the police service's reputation and support for policing.

16.3 In the case of a misconduct inquiry what does the leader have to do?

Sergeant and inspector leaders should make themselves fully aware of what they have to do should a misconduct or disciplinary matter arise (sometimes without immediate prior warning). Lack of knowledge could lead to undue delay in tackling issues, continuance of a problem, loss of evidence, embarrassment and reputational damage for the leader.

Sergeant and inspector leaders also have to appreciate that when they enter into misconduct proceedings their own actions will be under close scrutiny to establish what preventive action they could or should have taken. Additionally, it is of the utmost importance that misconduct proceedings are conducted fairly and properly and according to recognised procedures. Failure to follow procedural requirements could result in a case collapsing simply through a lack of competence and perceived fairness.

As well as knowing about what to do themselves when misconduct matters occur, sergeants and inspectors also have a duty to ensure that those who work under them are fully briefed on force misconduct policies and procedures. Being aware of the Standards of Professional Behaviour is particularly important in this regard (see section 16.5). Regularly refreshing memories during training sessions would be helpful.

16.4 Legislation and other professional considerations

Dealing with police misconduct has become very complicated indeed and is dealt with under a bewildering number of directions and regulations.

Police misconduct matters are dealt with, for instance, under:

- The Police Regulations 2003—the Regulations cover important matters such as:
  (1) restrictions on the private lives of members;
  (2) the business interests of members;
  (3) the discharge of probationers;
  (4) a duty to carry out lawful orders; and
  (5) testing for substance misuse.
- The Police (Performance) Regulations 2020—include matters of police performance and attendance for duty.
- The Police (Conduct) (Amendment) Regulations (2020)—set out the cases which the Director General of the Independent Office for Police Conduct can present in a misconduct hearing or an accelerated misconduct hearing.
- The Police (Conduct) (Amendment) Regulations 2024—the Regulations have an Explanatory Memorandum noting that chief officers should have a greater part to play in disciplinary proceedings, including dismissals. Proceedings for chief superintendent or below should be chaired by chief officers. Responsibility can be delegated to a senior officer, former senior officer or police staff member of equivalent grade.

Where more senior officers are concerned, for example chief officer or Deputy Commissioner, the chair will be His Majesty's Chief Inspector of Constabulary or a nominated His Majesty's Inspector. For independence and fairness, panels will have two independent panel members and an independent legally qualified adviser.

- A Home Office publication offers help under the heading *Home Office Guidance—Conduct, Efficiency and Effectiveness: Statutory Guidance on Professional Standards, Performance and Integrity in Policing* (Version 1.0 – February 2020).
- The College of Policing advises that Professional Standards Departments can play an important role in the maintenance of public trust and confidence which can be undermined by a failure to vet and manage misconduct and complaints or investigate counter-corruption activities effectively. It is, therefore, essential that such issues are dealt with openly and robustly in accordance with the Code of Ethics. Professional Standards include the following areas: counter-corruption, vetting, complaints and misconduct governance.
- The College of Policing Guidance for Ethical and Professional Behaviour in Policing and Guidance for Outcomes for Police Misconduct Proceedings are helpful.

16.5 Standards of professional and ethical behaviour

It is important that police leaders and managers and their staff should know what is required of them in terms of laid-down standards of professional and ethical behaviour. The Home Office Statutory Guidance on Professional Standards, Performance and Integrity in Policing, published in accordance with ss 87 and 87A of the Police Act 1996, lists Standards of Professional Behaviour as they are set out in Schedule 2 to the Conduct Regulations 2020:

> **Honesty and Integrity**
> Police officers are honest, act with integrity and do not compromise or abuse their position.
>
> **Authority, Respect and Courtesy**
> Police officers act with self-control and tolerance, treating members of the public and colleagues with respect and courtesy.
>
> Police officers do not abuse their powers or authority and respect the rights of individuals.
>
> **Equality and Diversity**
> Police officers act with fairness and impartiality. They do not discriminate unlawfully or unfairly.
>
> **Use of Force**
> Police officers only use force to the extent that it is necessary, proportionate and reasonable in all the circumstances.
>
> **Orders and Instructions**
> Police officers only give and carry out lawful orders and instructions.
>
> Police officers abide by police regulations, force policies and lawful orders.

Duties and Responsibilities
Police officers are diligent in the exercise of their duties and responsibilities.

Police officers have a responsibility to give appropriate cooperation during investigations, inquiries and formal proceedings, participating openly and professionally in line with the expectations of a police officer when identified as a witness.

Confidentiality
Police officers treat information with respect and access or disclose it only in the proper course of police duties.

Fitness for Duty
Police officers when on duty or presenting themselves for duty are fit to carry out their responsibilities.

Discreditable Conduct
Police officers behave in a manner which does not discredit the police service or undermine public confidence in it, whether on or off duty.

Police officers report any action taken against them for a criminal offence, any conditions imposed on them by a court or the receipt of any penalty notice.

Challenging and Reporting Improper Conduct
Police officers report, challenge or take action against the conduct of colleagues which has fallen below the Standards of Professional Behaviour.

These categories are expanded upon in the College of Policing's Code of Ethics (see also Chapter 5).

16.6 Misconduct—Home Office guidance

Often transgressions are of a very minor nature and require no more than a discussion between the leader and the person concerned. Nevertheless, that person should be aware of what they have done wrong, the consequences of their actions and what they need to do to return to the desired standard of performance.

The importance of the Home Office guidance makes it deserving of the close attention of sergeants and inspectors for here it is only possible to cover some of the important points it makes regarding disciplinary matters:

- The three main purposes for police disciplinary proceedings are to (i) maintain public confidence in, and the reputation of, the police service, (ii) uphold high standards in policing and deter misconduct, and (iii) protect the public.
- If the matter (if proved) would not justify at least a written warning, it is not appropriate for it to be referred for disciplinary proceedings.
- Disciplinary proceedings should not be used for matters of unsatisfactory performance, unsatisfactory attendance or gross incompetence.

- Gross misconduct is a breach of the Standards of Professional Behaviour that is so serious as to justify dismissal.
- Misconduct is a breach of the Standards of Professional Behaviour that is so serious as to justify disciplinary action.
- Disciplinary proceedings should only be used when there is a breach of the Standards of Professional Behaviour that justifies at least a written warning and constitutes what can be considered misconduct. This is distinct from dealing with less serious breaches or low-level conduct issues that can be addressed by line managers and supervisors, for example as Practice Requiring Improvement through the Reflective Practice Review Process.
- A written warning should be seen as a significant sanction and one that necessarily has an impact on the professional record of a police officer and should be taken seriously as a meaningful sanction where misconduct has been proven.
- The Reflective Practice Review Process for Practice Requiring Improvement should be used for underperformance or conduct not amounting to misconduct or gross misconduct, which falls short of the expectations of the public and the police service, as set out in the Code of Ethics and there is an opportunity for an officer to learn from an incident to improve their actions or behaviours.
- All persons serving with the police are under a duty to report any improper conduct and to not remain silent if they witness or become aware of an area of concern about the behaviour or actions of another person serving in policing. This duty extends to reporting both the improper conduct of colleagues as well as organisational impropriety, where it is found.
- Police officers are under a specific duty as set out in the Standards of Professional Behaviour contained within the Conduct Regulations to challenge and report improper conduct. This responsibility is set out and applied in the Code of Ethics and as such applies to all persons who serve in policing, irrespective of their role or status.
- Every police force has internal guidance and procedures for raising concerns or challenging improper conduct through line management channels and chains of command, force-based reporting routes (both open and confidential reporting lines) or directly with Professional Standards Departments. Normally, any allegations or matters to be raised should be made through these internal routes within force. Additionally, reports may be made directly to the Independent Office for Police Conduct.
- When an allegation suggests that a person serving with the police has acted in a manner that would justify the bringing of disciplinary proceedings or could amount to the commission of a criminal offence, the appropriate authority is under a duty to take action to assess and potentially investigate the allegation which could lead to proceedings being brought against an individual against whom the allegation has been made.

16.7 Misconduct—preventative action

If sergeant and inspector leaders are to be successful in encouraging good behaviour, they need to ensure that the ways in which they behave are beyond reproach. They should be fully conversant with disciplinary regulations including the Reflective Practice Review Process and the Code of Ethics.

Preventative action is aways desirable and it is up to the leader to create an environment conducive to harmony and good work but also an environment where people exercise self-discipline and are respectful to others. However, when a leader is required to act on a misconduct matter they must act swiftly to stop the continuation of the problem.

It is hoped that sergeant and inspector leaders will be able to deal with most minor infringements on an informal basis and as part of everyday supervisory practice. Leading by example, enforcing desired standards of behaviour and working should help with keeping good discipline. This is especially so if the leader makes clear inappropriate behaviour is totally unacceptable and will be dealt with expeditiously.

Sergeants and inspectors would be assisted if officers they command were encouraged to report misconduct amongst colleagues as soon as it becomes apparent and before untold damage is caused. This depends largely upon an ability to inspire trust and in instilling a moral obligation for officers to disclose the unprofessional behaviours of others.

KEY POINT – CONSEQUENCES OF FAILING TO DEAL WITH MISCONDUCT

Misbehaviour and indiscipline in the police service can have serious consequences, including the loss of public esteem, damage to individual and team morale and a failure to complete set objectives. Untoward actions must be dealt with expeditiously and fairly in order to remedy situations and to get individuals to comply with professional ethical standards. Often examining improper behaviour can lead to beneficial changes to procedures and improved team relationships. A failure to tackle misbehaviour is likely to be an indication of poor leadership.

16.8 How does a leader measure whether misconduct or disciplinary action has been successful?

A leader will know whether a misconduct or disciplinary matter has been resolved satisfactorily when the conditions that caused misconduct in the first place no longer exist. In other words, things have returned to normal and accepted standards of behaviour and performance have been resumed and maintained unless, of course, an officer has been required to leave the police service.

References and further reading

ACAS (2015), Code of Practice on Disciplinary and Grievance Procedures <www.acas.org.uk/acas-code-of-practice-on-disciplinary-and-grievance-procedures> accessed 22 May 2025.

ACAS (2020), *Guide to Discipline and Grievance at Work* <www.acas.org.uk/acas-guide-to-discipline-and-grievances-at-work> accessed 22 May 2025.

College of Policing (2022), *Outcomes for Police Misconduct Proceedings—Updated Guidance* <https://assets.college.police.uk/s3fs-public/2022-08/Guidance-on-outcomes-in-police-misconduct-proceedings.pdf> accessed 22 May 2025.

College of Policing (2024), *Guidance for Ethical and Professional Behaviour in Policing* <www.college.police.uk/ethics/code-of-ethics/guidance> accessed 22 May 2025.

College of Policing (2024), *Professional Standards—Guidance Overview* <www.college.police.uk/app/professional-standards> accessed 30 May 2025.

Home Office (2020), *Guidance—Conduct, Efficiency and Effectiveness: Statutory Guidance on Professional Standards, Performance and Integrity in Policing, Version 1.0.* <www.gov.uk/government/publications/policing-professional-standards-performance-and-integrity> accessed 22 May 2025.

Independent Office of Police Conduct (2020), *Statutory Guidance to the Police Complaints System* <www.policeconduct.gov.uk/publications/statutory-guidance-2020> accessed 22 May 2025.

17

Communications—general discussion

17.1 What is meant by the term 'communication' and what forms of communication are open to a leader?

The word 'communication' is widely used to cover a number of differing interpretations. Of course, we all communicate with other people every day, in different situations, throughout our entire lives. We do not just communicate orally as we use our whole body to transmit messages successfully. The more that we understand and practise the various established communication methods, the better we become at transmitting messages successfully. This, in turn, leads to desired outcomes.

17.1.1 Adler and Towne's communication model

From the outset it is worth looking at Adler and Towne's (1978) very useful communication model (see Figure 17.1) which explains basic communication difficulties.

Figure 17.1 The communication model (Adler and Towne 1978)

Source: Adler/Towne, Looking Out Looking In, 2E. © 1978 Wadsworth, a part of Cengage Learning, Inc. Reproduced by permission. <http://www.cengage.com/permissions>.

The information which follows helps to interpret the model.

- Communication originates with the 'Sender' as a series of mental images (ideas, thoughts, pictures and emotions) which he or she wishes to transmit to another person.
- The Sender needs to 'transpose or translate' images into symbols ('Encoding'); that is, words, pictures, sounds and 'sense information' (e.g. touch and smells) that the 'Receiver' is able to understand.
- After Encoding, the Sender needs to communicate the message to the Receiver, for example by way of face-to-face verbal contact, telephone, printed materials or visual media. Other 'Channels' include touch, gestures, clothing and the physical distances that exist between the Sender and the Receiver.
- When a message reaches a Receiver, he or she has to 'Decode' it by sensing and interpreting the symbols and turning them back to images, emotions and thoughts that make sense to him or her. When the Decoded message matches exactly what the Sender intended then effective communication takes place.
- Effective communication is a very desirable goal but it is very hard to achieve. This is because people are different, with different backgrounds, experiences

and emotional responses which affect the ways in which they interpret messages and attach meaning to them.

- 'Physical Noise' stands in the way of good communications, for example an excessively hot or cold environment or noise itself.
- 'Psychological Noise' relates to factors that restrict a Sender or a Receiver's ability to express or understand messages clearly, for example people with limited vocabularies. Additionally, Receivers may 'Filter' messages with which they disagree and enter into a defensive mode rather than trying to interpret a message correctly.
- As the number of people involved in the communication increases, so does the potential for misinterpretation.

Specifically, sergeants and inspectors and other police leaders have to communicate effectively with officers under their command, peers, seniors, other agencies and, of the greatest importance, members of the public. A competent leader requires first-class communication skills and without them he or she is unlikely to be successful either with followers or the completion of expected results. Metaphorically, as blood flows through our bodies so good communications flow through the corporate body of the police service serving all its needs and ambitions.

Differing circumstances demand different methods of communication, and the leader must select the best approach and the best method of communicating given the prevailing circumstances. Methods might include, for example, face-to-face discussions, emails, letters, memoranda, reports, telephone conversations, video conferencing and large briefing or debriefing sessions.

Poor communications are likely to frustrate and irritate recipients. Communicating really well is a very difficult thing to do and takes time, training and experience. In fact, learning to communicate well is a lifelong process. Perfect communications do not appear to exist for often what appears to be a simple and easily understood message comes up against some unforeseen barrier. This does not mean that the leader should not try to reach the ideal situation by sharpening and honing his or her skills to remove as many barriers as possible to effective communication.

17.2 **Communication—different levels**

It is of great importance that sergeant and inspector leaders appreciate that whilst communications operate at many different levels there are two major levels in the workplace that require emphasising and managing.

17.2.1 **'Official' and 'social' communications**

One level of communication includes, for example, the passing of strategic and tactical information, instructions and directions. 'Official communications' usually and rightly receive a great deal of attention because of their operational significance. However, whilst personnel do pay due regard to what they are required to do there is another level below this official level, which operates at a 'social level'. Whereas official communications are usually highly structured, social communications are unstructured. The social level can be extremely powerful and whilst bearing distinct benefits it is also able to undermine the official level if left unmonitored and unchecked.

This social network has a number of names and facets. For example, there is 'the grapevine'—bearing both true and untrue messages and half-truths. Then there is the 'rumour mill'—a set-up that fosters both positive and negative views and propaganda. Finally, there exists 'the canteen culture'—a means of discussing all moans, groans and negative observations (but positive ones too and not just in the canteen) in what they would regard as a leader- and manager-free safe environment. The actual workplace is itself a place where social interactions take place—probably more than anywhere else.

It must be emphasised that the social network has a really good side. Discussing things—for instance, holidays, who has won the lottery, who has just got married and the arrival of a new child—can draw team members together in a positive way that helps to build harmony and synergy. *A leader should not exclude him- or herself from this social level.* However, it requires careful regulation and it can also reveal valuable information that people are happy to voice to a sensitive leader.

To combat negative communications, the good leader recognises the importance of having an open communication system based upon mutual trust. An open system ensures that staff are informed of what is going on and are able to contribute their views, ideas and suggestions without fear of recrimination. An open system also involves giving and receiving feedback and inviting and answering questions no matter how difficult it is to do so.

17.3 Specific skills that a leader can learn to greatly enhance the communication process

Excellent communications and the acquisition of the necessary skills to become an effective leader are very important. This is why Chapters 17–26 are devoted to oral and written communications.

17.3.1 Communication—overarching considerations

To help good communications in a wider sense, a leader requires a wide vocabulary. A large vocabulary offers the opportunity to express mood, opinions, ideas and suggestions in the most appropriate way. An extensive choice of words enables us to exert influence for ourselves and for others. Also, a leader needs good comprehension skills and the ability to summarise succinctly as these skills help with message clarity and understanding. Additionally, a leader should learn how to apply these and other skills to best advantage. Finally, the leader has to be aware of the appropriate behaviours that greatly aid success when communicating with others. These attributes apply to both spoken and written words.

17.3.2 **Essential communication skills**

The leader can do much for him- or herself by reflecting upon and learning from experiences. However, there are *specific skills* that can be learned, which will greatly assist with the communication process. These are:

- the interpersonal skills—basic tools of communication;
- assertiveness skills—based on mutual respect but also good for difficult people and difficult situations;
- transactional analysis skills—good for understanding and dealing with different behaviours;
- feedback skills—essential for learning and self-development;
- briefing skills—to ensure effective briefing sessions and operational efficiency;
- debriefing skills—to ensure effective debriefing sessions and increase learning for investment in future operations;
- influencing skills—to assist in gaining participation, cooperation and satisfactory outcomes;
- meeting skills—to maximise the benefits to be gained from meetings.

17.4 **How can a leader test the effectiveness of team communications?**

Sergeant and inspector leaders need to plan and establish an effective communication system that ensures that information flows in all directions and that ideas and suggestions for the future are not lost. One-to-one contact is really important in this regard but so also is the holding of regular team meetings. These should operate with an agenda and with notes or minutes being taken (see also Chapter 26, 'Meeting skills'). Meetings should be timed for when it is operationally acceptable and should not be cancelled on a whim but only for important operational or other equally significant reasons. Additionally, regular, structured event debriefs (Chapter 23, 'Communications—debriefing skills') and honest feedback (Chapter 21, 'Communication—feedback') are very valuable.

Equally important is the need for a leader to create an environment where people are not afraid to put forward their views and, where necessary, they are able to seek clarification of facts. Continuous dialogue should be encouraged in order to identify problems before they become catastrophes and to stimulate interest, participation and progress.

The test for team communications is that team members are well informed and know what to do and how to do it in a manner leading to team efficiency and effectiveness with the minimum of mistakes or mishaps. In qualitative terms, team participants and other concerned parties, including members of the public where appropriate, should be asked how effective they think communications are. They should also be invited to give examples of good and bad experiences whilst offering suggestions for improvement. A quantitative appraisal involves measuring actual outcomes against desired outcomes (task and objective completion). There are many reasons why objectives are not completed satisfactorily, and these would have to be identified, but poor communications may well loom large in any examination of the facts.

17.5 How will a leader know that he or she personally has good communications with others?

First, a sergeant or inspector leader needs to critically and conscientiously examine his or her own performance linking this to the satisfactory completion of tasks and objectives, but also to team successes or failures. Part of this process involves seeking feedback from individual team members but also from the team as a whole (and people outside the team if this is appropriate). This should disclose any overall communication difficulties. Also, however, the leader should openly ask for a critique of his or her communications with others dealing with responses in a non-defensive way. Although it should be made clear that criticism should be offered with respect and be based on the facts, it is not always easy to accept. That said, team members are likely to respect a leader willing to subject him- or herself to scrutiny in the same way that they themselves are scrutinised. The point of all feedback is to learn and improve and it should be seen as a thoroughly normal and non-threatening practice.

References and further reading

Adler, R. B. and Towne, N. (1978), *Looking Out Looking In* (2nd edn, New York: Holt, Rinehart & Winston).

The Pfeiffer Library Volume 25 (2nd edn, 1998, © Jossey-Bass/Pfeiffer; with the kind permission of John Wiley and Sons Ltd, West Sussex, England).

18

Communications—interpersonal skills

18.1 What is meant by the expression 'interpersonal skills'?

Usually the term 'interpersonal skills' is used to describe how people use their oral skills to communicate in a positive and effective way with other people. As mentioned in the previous chapter (Chapter 17, 'Communications—general discussion'), a good leader must possess first-class interpersonal skills if he or she is to communicate well with all manner of people in all manner of situations. He or she will have to liaise with seniors, peers, juniors, agencies and members of the public in a professional way which gets a message across clearly without causing offence and resentment.

This chapter uses the expression 'interpersonal skills' to explore the basic communications building blocks upon which all other refinements rest.

18.2 Barriers to effective communications

A number of things stand in the way of good communications and these include, for example:

- a poor grasp and use of the most important interpersonal skills;
- not knowing fully the subject to be discussed and failing to prepare for important conversations, discussions or meetings whether on a one-to-one basis or with a group of people;
- anger, passivity, intolerance, discrimination and bias, stubbornness, inflexibility and an unwillingness to compromise;
- a failure to learn from both good and bad experiences through self-examination and feedback from others.

18.3 Interpersonal skills in detail

The skills essential to first-class communications are included in the following sections.

18.3.1 Empathy

Empathy involves trying to understand how another person feels and why they hold a particular point of view or behave in a particular way. By creating empathy, you will show that you are sensitive to the needs of others. You may not agree with a point of view; however, you should try to understand it in order to seek a modification of your own stance or achieve a mutual compromise. Of course, you may have to ignore a point of view in certain situations but you cannot properly discard an opinion without first having considered the possible reasons for it.

The important thing to remember about empathy is that it amounts to *an attempt* to understand how someone feels. For example, it is impossible for a white person to know how exactly a black person feels and vice versa. Equally, it is impossible for a man to understand how a woman feels and, again, vice versa. However, empathy may be able to bridge the communications gap between perception and reality.

Empathy does not amount to sympathy. Sympathy may incorrectly colour judgement and it may be seen as patronising.

18.3.2 **Words**

Words—obviously words are important to oral communication as they form the bedrock upon which good communication rests. However, a narrow vocabulary or a misunderstanding of words or subtle differences between words can limit the ability of a person to communicate effectively. A narrow vocabulary may lead to a person being overwhelmed or outmanoeuvred by someone with a much wider vocabulary using words in a sophisticated and articulate manner.

18.3.3 **Body language**

Body language—having said that words are important, arguably body language is just as or even more important. Body language is a natural part of being human and is central to human behaviours, feelings and communications. It is very difficult to mask body language, especially for any length of time. However, body language can be controlled in contrived situations so as not to betray what a person is really thinking or feeling. For example, when negotiating with others for some advantage we may try to hide our real feelings which may, for instance, be ones of delight or despair. This is so as not to betray a belief that we are perhaps winning an argument or revealing a weakness. Also, as a further example, at selection interviews we may try to give the impression that we are cool, calm and collected by adopting a still, calm posture, with good eye contact and slow, measured language whereas in reality we may be anxious and nervous.

Looking further at selection interviews, body language often indicates a conflict between answers and what a person really believes. For example, with a difficult question a candidate may fidget uncomfortably or show agitation by suddenly altering their passive, controlled posture to adopt a much more animated approach. This should, of course, invite a shrewd interviewer to find out the reasons for the change.

It is essential that good communicators watch body language closely to see whether it supports what is being uttered and implied. However, as it is difficult to interpret and people may hide their true feelings or beliefs, interpretations should not be assumed but checked by the use of open questions (see section 18.3.7).

18.3.4 **Voice tone**

Voice tone too has great importance in interpersonal communications. Voice tone helps to punctuate our communications. For example, a loud voice may be used to emphasise determination or it may be used to overwhelm opposition to a particular point of view. A quiet voice may indicate passivity and an inability to combat more aggressive personalities. Equally, it may indicate quiet resolution. A well-moderated voice may indicate a calm, confident, professional approach. However, none of these assumptions must be permitted as some people naturally speak quietly or loudly as part of their personalities. Where voice tone does appear to underline a particular belief or behaviour, it should be checked—again by the use of questioning. Finally, rise and fall in voice tone adds character and interest to conversations and prevents presentations becoming stilted and boring.

18.3.5 **Listening**

Listening is vital to understanding a particular communication. Many people do not listen properly as is evidenced by the frustration others feel at not being able to get their message across to inattentive people who, as a consequence, may appear to be insincere and disinterested.

Listening involves:

- remaining silent while others talk;
- concentrating hard, focusing and listening intently to what is being said;
- showing that listening is taking place through, for example, good eye contact, nodding the head, asking questions and seeking clarification;
- checking that a message has been correctly received by repeating back important pieces of information and summarising what has been said (see section 18.3.11) where appropriate.

18.3.6 **Note-taking**

Note-taking is a writing skill, but it is a useful aid to listening. It is difficult during a long discussion to remember everything that is said, therefore notes amount to a valuable aide-memoire.

Note-taking should be done openly and preferably in agreement with the other party (who should also be invited to keep notes if they wish to do so).

Most people are happy for note-taking to take place provided that they can see that it is to their advantage to do so. A word of warning though: there is a danger that note-taking will obstruct the ability to listen properly, which is why notes should comprise key or bullet points only.

18.3.7 **Questioning**

Questioning is at the very heart of good communications. Questions can be asked to seek information, clarify issues and interrogate the facts.

Open questions—using, for example, the words *what, why* and *how*—are good for gaining information. This is because they leave matters open for a full answer whereas closed questions (see later) do not. The following list offers useful examples of open questions:

- What are you going to do?
- Why are you going to do it?
- Who is going to do it with you and why have you chosen them to assist you?
- How will you perform the task?
- What resources will you require?
- What will happen when you have completed the task?
- How will you know that you have been successful?

This series of open questions seeks information and important facts in a logical fashion whilst discouraging one-word or one-sentence responses. They encourage dialogue and participation and help to remove ambiguity.

When interrogating the facts in many different situations, one of the most common mistakes made is not to pursue answers with more open questions to establish deeper meanings and behaviours.

Closed questions are good for gaining specific answers and verifying facts but their use invites limited responses. They often act as a good prelude to open questions and may be used in conjunction with them. The following is an example of a closed question:

Question: 'Are you aware that you should start work at 9 am?'
Answer: 'Yes.'

The answer does not reveal much but, for instance, in a 'being late for work' misconduct investigation it does show that a person did know when they should appear for work. The use of follow-up open questions should then establish why the person was late for duty.

Leading questions invite contrived responses because the responder often supplies the answer that the question prompts or that the questioner expects. For example:

Question (Boss): 'Do you like working here?'
Answer (Member of staff): 'Yes.' (Even if untrue because it might be foolish to answer otherwise.)

Trick questions—designed to catch people out—are manipulative and disrespectful and should not be used.

Hypothetical questions—famously used by selection interviewers—are good for testing knowledge and responses to possible problems. However, they are not particularly effective substitutes for practical exercises.

18.3.8 **Help from Rudyard Kipling**

Usefully, Kipling (1902) offers some sound advice on asking questions (open and closed) in one of his poems:

> I kept six honest serving-men
> They taught me all I knew
> Their names are *what* and *why*
> And *when* and *how* and *where*
> And *who*.

The sergeant and inspector leader may be surprised by how many times this wise combination of questions (used in any order and perhaps supplemented by other questions) can be found to be useful. For example, when exploring a team member's proposal for driving a new task and objective a leader might ask:

- *What* do you intend to do and *what* will the benefits be?
- *Why* do you want to do it?
- *When* will you start and finish the task?
- *How* will you complete the objective? *How* long will it take? *How* much will it cost? *How* will you measure success?
- *Where* will you work and *where* will you find the resources you need?
- *Who* is going to help you?

Of course, this is a very simple set of questions, but Kipling does offer a *memorable* framework for action in the same way that a mnemonic does.

18.3.9 **Silence**

Silence—it seems strange that silence should be included in the interpersonal skills repertoire. Silence can be both helpful and coercive. Silence is helpful when a speaker is giving someone time to reflect upon what has been said; it is coercive when it is prolonged, making a person feel uncomfortable and therefore prone to say something that he or she might later regret.

When listening intently, a listener should be silent most of the time and intervene only for points of clarification, etc.

18.3.10 **Clarifying**

Clarifying involves establishing whether a listener has heard correctly and is in command of the facts. Sometimes a person delivering information might realise through body language that a person has not understood a particular message. Then he or she should seek to clarify the situation by reissuing a message. When doubt exists, matters should be clarified through the use of questions and by inviting or delivering summaries (see the following section).

18.3.11 **Summarising**

Summarising is a very important communications skill because it helps to ensure that a message has been correctly delivered in the manner in which it was intended.

Summarising enables a leader to establish whether he or she has received a message correctly or passed a message on correctly to someone else. By asking someone to repeat a message, the leader can find out whether they have fully understood what has been said. If not, then the leader can correct any misunderstanding. Equally, a person can ask the leader to summarise what he or she has said to create a proper understanding.

Summarising is essential when people have been asked to take a particular course of action after the issuing of important operational directions or after, for example, corrective misconduct or disciplinary investigations.

18.4 **How can a leader improve his or her interpersonal skills?**

Learning how to communicate in the most efficient and effective manner is a lifelong task because of the complexity of language and the many responses that human beings are able to generate. First, a leader's ability to communicate well is likely to be enhanced by him or her recognising the importance of communications to their roles. Second, a leader should consider each significant transaction carefully to find out what he or she can learn from the experience. Third, leaders can learn from soliciting feedback from others including members of the public. Fourth, leaders can study aspects of communications that will help to greatly improve their ability to relate to others. This 'toolkit' seeks to aid this process.

Reference and further reading

Kipling, R. (1902), *Just So Stories (The Elephant's Child)* (London: Macmillan).

19

Positive communications—assertiveness

19.1 What is assertive behaviour and how will behaving assertively benefit the leader, those he or she leads and the public?

Often people misunderstand the nature of assertive behaviour, associating it with aggression and this is not the case. Behaving assertively means acting positively and with considerable skill to reach the best possible outcomes for all concerned.

Assertiveness skills are possibly the most important communication skills that can be acquired for success in both work and social situations. The principles of assertive behaviour are easy to understand but the associated skills are difficult to exercise with confidence. Mental agility is an essential ingredient, and much practice is likely to be required before a high standard of competence is achieved.

Assertiveness recognises that all individuals are important human beings who should be treated with respect and courtesy. Each person is valued in his or her own right, is worth listening to and always has something to contribute to discussions and deliberations.

Assertive people are happy to compromise and work towards a situation whereby all parties win and no losers exist. If necessary, they are prepared to concede their position if this is the right thing to do, or it is for the greater good.

Additionally assertive people:

- are honest in their dealings with others;
- forthright in stating things as they are and open with their transactions, avoiding misleading or deceiving statements or suggestions;
- say what they really want to say but in a diplomatic and sensitive fashion.

Behaving assertively will help a sergeant and inspector leader to communicate successfully and without aggravation at all levels of contact. This is because it is based upon forethought, respect and sensitive application. This is particularly important with regard to police contact with members of the public in many different situations, some of which are difficult to manage.

19.2 If a leader is not assertive does this matter?

Being based upon respect for others and a spirit of compromise, assertive behaviour by sergeant and inspector leaders is likely to result in good professional and personal relationships with team members, colleagues, external agencies and the public. Also, assertive behaviour is likely to entail positive outcomes and in establishing good grounds for important transactions in the future.

Assertive behaviour amounts to a desirable mode of expression. There are alternative modes—passivity and aggression, and we shall explore these now to see how they measure up against assertive behaviour.

19.2.1 **Passivity**

Passivity—passive people tend not to like conflict or confronting people and situations that perhaps they should confront. If a leader adopts a passive role, he or she may be seen by seniors, peers and team members as weak, indecisive and afraid to tackle issues such as team conflicts and inappropriate behaviour. Passivity may also, through inertia or a timid approach and the avoidance of people problems, damage team harmony, synergy and efficiency and effectiveness whereas positive and inclusive assertive behaviour would have a much more positive effect. Passive behaviour in the public arena, exhibited perhaps in a failure to react professionally and decisively, may lead to a consequent loss of respect for the police.

19.2.2 **Aggression**

Aggression—aggressive behaviour may achieve short-term gains but medium and long-term damage to the aggressor. Aggression may be seen as bullying. It may also be aligned to autocratic leadership. In any event, team members and others are not likely to want to communicate with an aggressive leader even when important issues are involved. When communications break down between a leader and team members and other colleagues, again team harmony, synergy and efficiency and effectiveness are likely to suffer. If a leader is aggressive towards the public this is likely to result in anger, resentment, frustration, reputational damage for the individual and police force concerned and the withdrawal of public support and cooperation.

19.2.3 **Making choices**

Of course, these modes of communication are not confined to leaders but are open to all of us. We all have choices, and we can decide what we want to do. Hopefully, the case for being assertive has been proven. Aggression is never a good option because of its negative connotations. However, some people choose to be passive even if there are downsides; for example, managing an extremely heavy workload because of an inability to put forward reasonable objections to work allocation. Often passive people are likely to be passive because it removes undue angst, and they consider that the disadvantages are worth bearing to avoid painful conflict. Assertive leaders try to encourage assertive behaviours in team members and others by inviting passive people to participate in team matters and challenging aggressive behaviour. Additionally, there are occasions when leaders choose to be passive because it seems appropriate at the time and passivity is seen as a prelude to a later assertive intervention.

19.3 **What does a leader have to do to be assertive?**

Often assertive people are described as confident. If this is the case, this is because they know what they are doing and how to do it in the most effective manner. Assertive behaviour draws heavily upon two concepts, and they are 'rights' and 'responsibilities'.

19.3.1 **Rights**

To be assertive a leader has to recognise his or her 'rights'. An assertive person does not proceed unless he or she is certain about the position they are adopting. The golden rule is: if you are unsure, do not proceed until such time as you know whether you have the right (the basis) to do so. Breaking this rule could lead to embarrassment and a stalled transaction. The assertive leader also makes him- or herself aware of the rights of others. This not only offers a planned and considered way forward but also opens the way to avoiding arguments and achieving a compromise where appropriate.

Rights come in different forms. You may as a member of the public have the right, for example, to:

- vote;
- state education;
- free national health care.

In the workplace, there will be the 'right' to benefit from, for instance:

- employment legislation;
- health and safety protection;
- discrimination legislation.

Most employers (including the police service) create a host of other rights by way of written policies (e.g. training and development opportunities). However, rights also take a looser form, which an employer would doubtless regard as at least a moral 'right'. For instance, the right to:

- be treated with respect;
- ask questions and express doubts;
- disagree;
- offer ideas and suggestions;
- give and receive feedback;
- be treated in the same way as everyone else in terms of fairness, advantages and other such considerations.

19.3.2 **Exceptions attached to rights**

Many rights, if not most, carry exceptions or limitations. These include, for example, the right to vote which is limited by younger people being unable to vote until they reach qualifying age and the right to trial by jury which does not apply to all offences.

19.3.3 **Responsibilities**

Rights do not come alone—they are accompanied by 'responsibilities'. For example:

- if you have the right to vote then you have a responsibility to vote;
- if you have the right to a state education then you have a responsibility to make an effort to learn and to contribute positively to the learning process;
- if you have the right to free national health care then you have a responsibility to attend appointments on time and assist the recovery process.

Similarly, in the workplace:

- if you have the right to be treated with respect then you should treat others with the same respect;
- if you have the right to ask questions and express doubts then you should ask relevant and well-considered questions and explain fully why you have doubts;
- if you have the right to disagree then you have the responsibility to state the reasons why you disagree;
- if you have the right to offer ideas and suggestions then you have a responsibility to provide sensible and well-thought-out ideas and suggestions;
- if you have the right to be given and receive feedback then you have a responsibility to accept, consider and act upon feedback, where justified, in a non-defensive manner; in giving feedback you should rely on the facts and evidence and not personality;
- if you have the right to be treated fairly and be offered available advantages and considerations then you have a responsibility to treat others fairly and not deny them advantages and considerations.

When policing:

- as a police officer, if you have the right to enforce the law then you have a responsibility to do so professionally, correctly, courteously and without discrimination.

19.3.4 **Rights for police sergeants and inspectors and other police leaders**

With regard to police sergeants and inspectors and other police leaders, a list of rights for a leader might include, for example, the 'right' (with 'responsibilities') to:

- lead (in an efficient and effective manner);
- plan (involving team members in the planning process);
- make administrative and operational changes (not on a whim but sensibly and with the help and support of team members);

- motivate team members (taking into account their individual abilities, aspirations and needs);
- delegate work (provided the person is able to take on the task, with training and support being provided where necessary);
- coach, train and develop team members (taking into account job needs, individual aspirations and abilities while soliciting their full cooperation);
- give and receive feedback (relying on facts and evidence and not personality when offering feedback and avoiding a defensive reaction when receiving feedback);
- investigate misconduct and matters (in a fair and honest fashion);
- be treated with respect (while respecting others).

19.3.5 **Rights for team members**

A list of rights for a team member may include, for instance, the right (with responsibilities) to be:

- led in an efficient and effective manner (but coupled also with a duty to follow);
- treated with respect (while respecting others—often rights are of a mutual nature);
- consulted and have one's ideas and suggestions listened to (with ideas and suggestions being made sensibly and thoughtfully);
- given feedback as a means to learn and improve (and to take on board suggestions for improvement);
- able to give the leader honest feedback (in a factual and constructive manner);
- trained (making positive contributions to the learning process);
- developed and given opportunities to fulfil one's potential (offering one's own ideas and suggestions on how to proceed);
- treated fairly and without discrimination (treating others in the same manner).

19.4 **Ways for the leader to improve his or her assertiveness skills**

A leader is best able to improve and hone his or her assertiveness skills through:

- training and development programmes, which cover communication skills in their many and varied forms;
- constant practice with self-review and feedback from others;
- meaningful, critically evaluated experience.

19.5 **Assertiveness—helpful tips**

The tips that follow should prove helpful in the competent use of assertiveness techniques.

(1) A cardinal principle when being assertive is to rely on what a person says and does rather than upon their personality. This will reduce the chance of prejudice and conflict and leave the way open to concentrate upon facts and issues.

(2) One way of acting to resolve a situation is to list the rights that all parties have and then prepare a clear objective for success to act upon. The leader should consider the desired outcome for him- or herself and others involved, bearing in mind the need for compromise and agreement wherever possible.

(3) Having decided upon a course of action, a leader requires a positive frame of mind and the removing of mental barriers to progress and feeble excuses to act. It is easy in difficult circumstances to falter but then courage and determination should seek to remove all obstacles that stand in the way of success.

(4) The leader should run through an intended course of action to be taken before meeting another party or parties. It is surprising how much pre-planning and knowing how to start proceedings contributes to confidence and success.

(5) Negative behaviour and negative remarks should be avoided. The assertive sergeant and inspector leader would do well to remember that aggression breeds aggression and in the long term it achieves little or nothing. Similarly, passive behaviour may mean that an unscrupulous party might take advantage of passivity. The goal should always be subject to mutual respect and a 'win-win' situation for all concerned.

(6) It is important for the leader to use his or her interpersonal skills to full advantage with good eye contact, listening intently, clarifying areas of uncertainty, asking questions and watching body language closely to see if it agrees with what is being said in response. The sergeant and inspector leader should use his or her own body language and voice tone to show confidence (achieved through good preparation and certainty) and to punctuate proceedings in order to emphasise points and create interest.

(7) The leader should not be afraid to express feelings, for example annoyance, frustration or disappointment, rather than suppress them—this is not a sign of weakness. How one feels is a matter of fact and a powerful way of communicating especially if the other party is sensitive and empathetic. More positive feelings such as pleasure may also be expressed.

(8) Sometimes aggressive or bad behaviour may be disorientating, leaving a leader uncertain what to do. In such circumstances, the leader should take time out to think and plan (perhaps a day or even more) and then re-engage with the problem. Additionally, if a leader is engaged in complex discussions and wishes to consider important issues further then he or she should politely seek an adjournment.

19.6 Encouraging and adopting assertive behaviour

It cannot be overstressed how important to good relationships assertive behaviour is, for it underpins all that police sergeants and inspectors wish to achieve as leaders.

KEY POINT—ENCOURAGING ASSERTIVE BEHAVIOUR

Assertive behaviour and assertiveness skills are very necessary communication skills not just for the sergeant and inspector leader but for team members too and they are absolutely essential to the dealings police have with the public. The skills are critical to handling conflicts, including between team members themselves, positively and respectfully and without damaging any individual's self-esteem. Therefore, a leader should encourage assertive behaviour in all team members to create a positive atmosphere and positive results in the workplace. This can be done by providing an example, through training, by encouraging assertive responses and by creating an environment where everyone feels valued.

19.7 Passivity, aggression and assertiveness compared

Alberti and Emmons (1970) compare relationships between passivity, aggression and assertiveness very well by noting:

- 'Non-assertive behaviour—denying one's own rights'.
- 'Aggressive behaviour—denying the rights of others'.
- 'Assertive behaviour—acknowledging your own rights and those of others'.

19.8 How does a leader know that he or she is in fact assertive in his or her dealings with others?

A leader will know whether he or she is assertive by way of:

- critical self-analysis—learning from each engagement in order to enhance interpersonal skills and acquire the power to communicate even more effectively;
- tasks and objectives and results being successfully achieved;
- honest feedback from others—including juniors, peers, external agencies and members of the public.

19.8 How does a leader know that they are assertive in their dealings with others?

References and further reading

Alberti, R. E. and Emmons, M. L. (1970), *Your Perfect Right: A Guide to Assertive Behaviour* (San Luis Obispo, CA: Impact Publishers).

Langrish, S. V. (1986), 'Assertiveness Training' in Cary L. Cooper (ed.), *Improving Interpersonal Relations* (Aldershot: Wildwood House).

20

Communications—modes of behaviour and transactional analysis

20.1 What is transactional analysis and how will understanding it enhance a leader's ability to communicate well?

The term 'transactional analysis' is rather forbidding and a bit off-putting. This is because it is closely linked to the world of medicine. Dr Eric Berne developed the concept of transactional analysis in the USA in the early 1950s as a way of approaching clinical psychotherapy. However, it transpired that transactional analysis offered an excellent opportunity for understanding how we communicate with others and how they communicate with us. It enables us to understand the positions we and others adopt and to modify our behaviour accordingly. It is a valuable communication skill that is complementary to the use of our interpersonal and assertiveness skills.

Transactional analysis in its entirety is a complicated subject. It requires thoughtful contemplation, sensitive application and plenty of practice to gain competence. This chapter therefore merely seeks to highlight some of the important principles of transactional analysis and apply them to our daily (and police) communication processes in a fairly simple way.

Despite its complexity, it is relatively easy to grasp an understanding of the powerful nature and usefulness of transactional analysis in the communications process fairly quickly. It is emphasised that transactional analysis should be used as a means to develop relationships and not damage them through calculated manipulation.

20.2 The process of transactional analysis explained within a police context

To begin to understand transactional analysis we need to identify and consider the three *Ego States* and other facets of transactional analysis so important to the process.

20.2.1 Parent State

The *Parent State* reflects the position of most parents who have the difficult task of raising their children to become well-balanced, decent adults. Parents love and protect and defend their children against all harm. Also, they nurture, counsel and guide them and educate them to equip them for their lives ahead. However, they also point out what is right and what is wrong and they set rules for how to behave. They set parameters about what their offspring can or cannot do. All this helps in the raising of happy but responsible adults.

It is clear that the *Parent State* falls into two distinct parts—the *Nurturing Parent* and the *Critical Parent*. The *Nurturing Parent* is loving and supportive and concerned with protection and development. The *Critical Parent* exercises control over his or her children and sets rules that govern their morality and behaviours. The *Critical Parent* also defines what children should do and how they should do it and under what rules.

We all share the *Parent State* and we draw upon it regularly throughout our lives. For example, police officers may draw upon their nurturing side when counselling distressed colleagues or supporting members of the public involved in tragedy or trauma. Sergeant and inspector leaders may use their nurturing side too when seeking to enhance the potential of team members. Equally, they may draw upon their critical side when carrying out internal misconduct investigations or enforcing the law in the public arena.

Some people may be rounded *Parents* using both sides of the mode to advantage, but others may be much more of one mode than the other. For example, a police officer may spend virtually all his time in the critical mode. Thus, he or she may be seen as precise, correct, unbending and unfeeling. On the other hand, a police officer dwelling largely in the nurturing mode may be regarded as too involved, for example, with team members' welfare or the undue concerns of members of the public whilst not paying too much attention to structure, order and discipline.

20.2.2 **Adult State**

The *Adult State* is that part of us which is rational and methodical and the adult in us endeavours to base decisions upon evidence and facts rather than feelings. The *Adult* patiently plans, taking into account external factors but also messages from all of his or her ego states. These might include, for example, strictures from the *Parent*, the needs of the *Child* (see the following section) or past good or bad *Adult* memories or outcomes. The word '*Adult*' could be misleading in that it implies maturity but such may not be the case.

The *Adult State* appears to be a very desirable state with its rational approach to issues but, although the state may yield many advantages, it may also be seen as boring and predictable. Sometimes when dealing with police misconduct proceedings and lawbreakers a sergeant and inspector leader has to bring both the strictures of the *Critical Parent* and the rational approach of the *Adult* to the fore.

20.2.3 **Child State**

As with the *Parent State*, we should be able to easily identify with the *Child State* and its many and often complex attributes. Children tend to be fun-loving, curious, imaginative, inventive and spontaneous and frequently acquiescent. But they also have another side where they can be mischievous, naughty, capricious and intent on rule breaking. They can also be difficult to manage and not at all acquiescent.

Similarly to the *Parent State*, the *Child State* splits into two distinct modes—the *Adapted Child* and the *Free Child*.

The *Adapted Child* seeks to accommodate people in control or having authority over them by being, for instance, submissive, compliant and non-combative. However, the *Adapted Child* may take an alternative tack. He or she may be, for example, rebellious, hostile and difficult to manage. Implicit in the mode is the implication that the *Adapted Child* changes to suit circumstances. We all have the complete *Adapted Child* within us but we may lay more emphasis on one side of the mode than the other.

The *Free or Natural Child* is not hostile but is, for example, joy-loving, untroubled, inquisitive, creative and able to do things instinctively. Such a motivational person should be an asset to a team leader and team mates but, of course, even the *Free or Natural Child* will be subject to the pressures of other modes of behaviour.

20.2.4 **Little Professor State**

The *Little Professor* state is reminiscent of the *Free Child* in that *Little Professors* are inquisitive and creative and are often inspired to do things. However, the downside is that despite these benefits a *Little Professor* can be deviously manipulative. Although the positive aspects of this mode should be used to advantage, sergeant and inspector leaders should be alert to the possibility of behaviour which might seek to undermine their position.

20.2.5 **Contamination**

Contamination occurs when the strengths of the *Adult State* are interrupted by the interventions of the other states. For example, the *Adult*'s ability for rational thinking may be challenged by the prejudicial experiences of the *Parent* or the make-believe behaviour of the *Child*.

Operational police officers regularly come up against all the states during the course of their duties. With careful observation it is possible to quickly identify which specific mode a person is adopting and react accordingly. Experienced officers will know, for example, that when being reported for offences or being arrested members of the public may either be submissive or try to change circumstances through angry hostility (*Adapted Child*). With the police officer starting out in *Parent* mode it might be advisable for him or her to then adopt the *Adult* mode and try to get the person concerned to do the same. A police officer should avoid being dragged down to the rebellious *Adapted Child* mode and possible conflict.

In the workplace, people also reveal all the modes and their attendant behaviours with good or bad outcomes. But behaviour changes regularly and often rapidly and it is rarely if ever static. These changes do not exclude a leader who should explore the effect he or she has on others with a view to perhaps modifying his or her own behavioural patterns. Transactional analysis methodology is very good for investigating team disharmony and returning the team to efficiency and effectiveness.

20.2.6 **Excluded states**

Excluded states—the ideal situation is to choose from the different states whilst reducing dysfunctional behaviours. Some people, however, may deny one or two of the states. This makes them predictable and perhaps uninteresting. Imagine someone stuck in a *Critical Parent* mode where they may be seen as severe, authoritative and unapproachable. Similarly, a person inhabiting the *Nurturing Parent* mode might be regarded as overprotective and smothering. The constant *Adult* could easily be regarded as unimaginative and tedious. The *Adapted Child* may appear submissive, passive and lacking backbone. Alternatively, he or she could be regarded as troublesome and at times poor company. The *Free Child* might be regarded as immature and a bit of a pain.

20.2.7 **Life Positions**

It is suggested that there are four *Life Positions* (Ernst 1971). We may have a preference for a particular position, but it is possible to change positions. The positions are:

- *I'm not OK but you are OK*—people who adopt this position may have feelings of inadequacy when compared with others. Equally, they may undervalue not only themselves but also what they have to contribute. They may avoid tackling difficult people and difficult situations.
- *I'm OK and you're OK*—people in this position respect themselves and others and seek to work in harmony and cooperation. They tend to be optimistic and happy. They will tackle problems in a positive fashion.
- *I'm not OK and you're not OK*—those who occupy this position adopt very negative attitudes and see most things as pointless. Their outlook is confused and aimless.
- *I'm OK and you're not OK*—people fitting this position may appear smug and self-satisfied, although there may also be feelings of anger. Additionally, they may have feelings of being superior to others and as a result look down upon them. In their search for power and status, they may bulldoze others aside.

It seems clear that the best situation is *I'm OK and you're OK*. The frame of mind that supports this position ensures respect for oneself and for others. This is likely to lead to good relationships and positive results. However, Harris (1995) states that '[w]e do not drift into a new position. It is a decision we make.' Therefore, the good sergeant and inspector leader should be aware of all the positions and be ready to make positive interventions where possible. This is so as to make appropriate workplace counselling, motivational and problem-solving contributions where necessary with the ambition of raising people to the best situation possible.

KEY POINT—LIFE POSITIONS AND THE IMPERATIVE TO ACT

Transactional analysis *Life Positions* identify many of the features to be found in almost any team anywhere and they are usually pretty obvious to the sensitive and discerning sergeant and inspector leader. If a leader wants a happy and productive team fully able to reach its objectives then it is imperative that he or she does not ignore negative behaviours. These must be tackled quickly and decisively and with full regard for individual feelings. Where necessary, help from others may be required, for example from human resource experts, professional counsellors or GPs.

20.2.8 **Strokes**

Strokes—the concept of strokes relies on a belief that people need recognition, which can take many forms. A positive stroke may be oral (praise) or physical (a warm smile). A negative stroke amounts to a 'put down'.

20.2.9 **Stamps**

Stamps (or trading stamps) are emotions that we collect, sometimes over a long period of time, and then cash them in, often with devastating results. For example, a series of events may build up anger in someone to a point where it can no longer be contained and it is then that it is vented upon unsuspecting and bewildered colleagues. Equally, we may store up resentment, jealousy or other strong emotions. Obviously, emotional containment can harm the person holding resentments as well as the person at the receiving end of them. Stamps can harm relationships, team harmony and efficiency.

Operational police officers need to guard against venting upon members of the public and be aware that sometimes the public release their pent-up frustrations on police in a way that belies their normal behaviour.

Although very difficult, at times sergeant and inspector leaders should remain alert to the possibility of individuals storing up pressures so as to be able to offer help with issues and problems. The leader, by establishing trust and creating the atmosphere for regular, honest and open discussions both on an individual and team basis, would be enormously helpful in this regard as would regular one-to-one conversations with team members.

20.3 How does a leader use and develop his or her transactional analysis skills?

A leader should use transactional analysis skills alongside other sophisticated communication skills. He or she should use the combined skills to assess what may be underpinning certain behaviours and then adopt the right responses to them. As well as managing difficulties, transactional analysis skills may help in the development of desirable behaviours in team members. Further, it would appear that there is no good reason why team members themselves should not be acquainted with transactional analysis. This, of course, would make the leader the subject of analysis too by way of feedback, which if not treated defensively is good for leadership development.

A leader will develop his or her transactional analysis skills by constant use and by critical self-analysis of his or her performance which will also benefit from honest feedback from others.

References and further reading

Barker, D. and Phillips, K. (1986), 'Transactional Analysis' in Cary L. Cooper (ed), *Improving Interpersonal Relationships* (Aldershot: Wildwood House). Permission kindly given by Keri Phillips.

Berne, E. (1968), *Games People Play: The Psychology of Human Relationships* (London: Penguin).

Berne, E. (1975), *What Do you Say After You Say Hello?—The Psychology of Human Destiny* (London: Corgi).

Ernst, F. H. (1971), 'The OK Corral: The Grid For Getting-On With', *Transactional Analysis Journal* 1(4): 231–40.

Harris, T. A. (1995), *I'm OK—You're OK* (London: Random House).

21

Communications—feedback

21.1 What is feedback and what is its purpose?

Put simply, for the sergeant and inspector leader feedback involves commenting in a constructive, assertive way on the behaviours and performance of individual team members and the team as a whole. Also, it entails identifying and remarking on good progress and difficulties and tackling any obstacles to the completion of tasks and objectives. Importantly, giving feedback opens up a dialogue with those receiving it and this offers opportunities for discussing issues, which might not have otherwise been revealed.

Feedback helps with, for example, problem solving, learning, self-development, motivation, efficiency and effectiveness and an improved public service. More specifically, the purposes of feedback are to help with:

- establishing how well individuals and teams are progressing with their work and to identify any problems or need for assistance (efficiency and effectiveness);
- offering genuine, encouraging praise where this is deserved (reinforces good practice and is motivational);
- learning from errors and mistakes made (problem solving);
- identifying and dealing with any inappropriate behaviours (misconduct);
- establishing any coaching or other training needs (individual and team development);
- learning from successes and establishing the ingredients for further success (planning);
- spreading good practice to others within and outside the team (to police service and public benefit);
- encouraging honest, open and forthright communications with individuals and team members (multiple benefits including an improved service to the public).

Another way of looking at the importance of feedback is to consider what the situation would be like in the workplace if it were not given. Observations might reveal, for example, a team with poor communications, where issues are not identified, ideas not sought and problems not solved. Team members may not be as highly motivated as they could be, and the team might operate on a plateau rather than strive for improvement. This could result in a poor service to the public and possibly removal of the leader and team reconstruction.

21.2 How does a leader offer feedback to individuals?

Feedback is a non-hostile method of communication and exploration. The principles that support it apply not only to individuals but also to teams and even members of the public.

Interestingly, the Chartered Management Institute (2013) notes the possible responses to feedback that a manager/leader might receive:

- 'difficulty in accepting responsibility for behaviour';
- 'fear of making mistakes';
- 'difficulty with uncertainty and change';
- 'assuming that "others know best"';
- 'self-doubt and lack of confidence';
- 'reluctance to set personal goals for development';
- 'suspicion of "experts" and those in positions of authority'.

It would be easy to add to this formidable list of possible responses which might, for example, include anger and disinterested passivity or outright hostility.

All these issues can be tackled by the conscientious leader who seeks to establish an environment where people feel free to discuss issues, including aspects of change and personal matters, openly and honestly and without fear of recrimination or retribution. The leader should also create a learning environment where feedback is seen as a means to self-improvement as well as team efficiency and effectiveness.

When offering feedback to individuals the leader should bear the following in mind.

(1) Generally individuals seem to prefer being given feedback in private especially if it has negative connotations. If there are lessons to be learned that go beyond individual sensitivities, these can be formulated in directions and policies without reference to the person or persons concerned.
(2) Seek, in all cases, to offer elements of praise if the circumstances warrant such a course of action. It would not be right to offer artificial or false praise. The purpose of praise is to recognise those things that a person has done well and to set the positive aspects against the negative ones. Indeed, the positive features may heavily outweigh the negative aspects. Additionally, praise at the outset will help to create an atmosphere conducive to the reception of matters that are harder to accept.
(3) Never seek to subject the person receiving feedback to personal abuse. Personal abuse is likely to cause resentment, anger and resistance to change. Any remarks must concentrate on observable behaviour and aspects of performance for which there is evidence. In short, concentrate on performance and not personality. The use of facts will bring credibility and objectivity to proceedings. The facts will also bring strength to a well-prepared case because they are hard to refute.
(4) Invite individuals receiving feedback to comment on its validity. A person delivering feedback must listen carefully to what the person receiving it has to say. If necessary, the person giving feedback should be prepared to change his or her position in the light of new facts offered by the respondent.
(5) Where appropriate, ask the person gaining feedback to consider the consequences of what they have done. Consequences might include, for example, failure to complete tasks and objectives, public dissatisfaction or even a misconduct investigation.

(6) Ask the person who is the subject of the feedback to generate solutions to any perceived problem. This course of action helps the individual concerned to think about the full nature of a problem. Also, the person is being empowered to solve the problem him- or herself and this is good for self-esteem. When a person is able to generate his or her own solution to a problem, he or she is more likely to implement it and make sure that it works. Of course, if the person involved is unable to solve a problem the person giving feedback can steer him or her towards a workable and desirable course of action. On occasions, the person offering feedback may have to direct that a certain course of action be taken. However, given the earlier comments, such directions may not offer the best way out of difficulties.

(7) Provide any appropriate help or training that the individual concerned requires to deal with problems identified. Where personal problems exist, the leader should seek appropriate help through, for instance, the Human Resources Department.

(8) Invite the person receiving feedback to summarise what has taken place along with any remedial measures that need to be taken. Summarising offers an opportunity to check understanding and to make certain that the person concerned then follows the correct course of action.

(9) Make sure that the person receiving feedback fully understands the consequences of a failure to correct mistakes. This advice is especially important in misconduct cases.

(10) Monitor what then takes place to set time limits so as to be certain that errors are eliminated, efficiency and effectiveness are achieved and the person concerned learns from the experience. If necessary, further discussions between the person offering feedback and the person receiving it should take place. Substantial improvements in performance will justify the giving of praise by the leader who gave the feedback.

21.3 How can a leader use feedback skills to debrief team work and projects?

A leader should deal with feedback at team level using the principles outlined in the previous section. Exploring the progress and completion of tasks and objectives should be a permanent feature of regular team meetings. Individuals should not be embarrassed in any way but where there is a collective responsibility this may be explored with the entire team without concentrating on individuals. However, some individuals may voluntarily put themselves up for scrutiny and such an action should be respected and appreciated. Projects and major operations should be explored in much the same way, but see also Chapter 23, 'Communications—debriefing skills'.

21.4 How can a leader invest feedback into the learning process?

Feedback fits into the notion of a 'learning culture'. A learning culture is a culture where learning is taken from both successes and failures. Learning helps an organisation to develop and grow by turning mistakes into investments. The investment is greatly increased if the ingredients of success and lessons learned from failure are collated and introduced into an organisation's learning programme.

A learning culture also involves passing information (knowledge) from one part of an organisation to another, including outstations. Learning can take place at all levels of an organisation and should form part of any communications strategy. This implies a well-thought-out structure, which allows the flow of information and the presence of a central coordinating function. However, there is no good reason why at a tactical level sergeants and inspectors should not record and pass on valuable information to team members, operational colleagues, training units and even senior management. Additionally, sergeant and inspector leaders should try to encourage reciprocal arrangements.

21.5 Should a leader encourage feedback from others?

A leader should not hesitate to invite feedback from team members or anyone else, including agencies who cooperate with police and the public at large. Feedback should help the leader to develop him- or herself as well as the team and show team members that he or she is not excluded from, but is part of, a very important communication process.

Reference and further reading

Chartered Management Institute (2013), *Managing Others: Teams and Individuals* (London: Profile Books).

22

Communications—briefing skills

22.1 Why is it necessary to brief people especially when an event may be small in nature?

An efficient member of police staff has to have a clear and appropriate written job specification detailing what is required of him or her and be well trained, coached and directed. Allied to these important considerations is a need for people to know what *exactly* it is that they have to do if they are to complete specific tasks and objectives successfully. Objectives may be fairly routine or part of major policing operations. If people are not briefed properly then in any work situation they are likely to make mistakes. This could result in an embarrassing failure to achieve sought-after outcomes and, in the process, damage the reputation of the leader and perhaps the police service itself.

To maximise learning, this chapter will concentrate on large-scale briefings resulting from major policing events involving, for example, the exercise of democratic rights to protest (public order), rioting (public disorder), major incidents such as a train crash or ceremonial occasions involving, for instance, the monarch. This does not diminish the importance of daily, operational requirements or the need for people to be made aware of what they have to do to satisfy the day's demands.

It does not matter if an operation is small scale or large scale—all people involved in it need to briefed so that they:

- know precisely what the objectives are and what the planner hopes to achieve;
- are aware of what they have to do, how they are going to do it and why they are doing it;
- realise what other people have been asked to do, why they are doing it and how it links in with what everyone else is doing;
- are alert to the possibility of certain risks and difficulties and how they might be managed;
- understand the command structure and various means of communication.

22.2 What does a leader have to do to carry out an effective briefing?

This book lays considerable emphasis on the importance of communications and using interpersonal skills to full advantage whilst making it clear how difficult it can be to pass on a message accurately because of differing experiences and perceptions (Chapters 17–25). The information that follows is designed to support the best use of a leader's communication skills.

When conducting a briefing session, a leader should do the following:

(1) Choose a briefing venue that is suitable for the numbers of persons assembled for the briefing and devoid of distractions including noise. Consideration should also be given to seating and general comfort including, where appropriate, refreshments, lighting and briefing aids such as PowerPoint and flip charts.
(2) Invite for briefing those persons whose roles are essential to an efficient and effective operation. With small-scale events, everyone involved may be able to attend a briefing. However, at large-scale events it may be possible only to invite key players who would then have to cascade information and directions down accurately to other participants.
(3) Prepare and be totally familiar with the material to be used at the briefing. This includes being clear about objectives and desired outcomes.
(4) Manage time effectively. The Chartered Management Institute (2013), in discussing group communication, notes the importance of setting time limits, being realistic about what can be achieved in the allotted time and being sensitive to the pressures on participants' time. Setting time limits (short rather than long) also encourages presenters to be brief and concise rather than rambling. Rambling presentations may encourage boredom, disinterest and inattention.
(5) Remember that reinforcement of a message is important if the full details are to be absorbed by the persons being briefed. Therefore, the leader should back any oral presentation with written instructions, diagrams and other important information and invite participants to take their own notes. Visually presented information (e.g. PowerPoint) will add to the reinforcement process as will summarising oral information at intervals but especially at the conclusion of a briefing.
(6) Ensure that those being briefed are made fully aware of what the objectives are and what will constitute a successful outcome, what they have to do, how they are going to do it and why they are doing it.
(7) Acquaint those being briefed with what their colleagues are being required to do, why they are doing it and how what they have been assigned to do fits in with their responsibilities and the actions of others.
(8) Make sure that people being briefed are aware of difficulties and risks and how these might be overcome or brought to the attention of the leader.
(9) Ask those being briefed to follow directions but be prepared to exercise initiative where a particular situation that arises requires it (exercising initiative in trying circumstances is a leadership matter).
(10) Make certain that those being briefed are fully aware of the command and communication structure including where the main control point is, who the controller is and how communications as a whole will work. (For police, the Gold (strategic), Silver (tactical) and Bronze (operational) command system will almost certainly apply.)

Additionally, the leader should exercise his or her interpersonal skills by the following:

(11) Watch the body language of persons receiving messages. Body language may indicate, for example, discomfiture at certain instructions, a failure to listen properly (lack of eye contact or talking to a neighbour while the briefing is in progress or gazing thoughtlessly out of a nearby window). Equally, it may show someone's eagerness to participate in formulating plans by expressing various views.
(12) Invite questions, for example to gain clarification or further information or additional instructions.
(13) Listen intently to questions, ideas, suggestions and doubts.
(14) Ask people (especially those with key functions), where feasible and appropriate, to summarise what they are being required to do. This will confirm whether a message has been accurately received. Failure to receive a message accurately may cause real difficulties subsequently.

The Chartered Management Institute (2013) mentions the 'group think' phenomenon where participants tend to conform to opinions supporting the majority view. On occasions, the majority view may be appropriate but on others 'group think' may lead to poor decision making.

Where briefings comprise a large number of participants it may be necessary for the leader to hold several briefing sessions. In such circumstances every effort should be made to brief key personnel with those they are working with so that a sense of common purpose is firmly established. It is essential that all briefings carry the same identical messages. This can only be assured if the leader personally attends each briefing session or, alternatively, all those carrying out briefing duties follow exactly the same script. However, there is a danger that interpretations may differ especially when responding to on-the-spot operational questions arising from those being briefed.

Every effort should be made to ensure that people are properly briefed before they leave the briefing area as a failure to absorb correct instructions could prove disastrous. The leader should emphasise that where people are in doubt they must ask for clarification.

22.3 How will a leader know that he or she has successfully briefed people to carry out a task or tasks?

A leader will know if he or she has briefed people properly largely by the end results—that is, whether an operation passes off successfully, although factors other than briefings can affect outcomes. For instance, unknown and unexpected developments or communications equipment breakdown. However, the level of a leader's briefing competence should be revealed by a post-operation debriefing session. (See Chapter 23, 'Communications—debriefing skills'.)

Reference and further reading

Chartered Management Institute (2013), *Managing Others: Teams and Individuals* (London: Profile Books).

23

Communications—debriefing skills

23.1 Why is it important for a leader to debrief events?

This chapter should be read in conjunction with Chapter 21 dealing with feedback and Chapter 22 concerned with briefing skills as both have a direct connection with debriefing skills.

Debriefing amounts to a feedback session and the process encompasses individuals, team and operational debriefs. This chapter concentrates on debriefing large-scale police operations following on, for example, from a rail crash, air crash, flooding, public demonstrations and serious public disorder.

All significant tasks and operations benefit from debriefing methods including those that go well. Failing to debrief any event, and especially significant events, is unwise given the loss of valuable experience and learning that may occur. An organisation or police force that fails to learn is likely to repeat its mistakes. Neglecting to debrief helps to maintain the status quo whereas debriefing opens the way to doing things differently, more economically and better.

23.1.1 Specific reasons for holding debriefing sessions

The purposes of debriefing are to:

- impartially and without attributing blame ascertain the degree to which events ran to plan;
- measure the efficiency and effectiveness of plans or arrangements;
- make immediate corrections or adjustments to existing procedures where necessary;
- note those things that went well and those that did not in order to embed the former and correct the latter;
- seek ideas and suggestions for improvement;
- utilise knowledge gained for future events and spread good practices to areas that would benefit from receiving them, for example divisions, departments, training and development units and other police forces;
- help the police service as a whole to offer the best possible service to the public.

23.2 The role of leaders in the debriefing procedure

Where the briefing of individuals, teams or others is concerned, briefing and debriefing are the built-in responsibilities of team leaders (for the purpose of this book—sergeants and inspectors). In this regard, leaders (at any level) are likely to be more successful if they are respected, honest, fair and seen as competent. The likelihood of success is enhanced if they show a willingness to tackle and see through problems and give credit and praise where this is earned.

Where the debriefing of major events of some magnitude is concerned, the responsibility for debriefing is likely to fall to a senior officer. However, he or she may wish to delegate the actual debriefing process to some other competent person or facilitator. This enables the leader to watch, listen and take notes without getting involved in the detail of the debriefing exercise.

23.3 Who should be invited to debriefing sessions?

Debriefing leaders should invite to debriefing sessions those people who contributed to the event or occurrence. Sessions should not be confined to managers, team leaders, supervisors and specialists but also include individuals (e.g. constables, detectives and civil staff) who carried out specific tasks. People who actually perform tasks are among those best able to suggest improvements to activities or procedures. Also, consideration should be given to inviting representatives from outside agencies involved with the event in question for their perspectives. Feedback from the general public should be considered where appropriate.

23.4 Briefings and debriefings linked

It is really important that all people in an organisation should know about the recognised briefing and debriefing processes. Having been properly briefed, people should be told that they may be asked to take part in a subsequent debrief. To this end, they should be encouraged to make their own notes when important matters arise during activities.

23.5 How does a leader carry out the debriefing process?

The debriefing session follows closely the format for briefing people and for ease of reference certain of the briefing elements are reproduced here along with other additional information.

When debriefing the leader should do the following:

(1) Choose a debriefing venue that is suitable for the number of persons assembled for the debriefing and devoid of distractions including noise. Consideration should also be given to seating and general comfort including, where appropriate, refreshments, lighting and briefing aids such as PowerPoint and flip charts.
(2) Plan debriefing sessions in advance taking into account what the objectives were and the extent to which they were or were not achieved.
(3) Invite for debriefing those persons whose roles were essential in carrying out the operation to be debriefed. With small-scale events everyone involved may be able to attend a debriefing. However, for large-scale events

it may be possible only to invite key players who should be instructed to consult with their colleagues before attending the debriefing session. Where appropriate, other agencies should be included in a debriefing session along with any views of members of the public where applicable.

(4) Manage time effectively, taking notice of the Chartered Management Institute's (2013) observation that with regard to group communication, it is important to set time limits, being realistic about what can be achieved in the allotted time and being sensitive to the pressures on participants' time. Setting time limits (short rather than long) also encourages presenters to be brief and concise rather than rambling. Rambling debriefs may encourage boredom, disinterest and inattention.

Additionally the leader should do the following.

(5) Based upon fact and evidence, clearly and succinctly outline what happened during the operation being debriefed, stating what the results of police actions were and what appeared to contribute to success or failure. Throughout this action the leader should carefully note any positive or negative reactions by those persons present so as to identify those who can help with opinions, ideas and suggestions.

(6) Exercise his or her interpersonal skills to full advantage, for example, by:
- giving non-threatening feedback and accepting feedback in return in a positive and non-defensive manner;
- watching reactions expressed through the use of body language and noting voice tone to detect emotion including anger and frustration and agreement (each to be explored and adapted to the learning process);
- expressing empathy with contributors especially with those who have experienced operational difficulties;
- offering praise where it is due;
- asking open, probing questions to establish facts and, where appropriate, to gain information or test views;
- listening carefully and paying full attention to what is being said;
- clarifying unclear messages and summarising regularly so as to maintain a common understanding of the point reached in discussions and also at the end of the debrief;
- asking those assembled to remark upon the quality of both the briefing and the debriefing sessions and inviting suggestions for improvement.

23.6 What should a leader do with information and ideas gathered from a debriefing programme?

After a debriefing session has taken place the leader may have to take some remedial action to correct continuing operational faults. It is vital that lessons should be learned, and valuable information not lost. Therefore, the leader should seek to invest what has been learned into policies and activities that support similar operations in the future. Where appropriate, new methods should be incorporated into training and development initiatives.

23.7 How will a leader know whether he or she is a good debriefing officer?

It is very important that the performance of leaders conducting debriefing sessions is measured so as to ensure competence and the best results. This can be done by critical self-analysis and by inviting constructive feedback from persons attending debriefing sessions. Having received feedback, the conscientious leader wishing to make genuine improvements should carefully consider and act upon feedback.

It is important to note too that feedback is not always sensible and without bias but no feedback should be dismissed out of hand. This would amount to very bad practice indeed. Where feedback is in doubt, the leader should ask its giver to justify remarks with facts and evidence. Another way of confirming or denying the quality of feedback is to seek the view of as many people as possible who were involved with the operational source of the criticism.

Reference and further reading

Chartered Management Institute (2013), *Managing Others: Team and Individuals* (London: Profile Books).

24

Communications—influencing skills

24.1 Looking at why influencing skills are essential for the effective leader

Leaders need to exercise influence over others and events as well as over, for example, team members, senior managers, agencies and others intimately involved with the police. This includes members of the public particularly at public meetings. Exercising influence helps to sell ideas and gain cooperation and commitment. It also encourages participation and support for workplace and policing interventions. It is important to remember, however, that making efforts to influence people does not mean failing to listen to and value suggestions and contributions made by others.

Where sergeant and inspector leaders are concerned it may be necessary, for example, to be able to influence team members who have to be persuaded that the leader's 'vision' is sound or that potentially disruptive change is worthwhile and can be successfully managed with their help. Also, a sergeant or inspector leader may have to persuade and convince senior management to adopt or support a certain course of action. Equally, the sergeant or inspector leader may have to persuade members of the public that certain policing plans and methods are sound.

The link between persuasion and influence is always present. Influencing is also about negotiating, in that people may be required to alter their views and adopt new ones. If this is the case, they may wish to gain some benefit in exchange for losses. In any event, it is unlikely that a person will be persuaded or influenced to change his or her position if they place themselves or others at a disadvantage.

It is worth noting specifically some of the reasons why leaders might wish to influence others. Reasons may include a need to:

- create sound relationships with team members, other police teams, peers and senior officers, based upon mutual cooperation and respect;
- build relationships with all manner of public bodies and institutions;
- motivate staff and team participants to improve efficiency and effectiveness and achieve objectives;
- agree mutually acceptable solutions with others;
- promote ideas and suggestions successfully;
- maximise one's potential and improve career prospects;
- maintain feelings of self-worth and of feeling valued;
- have considerable control over the direction of one's career and life.

KEY POINT—INFLUENCING OTHERS

Gaining influence with others and over events is a key leadership skill that requires the use of a whole bundle of interpersonal skills (as revealed in this book in the communication chapters). These include listening to other points of view, ideas and suggestions and showing sensitivity and empathy as well as being clear about desired outcomes and the needs of others. Sensible cooperation can increase support and impetus and widen the creative process so as to maximise effort and reduce costs and achieve the best possible results.

24.2 **How does a leader exercise influence?**

There appears to be little doubt that personality and attitudes play an important part in the ways in which we try to influence others. If we behave badly we are likely to get a hostile response. If we respect, value, esteem and cooperate with other people then we are more likely to achieve mutually acceptable results. *Success will then underpin future relationships and transactions.* This is because the ways in which we treat and esteem people are at the heart of good communications.

The following are important fundamental principles that form the basis for gaining influence. A leader should:

- be competent and credible in the area or areas in which he or she wishes to exert influence;
- be clear about what he or she wants to achieve and what success will mean—this usually entails having written objectives;
- remember the fundamentals of negotiation—be sensitive to what is taking place, the reactions and needs of others and the requirement that all sides should share in success and not feel cheated in any way.

In truth, influencing requires many interlaced skills; however, it is worth pointing out some of the important skills required.

- *Planning and objective setting*—planning relies on having a clear sense of purpose. Planning also offers an unambiguous way forward.
- *Asserting*—assertiveness is a key influencing skill because it offers a purposeful approach with respect for others. Being assertive means being honest, open and forthright and acting upon one's own rights but acknowledging the rights of others. Assertiveness helps greatly with dealing with hostility and unreasonable behaviour.
- *Negotiating* and assertiveness skills are intertwined. Negotiation is based upon a 'win-win' situation—seeking compromise and agreement and making concessions where appropriate.

- Using *interpersonal skills*—showing empathy, listening intently, adopting the right body posture and watching the body language of others and questioning—using open questions and probing with follow-up questions.

Added to these skills are the following:

- Offering carefully collected facts and presenting information logically in a clear and concise manner.
- Discussing the strengths of particular proposals and their merits and benefits and includes anticipating and planning how to deal with perceived difficulties and using reason to win people over.
- Recognizing, accepting and incorporating other points of view, ideas and suggestions, and giving thanks and praise for contributions where they are deserved.
- Believing in the concept and selling messages with sincerity and in an exciting, dynamic fashion; at the same time endeavouring to get others to buy into ideas and suggestions in a similarly enthusiastic manner.
- Selling messages—linked to *presentation skills*. It is no good having superb ideas if you cannot put them over to others. Presentation skills include careful planning, having clear objectives, good interpersonal skills and a logical narrative including facts and detail. Also required are strong reinforcement techniques; that is, an introduction, an exposition and a conclusion, plus visual aids and written handouts.

When endeavouring to influence others the leader should also:

- be patient with people and allow them to express their views;
- be devoid of emotional involvement, avoiding distracting and damaging confrontations;
- be straightforward, transparent and not manipulative;
- not exaggerate the benefits of an idea, plan or concept as this may damage their credibility—too many benefits may arouse suspicions quite unnecessarily and draw attention away from the really beneficial proposals;
- accept that it is a sign of confidence and strength to admit that something is wrong, for frank admissions add to credibility and things may be put right by accepting new ideas and suggestions where appropriate;
- refer to 'we' or 'us' rather than 'you' and 'I' when trying to get people to gain ownership in the process;
- seek evidence and facts politely, when people make unfounded allegations or spurious proposals;
- build alliances with those who appear to be supporting proposals or are open to persuasion.

24.3 **Some tips for leaders attending public meetings**

The following tips may help sergeant and inspector leaders and other police leaders attending public meetings:

- Be fully conversant with proposed plans and understand every detail of them. But do not regard them as 'set in concrete' and be open to ideas and suggestions put forward by those attending a meeting. If they see that you are flexible, that will add credibility to your ideas and they are more likely to accept plans to which they have contributed.
- At some contentious meetings you may receive a hostile reception. *The public are entitled to criticise police failures and shortcomings.* In these circumstances, you need to remain calm, professional, unruffled and non-antagonistic and show a willingness to listen and learn. You should try to anticipate problems and have genuine answers or solutions for them where possible. If you do not have the answers then commit yourself to finding them and coming back to the questioner or complainant concerned. You should admit where things have gone wrong but not dwell too much on the past, preferring instead to move on and make the changes that everyone wants.
- Sometimes people at public meetings wish to draw attention to their own specific and special circumstances which are difficult to respond to without further detailed inquiry. The circumstances in this instance also tend to obscure the main reasons for which the meeting was called. In such cases, grievances should be politely acknowledged with a promise that they will be dealt with outside the meeting.
- All relevant criticism should be listened to and responded to but where allegations appear to be unfounded or unreasonable the person making them should be required to produce evidence for them.
- Use interpersonal skills to full advantage and use empathy in particular to show that you appreciate how people may feel when they express, for example, anger, despair or disillusionment. You should listen intently, ask open questions where needed and thank people where they offer help or suggestions.
- Consider, where possible and desirable, asking those at a meeting to take an active part in reaching and enacting solutions. Involvement will bind police and public together in cooperation and keep the situation open to fresh initiatives.

24.4 **How will a leader know whether he or she is good at influencing others and events?**

Trying to gain influence involves a complicated bundle of planning and interpersonal skills, practice and experience. A leader is likely to struggle to achieve and maximise the benefits of objectives if he or she cannot gain influence, cooperation and help where it really matters. As with the application of other skills, a leader's ability to be influential should be judged by results, critical self-analysis and feedback from others.

References and further reading

Gillen, T. (1995), *Positive Influencing Skills* (London: Institute of Personnel & Development).

Johnson, R. and Eaton, J. (2002), *Influencing People* (London: Dorling Kindersley).

Murdock, A. and Scutt, C. (1993), *Personal Effectiveness* (Oxford: Butterworth-Heinemann).

25

Influencing skills—report writing

25.1 How can a written report be seen as an influencing agent?

Many people see report writing as an arduous chore. However, report writing is very useful for gathering ideas and suggestions and facts and evidence in order to present a particular point of view for consideration by others interested in outcomes and in perhaps approving the way forward. Therefore, sergeant and inspector leaders should not regard report writing as burdensome but as a means to gain and exercise influence.

Reports take many forms but all of these require careful research and consideration before facts, conclusions and recommendations are presented to readers. Poorly researched and badly structured and written reports are likely to have negative rather than positive results and reflect badly upon the writer.

25.1.1 Types of report

The number and variety of reports is extremely wide but might include, for example, reports:

- detailing suggestions on how to police local events with assessment reports being submitted at their conclusion;
- putting forward detailed observations and recommendations for policing major public events with the potential for disorder and extending beyond local considerations;
- looking at particular aspects of workplace efficiency and suggesting places where improvements might be made;
- designed to influence the agencies and other public bodies with whom the police have regular and meaningful contact;
- responding to all manner of queries, internal and external, about policing issues.

25.1.2 Different approaches to report writing

This chapter recognises that there are many ways of writing reports and that there is no 'one way' of doing so, although the writer must always remain true to the notion that reports should be clear in their objective, their content and their presentation. Therefore, sergeant and inspector leaders are advised to discover the various formats and ways of doing things required at the places in which they serve. This chapter does, however, set out a way of constructing a report in a logical and professional manner and the principles put forward and the framework offered can be adapted to suit a writer's particular needs.

25.1.3 **Problems with conveying messages accurately**

The writer needs to bear in mind the difficulty of conveying messages accurately and ensuring that they are interpreted in the way intended (see also Chapter 17, 'Communications—general discussion'). To achieve clarity of purpose, the writer has the considerable task of presenting information in an unbiased, clear, concise and logical way that as well as satisfying a set writing objective also recognises the needs of the reader.

25.2 **What are the barriers to effective written communications?**

The previous section hinted at the barriers to good report writing and there are many of them, including:

- *a failure to plan* and to be clear about what the report is intended to achieve resulting in a confused narrative and a confused reader. A writing objective is important (see also Chapter 10, 'Planning', section 10.2.6 on SMART objectives);
- *a failure to devise a suitable structure* for conveying a message or messages logically and clearly;
- *a failure to take account of the reader or readers* and what they already know, what is expected of them on receiving the report and how they are likely to react;
- *straying from the facts* and evidence and exhibiting bias and prejudice;
- *badly presented written work* includes a poor and confusing layout and inadequate presentation, which can lead to a failure to place emphasis on other important parts of a report through the use of, for example, headings, subheadings, diagrams and charts. Visual aspects are significant because they make the text inviting and interesting;
- *a poor vocabulary* leading to a lack of subtlety in word use and a loss of influence due to a failure to make the best argument possible;
- *poorly constructed sentences and paragraphs* including overly long sentences and overly long paragraphs;
- *bad spelling* and the use of unnecessarily complicated words when simpler, clearer words would do just as well;
- *the use of jargon,* acronyms, abbreviations and technical language. Jargon is a language developed between persons working in the same areas of interest (the police service has its own jargon). Jargon is acceptable within but not outside those areas. Once a lay person is involved in communications, normal English usage applies and not 'gobbledygook'—that is, indecipherable technical or confused writing;
- *poor punctuation and grammar* resulting in a loss of narrative impact;
- *a failure to logically link facts and evidence with conclusions and recommendations* for this can seriously undermine a report's credibility.

25.3 The report—important features

Section 25.2 presents important aspects of planning regarding, for example, having a planning objective, devising an appropriate report structure, considering the needs of the reader and creating visually attractive reports, which are well written and logical in their outcomes. The information which now follows is designed to augment these important principles.

25.3.1 Report design

Report design—to encourage the reader to want to read the report the writer must consider making it attractive and interesting and easy to explore. If the reader considers that a piece of writing is carelessly and inconsiderately put together, he or she may become hostile to its contents and think badly of the writer. This diminishes the writer's ability to influence the reader. In this regard the writer should consider:

- what quality paper to use and, where desirable, what sort of cover would be appropriate and how the report should be pulled together, maybe with, for example, metal staples or a plastic, spiral spine or a full book binding;
- what kind of type to use, for example 'Times New Roman', and which font size to adopt to help with both clarity and readability;
- making information easily accessible, for example by creating a table of contents, using plain language and reinforcing important information with headings, italics and diagrams whilst placing supportive but less important information in appendices or annexes.

25.3.2 The report front cover

The front cover of a report is the first thing a reader sees, and it is important that it should be eye-catching. This allows the writer scope for invention but not over-elaboration. A cover should be simple and contain a report title, the date of publication and the writer's details (including professional and academic qualifications).

25.3.3 The executive summary

An executive summary following the title page amounts to a brief but clear précis of the report's contents. Again, this is an important 'trailer' to the report itself. The busy reader will judge from the summary whether the report is worth reading at all. If he or she decides not to read the report then all of the writer's hard work goes for nothing. A précis should be as brief as possible and ideally not exceed half a sheet of A4 paper and definitely not one full page.

25.3.4 **The table of contents**

The report's table of contents should follow the executive summary. It should include the subjects covered in the various sections by way of their individual headings and subheadings and page numbers. The reader uses the contents page to measure the subject matter of the report and whether to read all the sections. Also, he or she uses the table of contents as a means to journey around the report from subject to subject.

25.3.5 **Numbering**

As a general rule, all of a report's pages should be numbered to match the table of contents. How a report is numbered is a matter for the writer. As an exception, the writer may decide not to number the executive summary. Many writers number the table of contents in the following way: (i), (ii), (iii), (iv), etc. These small 'Roman numerals' in brackets draw a distinction between the nature of the contents and the numbering of the report itself which should ideally be in 'Arabic numerals', for example: 1, 2, 3, etc. (Some people do not number the first page of the narrative, with the number 2 appearing on the second page (number 1 being omitted).) Appendices should be lettered A, B, C, etc.

The report's subject headings should be emboldened and numbered consecutively with Arabic numerals, for example: 1, 2, 3, etc. Ensuing paragraphs should be numbered to follow the subject headings thus: 1.1, 1.2, 1.3 and 2.1, 2.2, 2.3, etc (some writers further subdivide numbers and this is fine in helping to draw distinctions between various pieces of information, but numbering can if pursued even further become overcomplicated).

25.3.6 **Bullet points**

Writers use various types of bullet points as they are useful for highlighting certain topics in a list, for example:

Regular police street patrols are important because they—

- offer reassurance to members of the public;
- help to maintain the peace;
- deter criminals from committing offences; and
- enable officers to make arrests and report offences where the law has been infringed.

Although they can be visually attractive, bullet points do not always allow for quick reference. For example, if a writer wished to draw a reader's attention to 'deter criminals from committing offences' above during a discussion of a report, he or she would have to ask the reader to count 'three bullet points down' to reach the topic. The longer the list of bullet points, the more difficult this becomes, whereas sequentially numbered or alphabetically lettered points ((1) or (i) or (a)) would enable the rapid identification of particular points. However, when and where to use bullet points is a matter of choice and judgement.

25.3.7 **Reinforcement of information**

The process of reinforcing information provided is important because it is necessary to thoroughly embed a message and help the reader to understand what the writer wants from him or her. Aspects of visual presentation are important in this regard but so is a report structure which includes, for example, an *introduction*, an *exposition* and a *conclusion*. Each of these major inclusions should overlap to produce a binding, comprehensive message. For instance, an introduction states what is being done and why and how, an exposition draws together the facts and evidence and a conclusion analyses and presents a logical and reasoned outcome to be turned into equally logical recommendations.

25.3.8 **Words**

Words are obviously of great importance. The wider vocabulary the leader has, the better he or she will be able to express him- or herself. This is essential in both the oral and the written sense when seeking to gain influence. An inquisitive interest in words and especially their origins helps the writer to use them in the subtlest of nuanced ways adding greatly to the interpretation of true meaning. Wherever possible the report writer should try to use plain words rather than complex words. Bad spelling will damage the writer's credibility and the worth of any report.

25.3.9 **Sentences**

Shorter sentences enable the reader to take in information quickly and are ideal for report writing. Longer sentences may oblige a reader to backtrack in order to have a second go at grasping meaning. However, if every sentence were about the same length the text might appear staccato and a little uninteresting. Some sentences are necessarily longer but a mixture of sentences is likely to increase the reader's interest.

25.3.10 **Verbs**

Verbs give life and energy to written work. Where possible the writer should use active rather than passive verbs. When the subject of a verb performs the action described by a verb then the verb is deemed to be active. Conversely, when the subject of a verb receives or incurs the action of a verb then the verb is said to be passive. For example:

(1) Active verb (seven words)—
The police constable sounded the fire alarm.

(2) Passive verb (nine words)—
The fire alarm was sounded by the police constable.

The meaning of the two sentences is much the same. However, with the active verb example the emphasis is on the police constable whereas in the case of the passive verb it is upon the fire alarm. Writing with active verbs is more direct and there is usually a word saving over similar passive verb sentences. In this minor example the difference is two words. This means that there could be significant savings in a lengthy piece of prose.

25.3.11 **Paragraphs**

Paragraphs may consist of one or more sentences. Wherever possible a paragraph should be short and clear and be confined to the topic under discussion. A failure to construct paragraphs in this way may damage the logical flow of narrative and cause confusion. Also, the reader may be daunted by excessively long and forbidding paragraphs.

25.3.12 **Grammar**

Grammar is clearly very important, and a lack of competence may severely damage a writer's credibility. Grammar dictates the writing conventions that we all have to use when putting reports and other documents together.

25.3.13 **Punctuation**

Imagine a page of writing that appears without any form of punctuation whatsoever—not even a 'full stop' to indicate a conclusion. The reader would be put off by what would appear to be a single mass of information. Punctuation helps to create sense of what we write and give meaning and vitality to our prose. It follows, therefore, that the writer needs to be in full possession of fine punctuation skills.

25.4 **The report—a structure**

It is important that a report has a logical structure and the structure which follows is in keeping with the observations made in this chapter.

25.4.1 **Introduction**

The report introduction should include:

- why the report is being written, a brief synopsis of what the report contains and what it is intended to achieve;
- terms of reference and sponsor (if any);
- research methodology; and
- any other information deemed important and necessary.

25.4.2 **The report exposition, facts or findings**

The main body of the report should contain facts and evidence but not usually supposition or conjecture unless this can be justified. It should be based upon reason with the merits of particular pieces of information being discussed in full. The report should not stray from its writing aims or terms of reference. However, where the writer considers this to be necessary, areas for further research may be indicated. The content of the report should be produced in a logical and chronological form.

25.4.3 **The report conclusions**

The facts of the report should lead to logical and justifiable conclusions which should be expressed in simple but very clear terms. Individual conclusions should be cross-referenced with the appropriate paragraphs in the main body of the report.

25.4.4 **The report recommendations**

Again, the report's recommendations should follow on logically from the conclusions which themselves should follow on logically from the facts. (This reinforcement process adds impact to the report and the reader's awareness of what is required of him or her.)

25.4.5 **Appendices or annexes**

Appendices and annexes are used to remove information from the main body of the report to the back of the document. Information removed amounts to additional material that can be examined later at the reader's leisure. If it is of critical importance that material should remain with the body of the report. Appendices or annexes are usually produced in alphabetical order, for example: Appendix A, Appendix B, etc. They should be recorded at the end of the report's table of contents after the main subject headings.

25.4.6 **Speed reading**

Some busy people speed read reports and this process is aided by:

- a short introduction;
- a topic sentence at the beginning of each paragraph (i.e. a sentence introducing the subject matter under discussion in a clear and unambiguous way);
- headings and subheadings;
- emboldened, underlined and italicised words;
- a brief summary; and
- a brief set of recommendations.

25.5 **How will a leader know whether he or she is a good report writer?**

A leader will know whether he or she is a good writer if what a report is intended to achieve is in fact achieved. Additionally, he or she should review his or her writing skills as a result of experience and feedback solicited from others including a report's recipients either indirectly or directly.

References and further reading

Aitchison, J. (1994), *Guide to Written English* (London: Cassell).
Pythian, B. A. (1980), *English Grammar* (Sevenoaks: Hodder & Stoughton).

26

Meeting skills

26.1 Introduction

It is likely that many of us have experienced meetings that have been aimless in their purpose, unstructured and poorly controlled. Thus, meetings can amount to a frustrating, expensive nightmare, dominated by a few strong-minded individuals exercising control over the chair instead of the other way around. This chapter sets out to lay down some of the main principles essential for the running of effective meetings. The information provided concentrates on 'formal' chaired meetings but it can be adapted for sergeant- and inspector-run teams and other meetings, including public meetings.

Meetings take many forms but all require the sophisticated use of the interpersonal skills which this 'toolkit' covers at some length in the preceding Chapters 17–24. Acting as a chair will test a sergeant or inspector or other police leader's interpersonal skills to the full.

26.2 What is the purpose of a formal chaired meeting?

Put into simple terms, formal chaired meetings are convened to satisfy the specific reasons for which they have been called. Broadly, however, it is suggested that meetings are convened to:

- draw upon the expertise of those assembled to discuss issues;
- improve contact and communications between meetings members working together regularly;
- plan the way ahead;
- solve problems and create appropriate solutions;
- make decisions and allocate work;
- offer guidance and information;
- review, evaluate and validate the impact of decisions made and make adjustments where appropriate;
- provide an enhanced service for the public.

KEY POINT—MEETINGS ARE COSTLY

It is stressed that *meetings can be very time-consuming and expensive*. Therefore, they should only be called when other, perhaps cheaper and more appropriate, methods of resolving issues have been carefully considered.

26.3 Why are so many meetings time-wasters?

There are many reasons why meetings are ineffective and these include:

- being unclear about the reasons for holding a meeting;
- poor planning and a badly constructed agenda;

- poor chairing of the meeting including a lack of control of the proceedings;
- ill-prepared meeting members;
- meeting members who dominate meetings or who do not contribute at all;
- poor time keeping and overly long meetings often leading to tiredness and frustration.

26.4 **What is the role of the chairperson?**

The reasons why meetings are being convened must be clear otherwise people may have different views of what they are trying to achieve. They may, in such circumstances, pull in different directions causing conflict and confusion. Planning a meeting, and planning in general, requires the exercise of leadership skills. It is the job of the leader to make sure that people pull together to achieve a common objective. *The chair of a meeting is a leader* and participants act as team members.

A good way of helping to solve problems is to fall back on the experience, knowledge and skills of meeting members. Solutions are likely to emerge through a constructive dialogue and the pooling of expertise. It is a task of the chair of a meeting to encourage and develop ideas.

Meetings are a means to an end—increased efficiency and effectiveness, better policing and a better service for the public. They should result in tangible, beneficial outcomes. Therefore, it is important that when meeting members reach decisions they are acted upon. This presumes an integrated communication system which allows information to pass from meeting members to those responsible for enacting decisions and reporting back on progress.

26.4.1 **A chair's responsibilities**

The chair of a meeting has many responsibilities, for example he or she should:

- be absolutely clear about the purpose (aim) of the meeting for if he or she is unclear then so will the meeting members be unsure about what to do;
- set meeting rules governing processes and behaviours;
- ensure that the purpose of regular meetings is written down and given to meeting members along with the rules;
- decide the frequency and location of meetings and how long they will last;
- construct an agenda in the form of objectives (that support the purpose);
- appoint a minute secretary;
- select the right meeting members—that is, those people who can make meaningful contributions (membership may change from time to time depending upon the nature of the agenda);
- deploy a whole range of constructive interpersonal and problem-solving skills to get the best out of meeting members;

- allocate tasks with firm completion dates;
- evaluate and validate the practical outcomes of meeting decisions in the workplace or elsewhere including the public arena;
- evaluate through feedback the worth of each meeting in terms of the way it is run.

Additionally, the chair should set the rules for:

- the submission of papers for the attention of the minute secretary and meeting members;
- visiting speakers who, left uncontrolled, may dominate proceedings, including time allocations;
- the time limit for the publication of minutes;
- treating people who attend meetings without proper preparation;
- excluding meeting members for misconduct.

26.5 **How is an agenda put together?**

The chair should fix the agenda. It is *not* the job of the minute secretary to do so. That said, the minute secretary may (acting upon specific instructions) draft the agenda for the chair's approval. Responding to the chair's directions, the minute secretary may even prevent inappropriate items submitted by meeting members from appearing on the agenda. Equally, the minute secretary may question whether an item should be dealt with in another fashion by a meeting member (e.g. a series of telephone calls). However, the chair *must* take overall responsibility for the compilation and execution of the agenda.

The chair should be clear about what the desirable outcomes of the meeting are. Each agenda item should take the form of a measurable SMART objective. (See also Chapter 10, 'Planning', section 10.2.6.) Tasks in the form of mini-objectives flow from objectives. The chair should consider what the associated tasks are for they will help to guide discussions. The following is an example of an objective (in a shortened form):

> Objective: Reduce the overall overtime burden by 20%, by 31 December (year).
> Tasks:
> - discuss why there is a need to reduce overtime;
> - produce statistics to show how overtime is incurred and by whom;
> - test whether overtime is justified and set priorities;
> - discuss means of reducing overtime, for instance by stricter supervision, reducing workloads, acquiring additional help or investing in new technology;
> - decide on a way forward and allocate responsibilities (tasks for completion);
> - fix a review date for the monitoring of progress;
> - evaluate and validate outcomes.

A chair using this approach to agenda making helps to assist with establishing clarity of purpose, structure and time management. Time limits can be added as part of the SMART objective concept.

26.5.1 **Agenda format and procedures**

The agenda follows a well-known and time-honoured format as shown in the following example.

Date, Time and Place of Meeting

Agenda

1. Apologies for absence
2. Minutes of previous meeting
3. Matters arising
4. Item one—subject or topic
5. Item two—subject or topic
6. Item three—subject or topic
7. Any other business
8. Date of next meeting

Some meetings include standing agenda items. That is, the same item appears on the agenda each time a meeting takes place. Such items might cover, for example, security matters, health and safety at work issues or the monitoring of equal opportunities policies. It is perfectly acceptable to include standing items provided that they fall within the remit of the meeting and that their permanence is kept under very close review.

Apologies for absence—normally, when apologies for absence are recorded it is not necessary to note the reasons for absence. Absence is recorded to show that the person concerned is not involved in the decisions that the meeting makes. Similarly, if a meeting member retires early, the time of departing should be noted in the minutes. This should be done in a way that indicates how far they had got into the deliberation process.

Minutes of previous meeting—if the minutes have been circulated prior to the meeting then there is no need for the chair to read them out loud (Janner 1986). It is for meeting members to agree that the minutes are a correct record of proceedings. Although the chair should sign and date the minutes as a true account of what has taken place, he or she does not carry the sole responsibility for approving them.

Matters arising can turn into a confusing, lengthy, time-consuming debate. This is often caused by a misunderstanding of the purpose of matters arising. Matters arising should include significant issues emanating from the previous meeting. This infers that matters arising should be capable of being dealt with quickly. However, where it becomes apparent that substantial debate is still required it may be expedient to create a new agenda item.

Any other business is designed to accommodate urgent matters arising only after the agenda was fixed. Sometimes people will use 'Any other business' to drive through items when meeting members are tired and anticipating an early or scheduled close to the meeting. Important items can pass through under these conditions without the circulation of briefing papers and a proper discussion of the facts. The chair should make it quite clear that substantial non-urgent agenda items will not be entertained and must work their way onto the agenda in the normal approved way. Additionally, it is bad practice for the chair to invite each member (in turn) to state whether they wish to raise any issues under 'Any other business'. This unstructured approach can be time-consuming and is unnecessary.

Sequencing—sometimes agenda items are taken out of sequence. This may happen, for example, when a person wishes to make an important contribution before necessarily leaving the meeting early. If this happens, the minutes of the meeting should still reflect the order of the agenda.

Time issues—when fixing the agenda the chair must decide how much time will be allowed for each item. Time limits help to concentrate minds. A small allowance should be made to cater for any item that may unavoidably exceed its time allocation. Occasionally the cause of a meeting experiencing time difficulties lies with the lack of control exercised by the chair. Equally, the agenda may be unrealistic and have too many items on it for the time allotted. Items have to be prioritised before they are placed on the agenda to enable important items to be dealt with first. Often a heavy agenda is caused by the fact that the meeting members do not sit often enough. Difficulties such as these are a matter for the chair to resolve.

26.6 What is the role of the minute secretary?

The job of the minute secretary is a difficult one as well as being challenging and important to the successful running of a meeting. For example, it is the role of the minute secretary to:

- work closely with the chair of the meeting;
- direct meeting members to attend a given venue at a given date and time;
- where required and under the instruction and guidance of the chair, assist with the construction of the agenda;
- circulate an agenda and briefing papers prior to the meeting along with details of where and when the meeting will take place;
- take the minutes of the meeting;
- write up and circulate minutes after the meeting;
- file and care for meeting papers.

26.6.1 **The chair and minute secretary working together**

It is essential that the chair of a meeting and the minute secretary work in harmony and close cooperation. Given the background knowledge of the minute secretary and his or her importance to the proceedings, he or she should be positioned beside the chair at a meeting. This enables discussions between the chair and the minute secretary to take place where absolutely necessary. Basically, however, the minute secretary is a non-contributing member at the meeting.

Often the minute secretary has a memory of many meetings and acts as an important anchor for continuity, especially when chairs change on a fairly frequent basis. Because he or she is engaged in the regular recording of proceedings, the minute secretary usually has a recall of facts, and linking facts that might evade the memory or knowledge of the chair.

Additionally, with prior knowledge and respecting confidences, the minute secretary is often able to detect and transmit the feelings or positions of meeting members to the chair. Such information is invaluable in helping the chair to guide and control proceedings when meetings are in progress.

26.6.2 **The meeting venue**

The minute secretary should make sure that the meeting venue satisfies the comfort and other needs of meeting members. For example, arrangements should be made to eliminate unnecessary noise, provide a beneficial environment in terms of lighting and warmth, refreshments, writing materials (where appropriate) and table-top identification name plates.

26.6.3 **Minutes of meetings**

The chair and meeting members need to recognise that the task of taking minutes is a particularly onerous one and some people are unable to cope well with the role. The minute secretary has to make sense of what is being said and agreed often after, for example, heated debate and widely conflicting views. The situation is not helped by the fact that the interpersonal skills the minute secretary uses most are in conflict with each other. The minute secretary is required to listen intently but also take down notes, which detracts from the listening process. Where necessary, the minute secretary should seek clarification of statements through the chair.

Minutes should be brief and not over-elaborate or unduly long. They should record:

- the date, time and place of the meeting;
- the chair's particulars and those of the members present at the meeting;
- the people who were due to attend but did not attend the meeting;
- the approval (or otherwise) of the previous meeting minutes;
- any matters arising after consideration of the previous set of minutes;

- the agenda items in the order in which they are listed on the agenda even if they are taken out of sequence;
- the time of departure where people leave a meeting early;
- the differing views and discussions supporting a particular item and decisions reached;
- the agreed actions and who is to carry out the actions and by when they should be completed;
- the results of previous assigned activities.

26.7 Who should attend meetings and what role do meeting members have?

Deciding who should attend a meeting ought to be a relatively simple task. A basic principle suggests that only those people who can actively contribute to the purposes of the meeting should attend. People who cannot offer a meaningful contribution should be excluded and on occasions it may not be necessary for a meeting member to attend every meeting.

People who attend meetings must be prepared to make an active contribution to the proceedings. It is up to the chair to make sure that invited members are able to express their views. People who do not put forward their views may be letting down those people whose opinions they are supposed to represent.

It is the role of a meeting member to:

- submit briefing papers promptly in accordance with meeting rules relating to time, content and format;
- prepare thoroughly for meetings;
- arrive at meetings on time;
- make positive contributions to meetings in terms of oral and written submissions, suggestions, creative ideas and solutions;
- treat other meeting members with respect and combat improper behaviour;
- support the leadership of the chair;
- give honest feedback about the worth of meetings when required to do so.

26.8 Things a chair can do to get the best out of meetings

A chair can assist the progress of meetings by:

- telling meeting members why they are meeting, and what they are expected to achieve in terms of desired results;
- informing meeting members how long the meeting will last (to concentrate minds and manage time);

- introducing each agenda item separately, supplying background information, progress and facts, as appropriate;
- avoiding over-involvement in content (the chair is leader and facilitator and if he or she wishes to take a greater part in the detail of a meeting he or she should consider appointing another chair to conduct proceedings).

26.8.1 Using interpersonal skills and problem solving

The effective use of interpersonal skills by the chair of a meeting is critical to success. (See also Chapters 17–24 regarding communications and a variety of interpersonal skills.) In particular, the chair should listen intently, watch reactions and use open questions to interrogate and open up discussions. Additionally, regularly summarising the current state of proceedings helps to keep agenda items on track whilst at the same time maintaining a mutual understanding of what has so far been achieved. Importantly, summarising, especially when meeting members have reached a decision, greatly helps the minute secretary in constructing accurate minutes.

Problem-solving skills (see also Chapter 12, 'Problem solving') are essential to the successful handling and resolution of agenda items. To develop the best possible solutions the chair should tap into meeting member expertise and seek differing views, openly weighing one view against another. Probing, open questions should expose narrowly thought-out proposals and enlarge upon the potential of sound suggestions.

26.9 How does the chair manage the various interactions between meeting members?

Usually people attending meetings do behave in a supportive, self-disciplined and positive manner. However, on occasions people may behave in unexpected and sometimes inappropriate ways at meetings and it is important that chairs deal with aggravated behaviours promptly and decisively. To help to build good relationships leading to good meeting results, the chair should:

- assert his or her control of meetings at all times and never lose that control, otherwise confusion and perhaps disorder may occur;
- insist that points of view are based on facts and evidence and that personal attacks on other meeting members are strictly forbidden;
- deal quickly with rudeness, aggression and unlawful discrimination if necessary by excluding offenders from meetings and perhaps by way of misconduct proceedings;
- counter the impact of persistently strident individuals trying to force their views upon others and the power of meeting members who form an alliance to dominate proceedings—stridency and power may be diluted by inviting

contributions from everyone and testing the validity of all views against desired outcomes;
- encourage silent meeting members to make contributions to debates—silence should not be assumed to be a cover for lack of enthusiasm or knowledge;
- show that each individual's contribution is appreciated and valued.

26.10 How does the chair know that a meeting has been successful?

Measuring success in terms of the meeting process can be achieved by seeking feedback from meeting members at the end of each meeting. The chair should ask meeting members whether:

- the meeting was well run;
- time was managed effectively;
- everyone present felt able to put forward their views and suggestions;
- the meeting was worthwhile;
- meetings should be run at all in the future and, if so, how they could be improved upon.

One way of sharpening up the debate about the actual meeting and what it has achieved is to cost it in terms of wages/salaries spent, other costs (e.g. travel and accommodation costs) and facilities used (e.g. hire of a meeting venue and refreshment costs). Equally, 'opportunity costs' should be considered. In other words, what would meeting members have been able to do had they not attended the meeting?

Ultimately, the value of meetings should be judged against increased efficiency and effectiveness in the workplace/public arena. In other words, did a meeting's actions help police officers to do their jobs better and did the public benefit from the anticipated improvements to policing? This means looking beyond the agenda and demanding feedback on the value of the meeting's decision-making process. Success in this regard should not be assumed.

Reference and further reading

Janner, G. (1986), *Janner on Meetings* (Aldershot: Gower).

27

Self-development for the leader and encouraging leadership skills in others

27.1 Undertaking a leadership self-development programme

This leadership book is intended to help greatly with a leader's self-development especially with regard to the practical implementation of the checklists (toolkit) and the opportunity to learn from 'hands-on' experience.

27.1.1 Questions to ask

To assist with self-development plans the leader should consider the following questions:

- What exactly is it that I want to achieve in the future in terms of my career and my private life? For example: Do I want to be a better leader? Do I want promotion? Do I want a specialist role? Do I want to transfer to another police force to gain different experiences? Do I want to remain as I am and concentrate on aspects of my private life to create a better life–work balance?
- Am I willing and able to put in the required effort to reach my self-development and personal objectives?
- How does what I have achieved already tie in with what I want to achieve in the future? How experienced and competent am I now? Are my attitudes and behaviours of a desirable nature? Given my ambitions, what do I need to do to gain necessary additional knowledge and skills?
- What obstacles are there to my progress (e.g. lack of financial support for private studies, unhelpful managers or poor training facilities) and if they exist how do I overcome them?
- Who will help me to succeed with my objectives (e.g. my partner, my family, my team leader or my workplace colleagues)?
- Who might be willing to mentor and advise me?

27.1.2 The importance of feedback

Essential to the support of plans and ambitions is the need for regular, critical self-analysis and feedback from any source from which it may be obtained—including seniors, peers, juniors, outside agencies and, where possible, members of the public. (See also Chapter 21, 'Communications—feedback'.)

27.1.3 Learning cycle and learning styles

To get the best out of the educational process no matter what form it takes, a sergeant or inspector leader needs to take into account how people learn and in particular how they themselves learn.

Kolb (1984) explored the nature of learning styles. (See also Armstrong 2009.) His Learning Cycle is reproduced in Figure 27.1.

- *Concrete experiences*—may occur as a result of a planned activity or by accident.
- *Observations and reflections*—result from concrete experience and amount to an evaluation of the experience and what it means.
- *Formation of abstract concepts and generalisations*—amount to an attempt to formulate ideas and thoughts to manage similar situations in the future.
- *Testing implications of concepts in new situations*—means putting ideas and thoughts into practice giving rise to a new concrete experience. The new experience may prove to be successful or it could be unsuccessful, requiring a fresh rethink using Kolb's model.

This model usefully offers a method of systematically examining events and experiences in the workplace and complements other problem-solving techniques. (See also Chapter 12, 'Problem solving'.) It is absolutely necessary to carefully consider all stages of the model rather than miss any of them out.

Figure 27.1 Kolb's Learning Cycle (1984)

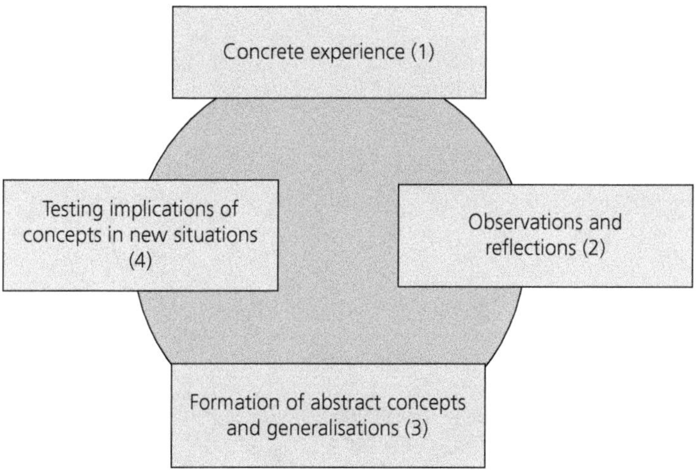

Kolb identified four learning styles:

- *Accommodators*—people who learn through doing things by 'trial and error'. They lay emphasis on the concrete experience and experimentation.
- *Divergers*—prefer tangible to abstract learning and reflection to active participation. They benefit from imagination and can see different aspects of a problem.
- *Convergers*—like to experiment with ideas in order to discover their practical applications. They try to establish whether a theory will work in practice.
- *Assimilators*—who enjoy creating theoretical models that integrate differing views and facts into a coherent explanation of events.

Honey and Mumford (1996) (again, see also Armstrong 2009) have drawn their own perhaps more straightforward version of learning styles:

- *Activists*—relish new experiences and new challenges.
- *Reflectors*—observe new experiences from different perspectives, collect data and then reflect on it and reach conclusions.
- *Theorists*—inclined to be perfectionists who take their observations and formulate logical theories.
- *Pragmatists*—keen to try out new ideas and new ways of doing things to find out if they work.

Figure 27.2 Learning styles (Honey and Mumford 1996)

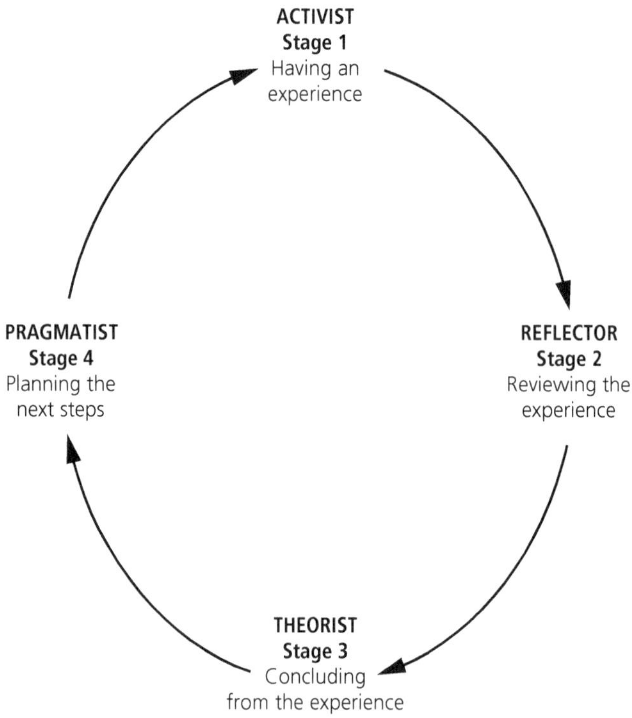

The Learning styles model illustrates how it is possible to have and review an experience to best dvantage. It suggests that individuals approach experiences in different ways. For example, some tend to review things in detail, or like to theorise, whilst others just want get on with putting things into practice. Different styles can work together but may cause conflicts between individuals.

It is necessary that leaders and, for example, trainers and coaches are aware of learning styles so as to be able to identify their own learning preferences and manage the learning styles of others. If leaders, trainers and coaches are unaware of their own styles they may try to impose their ways of doing things on others who learn differently. This may damage the learning process and perhaps cause anger and resentment.

Team leaders can establish learning styles by watching how people deal with workplace tasks and how, for example, they react at debriefing and problem-solving sessions. Additionally, they can simply ask people how they like to learn.

Different learning styles and different approaches translate directly to the everyday workplace. They can be the cause of friction especially when those styles clash; for instance, between Reflectors and Pragmatists. For example, a Pragmatist might want to rush off to do something immediately while a Reflector may wish to spend more time considering issues. It is, of course, possible too that a leader's style may clash with that of a team member. (This is an important leadership style issue.)

In operational circumstances, a sergeant or inspector leader can use different styles, and different talents, to great advantage by drawing upon the best of each individual. For example, it is right to consider issues fully and properly (reflection) but perhaps not dwell on them too long otherwise an important initiative may flounder (pragmatism).

27.2 Maintaining learning logs

Keeping a learning log (see Figure 27.3) has great advantages for the aspiring leader. A learning log amounts to a record of significant learning experiences. A log is not a daily diary nor should it become a chore that detracts from content and satisfaction. Entries in the log should be brief, clear and meaningful. The benefits of keeping a learning log include:

- improved workplace performance;
- the identification of training needs;
- continuous self-development;
- the gathering of evidence for staff appraisal interviews;
- obtaining evidence for job application forms and responses to questions at job selection interviews—including promotion interviews (expressing unique experiences from which real learning has taken place offers a distinct competitive advantage).

27.3 What does a leader have to do to encourage leadership skills in others?

Using the preceding paragraphs and information as a guide, the sergeant and inspector leader should endeavour to develop the leadership potential of all team members. However, some people are likely to prove more competent than others in the role. To assist in the development process the leader should do the following:

Figure 27.3 Example of a learning log

CONFIDENTIAL Learning Log Name .... Date		
Knowledge gained	**How knowledge was acquired**	**How newly learned competence will help in the future**
Learned about the importance of leaders or managers making timely assertive interventions. Obtained knowledge of how to deal with inter-team workplace disputes. Acquired an understanding of good team work and the importance of honest communications.	Two team members entered into a fierce row about who should do a particular job. One team member accused a colleague of interfering with their work and trying to take it over for their own gain. The second team member responded by accusing his/her team mate of stealing their responsibilities because they were interesting. The row degenerated in a show of mutual abuse. The two team members were unable to resolve their differences. Amazed and uninvolved team mates looked on in horror. A bad atmosphere was created and all team members stopped working. Factions supporting one or other of the antagonists appeared and work was disrupted for a lengthy period of time.	1. It is important that each team member should have written job specifications, and have clear explained objectives and roles that define the differences between them and other team mates. 2. Team leaders and managers should not allow disputes to fester but seek to resolve issues quickly through, for example, negotiation, issuing instructions and where appropriate orders (this is the least desirable course of action but may be entirely necessary). 3. Quarrelling team members should be asked to realise the consequences of their actions, for example lost production, team disharmony, misconduct proceedings and possibly dismissal. *Future use:* (a) I will provide sound leadership and set a good example. I will make sure that each team member knows what is required of them and how their duties fit in with the work of others. (b) I will encourage open, honest and forthright but respectful communications, where constructive feedback is welcome. This should help with dispute resolution but I will intervene where it is necessary to do so. (c) I will encourage the view that all team members have a responsibility to tackle difficult issues together but in a courteous, respectful and positive way. No person must subject another to personal abuse.

- Try to ascertain the levels of leadership competence that team members currently possess with a view to establishing areas for improvement or skills acquisition.
- Help to create a SMART objective-based self-development plan with time limits (see also Chapter 10, 'Planning', section 10.2.6).
- Provide opportunities to enhance skills through formal training programmes and on-the-job workplace coaching. Both should be part of a continuous joined-up process with overall skill development in mind. (Coaching does not require a 'professional' trainer as such because it is usually the person doing the job in question that provides the training. However, not all workers are good coaches—this is because work and training require a different set of competences and skills. Therefore, the leader should ensure that coaches do have coaching skills training to increase the chances of success.)
- Offer opportunities to develop skills, for example through delegating tasks with the authority to carry out actions without necessarily referring back to the leader continuously. The leader can also offer opportunities to take on new responsibilities to increase competence.
- Provide constructive feedback to learn from those things that go well and those which are not quite so successful.
- Be approachable when problems occur or difficulties are experienced.
- Keep performance under constant review and give advice and help where appropriate.
- Offer encouragement, particularly when the potential leader is under pressure, and praise for things done well.

27.4 **How will the leader know if he or she has been successful in developing leadership skills in others?**

A sergeant and inspector leader will know how well a potential leader is doing if he or she:

- conscientiously monitors and assesses performance, progress and results;
- receives evidence on performance based upon factual feedback from others;
- invites the potential leader to remark on their own leadership qualities, attributes and competence (and any additional needs);
- considers allowing the trainee leader to deputise in his or her absence or even while the leader is present where specific tasks are concerned.

A person showing signs of leadership potential may not be good at carrying out leadership responsibilities despite comprehensive training and opportunities. If this is the case, he or she should be told so in order that they may discuss and review their aspirations and the way forward.

References and further reading

Armstrong, M. (2009), *Handbook of Human Resource Management Practice* (11th edn, London: Kogan Page).

Honey, P. and Mumford, A. (1996), *The Manual of Learning Styles* (3rd edn, Maidenhead: Honey Publications).

Kolb, D. A. (1984), *Experiential Learning: Experience as the Source of Learning and Development* (Upper Saddle River, NJ: Prentice Hall). Used with the kind permission of Dr Alice Kolb.

Learning Styles Questionnaire. Copyright © 2006 Peter Honey, Published by Pearson Talentlens, a Division of Pearson Education Ltd.

PART TWO

Leadership—competence checklists (toolkit)

Checklist 1—Leader's leadership skills

(See Chapter 2, 'Exploring the concept of leadership')

Summary

A leader is required to take the lead in current circumstances but must also be able to look ahead and establish what is required in the medium and long-term future. A leader should create a 'vision' that others can be persuaded to adopt and then fulfil. Therefore, excellent change-management skills are very significant. The leader should also maximise team skills to full advantage, motivate followers and remove obstacles to progress. Planning and communication skills are of the greatest importance to an effective leader.

Toolkit

An efficient and effective leader should ensure the following:

- Exhibit high levels of professional competence and equally high standards of ethical behaviour, acting at all times without prejudice and discrimination.
- Behave in a way that treats individuals with respect and values what each person has to offer in terms of completing tasks and objectives.
- Carefully consider the best use of all available resources including people, and all manner of cost implications, so as to provide an efficient, effective and economic service to *the public who should always be the focus of police activity.*
- Take account of prevailing circumstances when making necessary plans for the immediate, medium and long term. This includes considering the stated aims of the police

service coupled to an understanding of, for example, political and social changes, public expectations and local needs. Additionally, perceived and real risks need to be taken into account and managed so as not to miss important opportunities for change.

- Draw up practical and workable plans based upon clearly understood aims, objectives, tasks and performance measures.
- Construct 'change plans' so as to manage necessary changes to achieve the aims of the police service and maximise benefits for the public, whilst at the same time taking into account the genuine concerns of those police and other persons involved with the changes.
- Use problem-solving and communication skills to remove any obstacles to the proper completion of tasks and objectives.
- Inspire and motivate followers throughout the good times and the bad times and encourage individual participation and contribution.
- Set an example by behaving correctly personally at all times whilst dealing with poor and unacceptable behaviour and misconduct in others promptly.
- Measure and evaluate results with a view to further improvement in the future.
- Seek to train and develop self whilst doing the same for team members as part of a progressive skills-enhancement programme.
- Learn from both mistakes and successes in equal measure but also champion team members when they are unfairly criticised or attacked.
- Share the 'fruits' of success with team members and others who have contributed to it but be prepared to be held accountable for things that go wrong.
- Regularly give and invite feedback as a means to improve job efficiency and personal competence.
- Identify and develop leadership qualities and abilities in promising team members whilst not ignoring the aspirations of others.

Checklist 2—Leader's team skills

(See Chapter 3, 'Leadership and team work')

Summary

A leader is unlikely to be successful without well-motivated and efficient team members acting harmoniously together.

Team members require clear roles and objectives and they must know what is needed of them and also their team mates.

The leader should develop and capitalise on individual strengths and abilities to maximise effectiveness.

It is important that a leader is aware of how teams form, perform and progress so as to be able to make appropriate leadership interventions.

Team communications are complex and require high levels of interpersonal skills from the leader.

Toolkit

Teams require the following:

- A strong, fair, competent leader will offer team members a sense of direction and be able to withstand and manage both success and failure.
- An inspirational leader will be able to motivate each team member to do their best even when progress is difficult.

- Clear written objectives should be commonly understood by each team member and performance measurements should indicate what success will look like.
- Team members should have job specifications and know what roles they have to fulfil and how their roles fit in with the roles of others.
- A leader should be able to match individual skills and abilities to individual tasks whilst encouraging leadership development through task allocation.
- A leader should be able to solve problems, make sensible decisions and remove obstacles to progress.
- A leader should involve team members in the decision-making process and value their ideas and suggestions to improve efficiency and effectiveness.
- A leader should be interested in each team member's welfare and aspirations and create opportunities for increased individual contributions and self-improvement.
- A leader should be prepared to give and receive honest, evidence-based feedback as a means to learn and improve personal and professional competence.
- A leader should praise and reward good work and be willing to share success with team members as well as the consequences for things that go wrong.
- A leader should act as a 'champion' who will support team members when things are not going well or when team members are being treated unfairly.
- Team members should recognise that there is a duty to follow as well as to lead.

Checklist 3—Leader's team audit

(See Chapter 3, 'Leadership and team work')

Summary

It is essential that a newly appointed leader of an established or new team should start well and illustrate at once all the characteristics of determined, competent leadership.

When joining a team, a leader needs to find out how well team members are performing by carrying out an audit. The following checklist assists with this very important task. The actions suggested can also be used for further periodic reviews and for setting up a new team.

Toolkit

On joining a team the leader should ensure the following:

- Be fully conversant with the relevant police force's aims, values and ambitions and public expectations of the police.
- Fully understand the team's objectives, tasks they have to perform, standards they have to adhere to and how performance will be measured.
- Become fully familiar with Tuckman's Team Development Model (1965) showing how teams develop over time, that is:
  - *forming* (getting together);
  - *storming* (experiencing problems and surfacing and dealing with difficulties);

- *norming* (understanding and accepting what is required);
- *performing* (doing what is needed well). The model is good for measuring team relationships and performance. But also it reminds the leader that as a new admission to a team he or she is inevitably going to upset the team's equilibrium. Equally, the arrival of a new team member can upset a team's balance. The use of good interpersonal skills is essential in these circumstances;
- *adjourning* (managing dispersal).

(Tuckman and Jensen 1977)

- Take note of Adair's Action Centred Leadership Model (1983). The model illustrates three elements that need to be kept in balance in order to be efficient and effective. That is:
  - *task needs* (which nearly always appear to dominate because tasks have a very strong link to production);
  - *individual needs*;
  - *group maintenance needs*.

Should any one component dominate then the other two components will suffer. It is a leader's job to keep these elements in balance by making necessary leadership interventions.

- Ascertain if each team member has a job specification and whether they know what they are doing and how their roles fit in with the roles of other team members.
- Establish what objectives and tasks team members have been given and how well they are completing them. Reasons for non-completion should be ascertained and praise given where earned. Problems should be resolved.
- Discover what training team members get and whether this is adequate for their needs. Construct training and self-development plans as necessary as part of an integrated and continuous training programme.
- Inquire into the state of team harmony by way of team meetings but also ask individuals separately:
  - how well they think that they and the team are doing and seek views on how performance might be improved;
  - to identify their strengths (and weaknesses too for development purposes) and what they bring to their work, what they like doing and their aspirations and ambitions;

  - what additional help they and the team need to improve team relationships and efficiency and effectiveness.
- Additionally, individually and at team meetings discuss:
  - police force requirements;
  - performance standards;
  - standards of behaviour;
  - service to the public;
  - the desire for cooperation, participation, honesty, openness and individual well-being and happiness.
- Lay plans to take the team forward and utilise communication, problem-solving and motivating skills to best advantage.
- Consider scheduling further reviews in the future.

Checklist 4—Leader's valuing, protecting and enhancing public esteem

(See Chapter 4, 'Valuing, protecting and enhancing public esteem')

Summary

Officers acting and behaving professionally, honestly and impartially are absolutely vital to the carrying out of their policing duties both efficiently and effectively. Ill-tempered and intemperate officers are unlikely to secure the support and cooperation needed from members of the public. Indiscipline, insensitivity and bad behaviour are not acceptable. Neither is criminality, which can have a hugely negative effect on how people regard police. Unfortunately, police officers who are not corrupt or undisciplined are unfairly tainted by miscreant colleagues. It is a responsibility incumbent on all good officers to drive out those who should not be in the police service.

Toolkit

When leaders are managing and encouraging ethical and professional behaviours they should:

- Ensure that their own attitudes and behaviours are beyond reproach, and that they act as respected role models.
- Adopt a strategic overview on the maintenance of ethical behavioural standards and make sure that officers know exactly what the police service requires of them.
- Remind officers of the dangers associated with the use of social media.

- Make clear to constables that it is their duty to reveal corrupt officers and not to safeguard them out of team loyalty.
- Create an environment, whereby the leader as well as team members are open to comment, praise and criticism. Encourage challenges to inappropriate behaviours.
- Be aware that sometimes individuals discriminate against their colleagues and may abuse and even bully them. Leaders must investigate the circumstances of misbehaviours and eradicate them, taking disciplinary action where this is necessary.
- Note that unhealthy cliques of officers working together can have a detrimental effect upon team members and harm its cohesion and performance. They should be broken up.
- Observe that briefings and debriefings are useful for discussing attitudes and behaviours in a non-threatening way. Briefings can mention desired behaviours when operational, and debriefings can make subtle references to behaviours. For instance, how did individuals perform and how did team members perform together?
- Influence and change attitudes and thus behaviour by highlighting examples of good behaviours.
- Take action where there are persistent complaints made against an individual officer by members of the public.
- Remember that most police officers are of the highest calibre and deserve encouragement and support at all times and praise where due. Good officers resent those who damage their reputation and that of the police force. Their cooperation is almost certainly assured but needs to be encouraged and directed to positive outcomes.
- Consider studying Chapter 20, 'Communications—modes of behaviour and transactional analysis', which should assist greatly in identifying how people behave and how to manage different behaviours.

Checklist 5—The College of Policing—leader's Code of Ethics

(See Chapter 5, 'The College of Policing—ethics, leadership standards, competence and values, and decision making')

Summary

The College of Policing has an important role in creating and fostering good practice in the police service. To this end, the College has produced a Code and Guidance on ethical behaviour, a set of leadership standards, and advice on competence and values and decision making. There is a lot for all police officers and staff to absorb. However, ethical practices will form a future bedrock for policing to the benefit of officers and public alike.

There are four components to Chapter 5 which will be covered separately in Toolkit form. This checklist offers help on embedding the Code of Ethics.

Toolkit

What sergeant and inspector leaders can do to support the Code of Ethics and the Guidance for Ethical and Professional Behaviour in Policing:

- Understand that the Code and Guidance are important but complex documents and that they require close and detailed attention if they are to be assimilated and be useful in directing and assisting officers under their command to put them into practice and embed them in the police culture.

- Recognise that although sergeants and inspectors are important agencies for ensuring that officers working for them are fully cognisant with the Code and Guidance, it is the job of *everyone* in the police service to understand them and make them a success in the workplace.
- Practice what they preach and review their own behaviours and seek to set a good example to the people they command.
- Review, with team members, the team's current state of behaviours with an emphasis on professionalism and public service and agree a way forward together. This will require tact, but discussions should run on the premiss that ethical requirements are non-negotiable, then prepare an action plan together and regularly review progress. Link the review with the Competency and Values Framework (see the associated toolkit entry).
- Test officers' knowledge and learning from time to time, on a one-to-one basis or as a group, particularly after significant incidents have occurred. Eventually, the Code should become synthesised into every fibre of the police service. However, officers should also be made aware of the disciplinary consequences of not applying the Code to their policing duties.

Checklist 6—The College of Policing—leadership standards

(Chapter 5, 'The College of Policing—ethics, leadership standards, competence and values, and decision making')

Summary

The College of Policing has an important role in creating and fostering good practice in the police service as a whole. To this end, the College has produced a code and guidance on ethical behaviour, a set of leadership standards, and advice on competence and values and decision making. There is a lot for all police officers and staff to absorb. However, excellent leadership is vital not only in embedding ethical practices but also in creating teams dedicated to public service and raising esteem for the police.

There are four main components to Chapter 5 which will be covered separately in Toolkit form. This checklist offers help on embedding leadership standards.

Toolkit

What sergeant and inspector leaders can do to support leadership standards:

- Thoroughly read and understand the standards and convey their essence to the officers under their command. Explain, for example, that the standards—

  (1) include all police officers, staff and volunteers;

(2) are designed to assist with leadership development, promotion and progression at all levels within the police service and in sequence they amount to a leadership progression programme;

(3) work in concert with the Code of Ethics and the Competence and Values Framework.

- Discuss with officers the fact that there are five staged organisational development levels:

  (1) foundations (constables);

  (2) first-line leaders (sergeants);

  (3) mid-level leaders (inspectors and chief inspectors);

  (4) senior leaders (superintendents and chief superintendents) and

  (5) executive leaders (currently working at, or aspiring to, chief officer level).

(a) to (d) include staff with equivalent levels of responsibility.

- Encourage and develop leadership practices in the officers they command for when on duty in the public arena they are de facto leaders. It is in the interests of individuals, the police service and the public that ethical, professional policing remains a constant factor.
- Measure progress against the desired standards and offer regular feedback and support. Sergeants and inspectors should seek the same help they offer their officers from those who supervise them.

Checklist 7—Leader's Competency and Values Framework

(See Chapter 5, 'The College of Policing—ethics, leadership standards, competence and values, and decision making')

Summary

As part of a drive to improve policing on a professional and ethical basis the College of Policing has produced a Competency and Values Framework which works in conjunction with the Code of Ethics.

There are four main components to Chapter 5 which will be covered separately in Toolkit form. This checklist offers help on embedding competency and values.

Toolkit

What sergeant and inspector leaders can do to support Competency and Values Framework:

- Read and understand the seminal importance of the Competency and Values Framework which works in tandem with the Code of Ethics. Discuss the framework with officers under their command; this is very important because each competency and value is accompanied by a list of example behaviours.

- Note that *values are described as beliefs* which are important to an individual and *which guide and motivate particular behaviours and actions*; competencies are behaviours (knowledge, skills or abilities) related to effective job performance.
- Understand that the framework can be used in performance assessment or when selecting applicants for a particular role; however, the behaviours should not be used in isolation or as a checklist for there are many ways in which an individual might demonstrate the required competencies and values.
- Appreciate that *competencies and values are associated with effective performance* in policing roles, and *everyone is expected to display the same values* regardless of their role or seniority.
- Observe that *all people have different strengths and preferences*, in terms of skills and abilities, and the Framework should be used in ways that allow for differing abilities, including those that stem from disabilities or neurodiversity.
- Note that behaviours can be observed, drawn to attention by a third party or arise from a complaint; this means that sergeants and inspectors should address poor behaviours with alacrity. Competencies can be imparted and enhanced in several ways, for example by informal and regular coaching or training courses.

Checklist 8—Leader's National Decision Model

(See Chapter 5, 'The College of Policing—ethics, leadership standards, competence and values, and decision making')

Summary

The National Decision Model devised by the College of Policing is suitable for the making of all decisions on an ethical and practical basis and is intended for use by everyone engaged in policing.

There are four main components to Chapter 5 which will be covered separately in Toolkit form. This checklist offers help on embedding the National Decisionn Model which includes briefing and debriefing procedures.

Toolkit

What sergeant and inspector leaders can do to promote the sophisticated and involved National Decision Model which requires close scrutiny:

- Study the model carefully with getting to know and implement its procedures in mind, and be prepared to explain and discuss it with officers under their command, noting that the model has an extremely wide range of applications, for example, it can be used in spontaneous incidents and planned operations, and by individuals or teams engaged with both operational and non-operational situations.
- Note that the Decision Model has six key elements:

(1) observance of the Code of Ethics and the Guidance for Ethical and Professional Behaviour in Policing;

(2) gathering information and intelligence;

(3) assessing threat and risk and developing a working strategy;

(4) considering powers and policy;

(5) identifying options and contingencies;

(6) taking action and reviewing what happened.

- Observe that the briefing and debriefing model is described thus:

(1) briefing and intelligence;

(2) individual and team tasking;

(3) delivery methods;

(4) debriefing;

(5) results.

- It is necessary for decision makers to record the decisions that they make as subsequently they may be asked to account for their actions before some form of inquiry.
- Briefing styles vary, but there are three key objectives to meet in any briefing:

(1) to ensure that the team has assimilated the relevant information contained within the briefing (random knowledge checks to confirm understanding are helpful);

(2) to ensure that individual members of staff understand their responsibility for the allocated task;

(3) to confirm there are sufficient resources to conduct the required tasks (this includes situations where staff may self-brief, for example at remote stations).

- Remember that when officers are being briefed it is essential that they are quite clear about what they are being required to do and why they are doing it; questions asked and ideas and suggestions offered should always be considered and acted upon where appropriate.
- Observe that structured debriefing sessions can add greatly to learning experience and the development of ideas and improved practices; however, effective debriefings rely heavily on encouraging openness, respectfulness, frankness and constructive suggestions for improvement. Also, no participant should be criticised for making genuine contributions, even if they are uncomfortable to accept.
- Review actions taken as a result of a briefing and consider the following:

(1) Were decisions proportionate, legitimate, necessary and ethical?

(2) Were decisions reasonable in the circumstances facing the decision maker?

(3) Were decisions communicated effectively?

(4) Were decisions and the rationale for them recorded as appropriate?

(5) Were decisions monitored and reassessed where necessary?

(6) What lessons can be learnt from the outcomes and how were the decisions made?

- Note that where the outcome was not as planned, if the decision was reasonable and proportionate in the circumstances, and made in accordance with the Code of Ethics, the decision maker deserves the support of their supervisor and that of the organisation.

Checklist 9—Leader's stress management and long Covid-19 considerations

(See Chapter 6, 'Leader's stress management and long Covid-19 considerations')

Summary

The stress response is designed to help cope with challenging and sometimes life-threatening situations. Policing is inherently stressful, but everyone is likely to suffer stress at some time or another. What may appear to be stressful for some is not a problem for others. Some people have their own ways of managing stress, but others may need help.

Sergeants and inspectors need to be able to pick up signs of stress in their staffs. They should encourage officers to talk to them when stress becomes a real issue. Sometimes people hold back from expressing concerns because of feelings of inadequacy. Sergeants and inspectors may offer help through their ability to influence workplace operating conditions. In some cases, inviting an officer to see medical practitioner will seem appropriate.

Long Covid is still a workplace feature. People permitted to work with long Covid should be closely monitored to offer additional support. However, an officer may have long

Covid without realising that this is the case. Symptoms may be masked by, for example, suspected workplace inefficiency and ineffectiveness. A confidential interview, convened by a sergeant or inspector acting without preconceived views, should help to identify causes, but where long Covid is suspected an officer should see a medical practitioner.

Toolkit

When managing stress sergeants and inspectors:

- Need to understand the body's biological response to stressful situations. It seems a forbidding task to learn about the autonomic, sympathetic and parasympathetic nervous systems. However, in simple terms, it boils down to the fact that if a person keeps drawing non-stop on their bodily resources, without taking time to replenish them, then they likely to suffer a severe and damaging bout of stress. Consider explaining the response to team members. Everyone has a responsibility for taking good mental and physical care of themselves.
- Should, when suffering from other than abnormal stress, do something to alleviate it straight away and encourage others to do the same. Sitting on stress problems can make them worse. Although other people can assist with helping to put things right, it needs the full commitment of individuals to put things right. Invite officers to examine their own stress issues and their resilience to stress.
- Need to adopt a management style that is professional, ethical and that is sensitive to what is happening around them. Additionally, endeavour to create an atmosphere whereby officers feel able to have open and frank discussions about work pressures and any excessive stress that is bothering them.
- Should recognise that although the police service is always under pressure excessive hours and shift work can cause stress in officers. Also, it is important that people are properly trained to do their jobs, that there is clarity of purpose and that individual objectives, workloads and deadlines are not unreasonable, with help being provided where possible. Sometimes people are unsuited to particular tasks but good at others. It is up to sergeants and inspectors to match skills to tasks.
- Should work to develop a team where it is recognised that everyone, including sergeants and inspectors, is likely to suffer stress at some time and that team members should be self-supporting—helping each other in a practical way with, for example, workloads and problems both professional and personal.
- Need to ponder that although it is usually businesses that are advised to take stress audits there are no reasons why team audits should not be taken with the cooperation of team members.

Sergeant and inspector leaders can cope with long Covid issues in the workplace by:

- Helping anyone who has been diagnosed with long Covid but who has been permitted to carry on working, perhaps with conditions attached. Additional support and reassurance may be necessary with regards to work allocation, the number of hours worked, fatigue, extra help with projects and monitoring progress.
- Remaining aware that some people may not know that they have long Covid or have decided not to declare that they may have it. Symptoms could become confused with other perceived causes such as inefficiency linked to a general poor performance, or they may be suffering operational stress. Sergeants and inspectors should then use their interpersonal skills to probe for causes in a confidential environment and, should they even suspect long Covid, refer the officer concerned to a medical practitioner.

Checklist 10—Leader's dealing with unethical behaviours and workplace ineffectiveness sometimes without obvious causes

(See Chapter 9, 'Dealing with unethical behaviours and workplace ineffectiveness') sometimes without obvious causes

Summary

It is for sergeants and inspectors to nurture individuals to maintain and increase personal and team efficiency and effectiveness to meet objectives. However, policing can be undermined by the unethical and perhaps criminal behaviour of some police officers and staff. Eliminating corruption and misbehaviour is a responsibility falling not just on sergeants and inspectors, but also on all members of the police service.

Most cases of inefficiency can be dealt with by sergeants and inspectors as a matter of managerial routine. However, an individual's performance can visibly drop for no apparent reason, and there may be reluctance to explain why. Ineffectiveness can have a wide range of causes, some of which can be dealt with by management interventions. Other causes, for example bullying and the presence of crime, are much more difficult to handle. Nevertheless, it is incumbent upon sergeants and inspectors to deal with all causes of inefficiency in an appropriate way.

Toolkit

In dealing with inefficiency and effectiveness in the workplace sergeants and inspectors should:

- Ensure that the officers they lead behave ethically and professionally in the effective discharge of their duties. They need to be aware of behavioural standards, be properly trained, and their abilities developed to reach peak efficiency. Sometimes performance may drop where, for example, someone is unsure about what they are doing, or they need to refresh existing skills or acquire new skills. These issues can be addressed by making management interventions such as mentoring and coaching.
- Remain alert to uncharacteristic drops in individual performance and maybe mood changes, i.e. from being happy and cheerful and communicative, to being withdrawn and sullen. If an officer is not forthcoming about the causes of their lapses the matter needs immediate attention, and an exploratory interview should be arranged.
- Note that exploratory interviews in this instance require a sophisticated and sensitive use of the interpersonal skills. Proficient use of the skills is a necessary attribute of policing. However, it may prove helpful to view Chapters 18–21 which discuss the use of the interpersonal skills.
- Choose an interview location where proceedings will not be open to interruption.
- Be concerned when interviewing not only with the welfare of individuals but also the reputation of the police service and the quality of service demanded by members of the public.
- Note that the causes of workplace inefficiency can be manifest and that they should expect surprises and therefore adopt a flexible approach. They should also note that stress at work can cause stress at home and vice versa.
- Strive to keep an open mind and stay focused on the task in hand and not allow the mind to stray as this may show disinterest and insincerity.
- As a prelude to questioning, put the interviewee at ease. Issues of confidentiality should be discussed where and when appropriate. Objectives should be explained, for example (a) to discover why performance levels have fallen, (b) to uncover any debilitating worries that they may have, and (c) to establish how they can help the interviewee to return to the required levels of efficiency.
- Encourage interviewees to take an active part in discussions, being able to ask questions, put forward ideas, suggest ways forward and point out stumbling blocks.
- Check progress with the interviewee at regular intervals in order to create a common understanding of what is taking place. This can be done by summarising or by asking the interviewee to do the summarising (especially important when agreeing solutions).

- Note that most interviews are likely to result in offering management support, for example with workloads, coaching and training, adjustments to hours of duty (helpful for instance, where officers have worrying family health issues). Matters of ill-health per se are a matter for medical practitioners to deal with although sergeants and inspectors may be able to offer valuable supplementary support.
- Remember that where criminal activity is involved, and in which the interviewee may be involved, the situation automatically warrants a criminal investigation. Similarly, if disciplinary issues arise, a discipline inquiry will be necessary.
- Wherever possible, involve interviewees in generating their own solutions which they are more likely to implement than those imposed upon them. However, conditions may be imposed if they involve compliance with behavioural standards, rules or regulations.
- Point out to an interviewee that if they refuse to cooperate with an inquiry then the consequences could be significant for them. For example, they may subsequently be required to leave the police service.
- Note that no interview should be left open-ended. Agreed activities should be recorded and given completion dates. Review dates should also be recorded with adaptations being made where necessary.

Checklist 11—Leader's treating people equally

(See Chapter 7, 'Treating people equally')

Summary

The importance of how people are treated cannot be overemphasised. Leaders have a moral and legal responsibility to treat all people including team members, colleagues, external agencies and members of the public equally. This means acting and behaving at all times fairly and without bias or prejudice with regard to, for example, race or sex *or any other unjustifiable false reason*.

This respect for people can be extended and enhanced by valuing each individual for their unique characteristics, talents and abilities. Insofar as team members are concerned, the leader should seek to discover, nurture and maximise each individual's potential and ambitions to the advantage of the person concerned but also to the work of the team itself and importantly the public at large.

Toolkit

Leaders must ensure that they themselves understand what is required of them with regard to:

- equality law and the provisions of the Equality Act 2010 ('protected characteristics' include: age, disability, gender reassignment, marriage and civil partnership, pregnancy and maternity, race, religion or belief, sex, sexual orientation);

- what the police service requires of them, their teams and all police personnel (including civilian colleagues) with regard to the ethical and professional standards of behaviour that they should adhere to when in contact with all manner of people including members of the public (Standards of Professional Behaviour issued under the Police (Conduct) (Amendment) Regulations 2020 apply).

Knowledge may be gained through, for example, policy statements, written instructions and training and by consulting with human resource experts and even by contacting the Equality and Human Rights Commission for advice.

- Leaders must ensure that team members too are aware of what is required of them but also they should be informed of the consequences of infringements of the law and police service directions. Infringements may, for example, lead to misconduct inquiries, discipline and even dismissal from the police service. Importantly, workplace misconduct amounting to discriminatory behaviour may result in the ill-health of a victim (including members of the public), poor team performance, demotivated team members and public dissatisfaction.
- Leaders should create an environment where prejudice and discrimination are seen as unacceptable and followers feel able to report transgressions without fear of recrimination. This requires a leader to be alert and inquiring as well as open, honest, fair and empathetic to the sensitivities and needs of team members and others.
- Leaders must deal with prejudice and discrimination without delay and not allow difficulties to escalate and become worse. Where necessary, they should seek the help of senior officers and human resource specialists.
- Sergeant and inspector leaders should continuously monitor the progress of equal treatment practices and initiatives and not assume that problems will never arise. This involves 'walking the shop floor' to see what is happening first-hand and encouraging people to reveal problems where they exist.
- Leaders should take into account that teams will contain unique individuals who together offer a wide range of abilities and perspectives. Their individual and joint contributions to the work effort should be welcomed and valued. Every effort should be made to ensure that all team members are able to contribute to team objectives with any impediments or intolerances being removed so as to create team harmony.
- Leaders should encourage team members to value each other and to help each other achieve their aspirations. Encouragement is dependent upon the leader creating an environment where professionalism and respect for self and others are highly prized.
- Leaders should remain alert to the huge benefits that can result from equal treatment and managing diversity in terms of individual motivation and well-being, team cooperation and synergy, efficiency and providing the best possible service to the public.

Checklist 12—Leader's valuing diversity

(See Chapter 8, 'Valuing diversity')

Summary

Multi-cultural teams, a common workplace feature, are groups of people from different nationalities and cultures whose shared goal is to deliver for an organisation (in this instance the police service). In these teams some members have spent a significant portion of their formative years in different countries and have learned different values and demeanours. A vibrant mix of people with different perspectives can greatly enrich processes and outputs to the benefit of the public at large.

Teams are likely to hold people who are neurodivergent. Neurodivergence means having a neurology that differs significantly from typical neurology. It highlights that people naturally think about things differently and process information and learn differently as well. Neurodivergent people may have been undervalued in the past along with their ways of looking at things and they can add greatly to creativity and problem solving.

It is up to sergeants and inspectors to harmonise so many talents to increase and maintain team morale and reach and exceed set objectives.

Toolkit

To help multicultural and neurodiverse teams and all team members to reach their full potential sergeants and inspector leaders should:

- explain to followers what 'valuing diversity' means and find out what each individual aspires to achieve and has to offer and contribute and how they wish to be developed.

The leader should wherever possible provide opportunities for all followers to explore and develop their unique potential. (See also Chapter 15, 'Motivation');

- remember that it is their job to create harmonious teams and that diversity, in whatever form it takes, adds value to the creative and problem-solving processes;
- get to know each individual officer well to be able to participate with them in developing their potential by means of training, coaching and constructive feedback;
- develop and encourage an open communication system whereby everyone feels able to put across their point of view without fear of recrimination. This will help with team and workplace relationships and encourage participation and progress;
- note that members of multicultural teams may have some language issues that could affect their own well-being, communications with other officers and members of the public. Many individuals, with the cooperation of team members, will improve their language skills through experience. However, attending language training courses may help individuals to become more proficient;
- encourage team members to value and support each other. Intolerance and discrimination of any sort have no place in an effective team.

Checklist 13—Leader's planning

(See Chapter 10, 'Planning')

Summary

Planning is an integral part of a leader's job. Without planning skills or the willingness to plan properly a leader is unlikely to be effective.

Planning involves being clear about what is to be achieved after a risk assessment, establishing exactly what it is that has to be done and marshalling the resources and support for a project.

Crucially, it also involves setting 'SMART' objectives (Doran 1981) and allocating roles to fulfil the objectives. Objectives must remain under constant review with a flexible approach being taken to meet changing circumstances.

Toolkit

When laying plans a leader should ensure the following:

- Be clear about what is to be achieved and how it will be achieved. This involves having a clear 'vision' about what success will entail. In other words, what will have changed and to what advantage?
- Carry out a risk assessment bearing in mind operational, financial and reputational risks in particular. Too many risks may cause the abandonment of a project but most risks can be managed and mitigated or eliminated with foresight. Being risk-averse could be detrimental to making real progress.

- Marshal the support of key personnel and the support of those carrying through plans to fruition and gain the resources necessary to complete objectives (objectives should be tailored to match the available resources).
- Set SMART objectives:

S	Specific and stretching
M	Measurable
A	Achievable
R	Realistic and relevant and reviewable
T	Time-based or time-bound

More detailed information on SMART objectives is shown in 'Checklist 14—Leader's planning: SMART objectives'.

Objectives should remain under constant review with a flexible approach being taken to meet changing circumstances. However, completion dates should only be changed where absolutely necessary otherwise task completion indiscipline may occur.

- Agree the tasks that support objectives in a time-managed form. Tasks should be treated as mini-SMART objectives.
- Allocate roles and tasks to the people required to complete objectives, making sure that they know what is required of them and of others assisting them.
- Be prepared to tackle problems as they arise, seeking help from those working on objectives. Be prepared to be adaptable and imaginative using the ideas and suggestions of others. (See also Chapter 12, 'Problem solving'.)
- Agree quantitative and qualitative measures for success to be used to assess performance and results once objectives have been completed. Measures should include costs and time expended on projects.
- Debrief projects on conclusion to identify successes and what did not go so well with results and lessons learned being invested in future projects.

Checklist 14—Leader's planning: SMART objectives

(See Chapter 10, 'Planning')

Summary

Planning is a key leadership skill. Central to the planning process is the creation of SMART objectives (Doran 1981) for they offer structure and direction and the means for action and measuring results.

Toolkit

SMART is a mnemonic that assists the planner to remember and recall important stages in the objective-setting process thus:

S	Specific and stretching
M	Measurable
A	Achievable
R	Realistic, relevant and reviewable
T	Time-based or time-bound

SMART amounts to a 'bare bones' approach and the mnemonic can be expanded upon to great advantage, creating any number of worthwhile additions.

- *Specific*—objectives must be clear and unambiguous and not open to a number of interpretations. Objectives should be written down and explained to those who have the job of completing related tasks in order to create a common understanding of what is to be done.
- *Stretching*—not limiting team talent and innovation and being ambitious to maximise results.
- *Measurable*—measuring performance outcomes to ascertain whether an objective has produced the desired results. Measurements should be quantifiable (countable) and qualitative (seeking confirmation from those supposed to benefit from completed objectives). Cost and time implications should be measured too.
- *Achievable*—setting objectives that can be completed. There is no point in creating objectives that are fanciful and likely to fail through lack of forethought. Resourcing considerations include time available, personnel, competence and training implications and other work to be carried out simultaneously.
- *Realistic and relevant*—being realistic in terms of the scope of the objective and its relevance to the needs and aspirations of the organisation, its ambitions and the people it serves.
- *Reviewable*—exercising control and keeping progress under regular scrutiny to ensure that proceedings remain on track and any impediments to progress are removed.
- *Time-based or time-bound*—involves managing time to make a friend of it rather than an enemy. Striving for adherence to tight time limits for objectives and resultant tasks may not only get the job done quicker and save on resources but strict time constraints may also generate enthusiasm and energy.

Importantly, time limits and time milestones (staging points) are a strong form of control. However, when reviewing progress a leader may on occasions and out of necessity have to adjust time limits but this should never be done lightly.

Checklist 15—Leader's delegation

(See Chapter 11, 'Delegation')

Summary

Being able to delegate successfully is an important leadership function. A leader who does not delegate is likely to be regarded as a poor leader. Delegation is of the greatest importance if individual and team contributions are to be maximised, tasks and objectives completed and public service enhanced.

Toolkit

When delegating work leaders should ensure the following:

- Be clear about the reasons for acts of delegation and what is to be achieved; for example, to enhance individual skills, to widen the team's skill base and improve team performance, to spread the workload and relieve stress or develop leadership skills in others.
- Choose the right people to delegate to as some team members may be totally incapable, even with training, of taking on certain tasks, not because they are foolish but because of their aptitudes and preferences.
- Discuss the conditions under which the delegation is to take place before a task is attempted and listen to and address any concerns.

- Make clear to individuals what powers and scope they have to act—responsibility, authority and freedom to make decisions should be allowed otherwise the leader might just as well do the job him- or herself.
- Provide appropriate coaching or training for the individuals concerned.
- Offer total support to individuals, which includes giving advice, encouragement and ensuring that they do not suffer undue stress.
- Monitor the progress of tasks and assist with any problems that may occur where appropriate.
- Ensure that individuals learn from and receive praise for jobs well done.
- Remember that leaders cannot delegate accountability and are ultimately themselves responsible for things that do go wrong.
- Do not allow failure to inhibit delegation because when things do not go well, and indeed when they go right, lessons should be learned for the benefit of future acts of delegation.
- Where an instance of delegation brings forth successful results, the leader and the person achieving the results should enjoy the rewards together; it is not wrong for a leader to enjoy credit for leading people effectively.

Checklist 16—Leader's problem solving

(See Chapter 12, 'Problem solving')

Summary

Problems are a feature of everyday life whether in the workplace or socially. In the workplace when plans are laid they do not always go as anticipated and problems occur and difficulties appear regularly on an almost daily basis when carrying out routine administrative and operational policing duties. It is very important that a leader seeks to remove obstacles to progress to reach satisfactory conclusions in order to maintain efficiency and effectiveness and a first-class public service.

Toolkit

When solving problems a leader should ensure the following:

- Seek to prevent problems from occurring in the first place by, for example, carrying out regular 'spot checks' and agreeing, implementing and monitoring appropriate quality standards. And by encouraging team members to reveal problems before they turn into disasters and by discussing potential issues at regular team meetings.
- Be clear about what things will be like and what will happen when the problem has been solved. This should be put in writing and shared by all those concerned with outcomes.

- Separate the symptoms from the causes and then concentrate on the causes which should be put in writing to create a common understanding of what needs to be done to reach a solution. Diverting energy to tackling symptoms is likely to be wasteful of resources.

Consultation should take place with those intimately involved with the problem for they are often well positioned to offer sensible solutions thereby reducing effort spent unnecessarily on problem solving.

Seeking causes includes examining agreed standards to ascertain if a deviation from accepted practices has resulted in difficulties.

Examining symptoms and seeking causes require the application of logic based upon facts and evidence rather than supposition and guess work.

- Generate solutions using logical thinking. However, also try to be creative by challenging accepted traditional norms and by exploring seemingly illogical and irrational solutions which when tempered may become new and exciting ways of doing things.
- Try to identify creative contributors. Team members with ideas and suggestions pooled together may prove to be very useful. The leader should try to encourage people to think beyond normal parameters and confines. (See also 'Checklist 17—Leader's problem solving: brainstorming'.)
- Identify and test possible solutions before implementation. This will involve, for example, looking at competing demands elsewhere and costs in terms of time, personnel, equipment, accommodation and training.

'Pilot' schemes can be valuable for testing new approaches. However, often they appear to work because all the necessary resources and attention are provided during the experimental period. Conversely, however, during the subsequently approved widespread application of a pilot model in the workplace, results are sometimes not quite so good. This is because insufficient resources are made available because of other competing demands.

- Monitor the progress of solutions and make adjustments and adaptations where necessary.
- Compare actual outcomes with desired outcomes. Abandon unsatisfactory solutions and start the problem-solving process all over again.

Checklist 17—Leader's problem solving: brainstorming

(See Chapter 12, 'Problem solving')

Summary

Solving problems is an important part of a leader's role. In solving a problem a leader should endeavour to surpass the status quo to discover new and better ways of doing things and providing an enhanced service to members of the public. This involves creative thinking, which can be aided by involving team members in enjoyable, high energy, team-bonding, brainstorming sessions (Osborn 1963).

Hopefully, the rules laid down here for the sergeant or inspector leader to follow when encouraging brainstorming contributions should prove helpful. However, the rules themselves always remain open to adaptation and further improvement in the light of experience.

Toolkit

When running a brainstorming session a sergeant or inspector leader should ensure the following.

- Be absolutely clear about what the objective of the session is, what is to be achieved and what success will entail.

- Select a date, time and place when and where team members can give their undivided attention to what is required of them.
- Do not take part in the process of generating ideas as this may cause the exercise of undue influence over proceedings. Allow those assembled for the session the freedom to produce suggestions in an unhindered and unfettered way.
- Consider involving suitably qualified persons from outside the team who can bring unbiased and fresh views to the problem-solving issue.
- Appoint a skilled independent facilitator to conduct the session. He or she should help the leader to fulfil the session's objective without becoming involved in the detail of discussions or the decision-making process.
- Brief the *facilitator* who should tell participants what the objective(s) of the session are and what part they are to play in generating ideas. He or she should also set a time limit, for example 25 minutes to encourage responses, but eliminate unnecessarily long pauses and avoid continuance when the best ideas have long been offered. Further, the facilitator should explain to participants that they are free to make any suggestions that they wish no matter how unlikely they might first seem (this aids the creative thinking element of a session and originality), and that no one must subject anyone else to ridicule for a suggestion that they have made (this will help to kill a session off very quickly). Finally, team members may almost certainly find out that they can build upon the suggestions that others make.
- Help the facilitator who should not be encumbered by note-taking but lead discussions and manage time. The *sergeant or inspector* leader should engage a non-participating note-taker(s) for this purpose. Ideally notes should be displayed on sequentially numbered, large pieces of paper (perhaps using the flip-chart system) so that all may see the progress being made and allow for even more fresh ideas.
- Be aware that when a session appears to be faltering, the facilitator should stimulate responses by suggesting other avenues of inquiry and seeking the enlargement of ideas already put forward.
- Note that it is part of the facilitator's role to close the session at the agreed time unless ideas are still pouring forth (a matter of judgement). However, if a session loses impetus it can be closed down at any stage during the proceedings.
- At the end of the idea-gathering session, the sergeant or inspector leader should, with the facilitator's help, invite team members to place suggestions into categories, eliminate totally inappropriate ideas and identify really worthwhile suggestions in priority order.

- Having thanked participants for their contributions, the sergeant or inspector leader should later test the validity of good ideas against the session's objective taking full advantage of the best suggestions and implementing them where possible. However, the leader should bear in mind that brainstorming is not an infallible process and that the search for answers may require further research.

Checklist 18—Leader's coaching skills

(See Chapter 13 'Coaching skills')

Summary

Sergeants and inspectors should coach their officers on an 'informal' basis as a natural consequence of their supervisory responsibilities. Coaching on a one-to-one basis helps to develop officer competence and correct faults in the application of workplace practices. Ultimately coaching helps to increase officer efficiency and effectiveness.

Occasionally, it may be appropriate to offer a more intense form of coaching to be carried out on an individual basis because of (a) the need to train just one person, or (b) the complexity of the subject matter, or (c) to refresh skills particularly where someone is having difficulty with their application. Coaching may also be used to address behaviours that cause concern to supervisors.

Sergeants and inspectors need to recognise that although formal coaching has a high value it can be time-consuming and should be used with discretion.

Toolkit

The advice here applies to 'formal' coaching courses, but the same basic principles apply to 'informal' workplace coaching as well.

When conducting a coaching session a sergeant or inspector should:

- satisfy themselves that they have the competence to coach particular sessions;

- note that coaching tuition is usually directed at a single person to offer them undivided attention and maximise learning. More than one person will dilute the training. However, there may be occasions where two or three persons can train together especially if role play is beneficial;
- choose a suitable venue where coaching can take place without interruption or interference and any training equipment can be accommodated;
- use the SMART formula to fix aims (what a session is intended to achieve in terms of future performance) and objectives (against which a trainee's subsequent workplace performance can be measured);
- create notes to match the order of delivery. They will ensure session coherence and make sure that facts and important points are not missed out. The notes can also be used to create a timetable and a handout to be given to the coachee at the end of training;
- give a copy of the aims, objectives and timetable to the trainee before coaching takes place;
- make the coachee feel at ease and relaxed and able to fully participate in the process without feeling embarrassed. Training can be testing but there is no reason why it should not also be enjoyable for it encourages participation;
- remember that role play is an essential feature of most coaching sessions. Different scenarios can be rehearsed in a non-threatening environment. Trainer and trainee can swap roles to broaden experience;
- use their interpersonal skills to full advantage, for example by:

  (1) using a voice tone and body language that chimes with being supportive, patient and encouraging. Equally important is the coachee's voice tone and body language as it may, for example, indicate disinterest, uncertainty or confusion as well as eagerness and enthusiasm. (Negative issues need to be professionally addressed.)

  (2) asking open questions (which avoid one-word responses) for example, by using 'How', 'What' and 'Why' for they stimulate discussion. The coachee should be encouraged to ask questions and to mention when they are unsure about any particular matter and require clarification. Exchanges should be harmonious and productive;

  (3) summarising regularly to help a coachee to learn in stages with all parts leading to a composite picture. It also offers space for a coachee to confirm their understanding of what has transpired so far. It is useful to ask a trainee to summarise themselves at opportune moments. This will also help to test whether or not they have absorbed aspects of what they are being taught;

(4) allowing trainees to practise newly acquired skills as many times as they wish until such time as they feel that they have mastered them.

(5) monitoring trainee progress by witnessing the use of newly found competence in the workplace and offering further help where necessary. It is likely that mistakes will be made at first and these should be tolerated as part of the learning process. Mistakes can be eliminated through practice and experience.

(6) arranging a follow-up session to review progress with the coachee. Address any perceived difficulties and offer praise where this is due;

(7) reviewing a coaching session and inviting honest and candid feedback from the coachee allowing for improvements which should be ploughed into any sessions delivered in the future. Avoid defensive reactions to feedback.

Checklist 19—Leader's change management

(See Chapter 14, 'Leaders as agents of change (change management)')

Summary

Change is an everyday occurrence hitting the police service at both the strategic and the tactical levels. Change can be complex, arising, for example, on the strategic level from political, social and legal pressures and, most importantly, the need to lay plans to serve the public. However, a great deal of change (arising from strategy) is tactical, affecting the way policing is carried out in operational situations. Sometimes changes are large but quite often they can be quite small. Nonetheless, the actual management of change is a critical and sometimes very difficult process. Regardless of this fact, the leader who does not manage change effectively is likely to experience a loss of prestige, a demoralised workforce and incomplete or abandoned objectives and perhaps failure may result in a poor service to the public.

Toolkit

The efficient and effective management of change requires the following:

- Sensitive and positive leadership should be of the highest quality. Leaders need to be realistic, inspirational and persuasive, good at solving problems and first-class communicators able to deal with all manner of issues and concerns that change may bring.

- Ensure that the change process itself is well planned with clear aims and objectives and risk assessments. But also that the change plans lay special emphasis on the feelings of all those people experiencing the changes who will perhaps have different expectations and concerns.
- Make absolutely clear to people what is changing and why and the benefits it will bring whilst being truthful about any possible disadvantages.
- Manage the different and varying reactions to change. Some people welcome change but others do not. Those who do not are not necessarily reacting unreasonably and their concerns have to be addressed. The leader should seek to allay fears and put staff at their ease by being honest, open and truthful. Problems may be solved through consulting those affected by change and by making helpful leadership interventions where possible. However, on occasions people may wish to move to a new position in the police service or choose to leave the police force concerned and seek employment elsewhere. This is perhaps a point where human resource experts should be consulted.
- Pass information to staff to inform them of what is going on at all stages of the change. However, information is insufficient on its own. Communication involves seeking and acting upon the views and the ideas of others and implementing suggestions where feasible and desirable. This is a conscious and continuous act.
- Where team harmony, synergy and efficiency are lacking, try to find out why and seek to generate enthusiasm through involvement, skill utilisation and individual motivators.
- Train people to acquire new skills and competence to match changes. The absence of appropriate skills will have a negative result on both individuals and change plans.
- Monitor the progress of change plans. This requires flexible leadership, seeking honest feedback, problem solving and making adjustments where necessary. Staff concerned with implementing the changes are likely to know why problems occurred, their effects and possibly solutions.
- Completed changes should be embedded with the creation of behavioural and performance standards. The good performance of staff should be recognised and people praised and rewarded where possible.
- Continue to look ahead to the future with a view to anticipating further necessary changes on the horizon. Smooth progressive change is better than one-off large changes or enforced changes.

Checklist 20—Leader's motivation skills

(See Chapter 15, 'Motivation')

Summary

Maintaining a well-motivated team of followers is an essential leadership task. A leader is likely to fail if team members feel demotivated and demoralised. Dissatisfaction among team members means that tasks and objectives are unlikely to be successfully completed, resulting in criticism of the team and perhaps a poor service to the public.

Motivating followers is a complex and sophisticated task. This is because different people may be motivated by the same things but also by different things depending upon their own abilities and needs. *Each person has unique motivational requirements.*

Toolkit

When seeking to motivate people the leader should ensure the following:

(1) Consider workplace activities closely and seek answers to the following questions.

- Are team members aware of their roles and what they and others are supposed to be doing?
- Are set tasks and objectives being completed well and on time?
- Are the absence and sickness rates high and, if so, what are the reasons for this?
- Have team members accrued a high number of complaints for substandard work (includes complaints against police and misconduct proceedings) and, if so, why?

- How do others outside the team view team performance (e.g. other teams, senior officers and external agencies)?

If the answers are positive, this is a good sign that individual and team satisfaction is sound and worth building upon. If the responses give cause for concern, then corrective measures will have to be taken and motivational factors considered.

(2) Consult with team members on an individual basis so as to establish:

- what they are doing, how well they are doing it and what they have achieved in their jobs;
- what they like doing and what they can offer the team in terms of skills and competence;
- what suggestions they have for improvements and how they personally can help to enhance team harmony and productivity;
- what their aspirations and ambitions are and how they intend to help themselves but also what help they need.

This information added to that provided at point (1) should help the leader to:

- better understand how to utilise individual skills and motivators to enhance contributions to the team effort and greater efficiency and effectiveness;
- satisfy individual motivators, ambitions and aspirations through the creation of individual and team development plans to the benefit of each team member and the team itself;
- deal promptly with any inefficiencies and inappropriate behaviours identified so as to remove discontent and create the conditions for a fresh start.

(3) Additionally the leader should:

- review physical working conditions (e.g. building, furniture and equipment) to establish where any reasonable and affordable improvements need to be made;
- continuously encourage participation, involvement, ideas and suggestions for improvement whilst allowing as much individual freedom of action as possible;
- set up an effective communications system including, for example, regular daily one-to-one contact experiences (where possible and no matter how casual and brief), team meetings, and briefing and debriefing sessions;
- endeavour to make work as varied and interesting as possible for team members;
- provide the means for personal growth and advancement for individuals by creating self-development plans, coaching sessions and by offering responsibility through delegation;
- recognise good work by giving praise and encouragement;

- make sure that prejudice and discrimination have no place in the police service;
- ensure that policies and directions are clear and easily understood or where they are not make appropriate requests for clarification of content;
- remain aware of individuals' support and welfare needs.

Checklist 21—Leader's misconduct and discipline

(See Chapter 16, 'Misconduct and discipline')

Summary

Dealing with misconduct issues is one of the hardest things that a leader has to do, especially when coming up against very strong and dominant personalities. But a failure to act may discredit the leader and result in the persistence of inappropriate behaviour as well as creating resentment within the team and possibly a poor service to the public.

The leader should take action personally by setting a good example through education and instruction in order to prevent misconduct issues from arising in the first place.

In all instances of misconduct, the leader should act promptly and gather necessary evidence before it is lost. He or she should follow investigative procedures strictly as failure to do so may result in a negative and unsatisfactory outcome and criticism of their professionalism.

Persons who are the subject of misconduct inquiries should be treated fairly, properly and with respect at all times.

Toolkit

When dealing with misconduct matters the leader should ensure the following:

- The leader and team members should be fully aware of the professional, performance and behavioural standards required of them at all times. This is likely to involve training, being aware of force policies and directions and an awareness of the College of Policing's Guidance for Ethical and Professional Behaviour in Policing and Ethics and the agreed Standards of Professional Behaviour issued under the Police (Conduct) Regulations 2020. Reinforce knowledge of the necessary standards by regularly reminding team members of their obligations in this regard.

- Be certain of what to do when a misconduct issue arises—sometimes without notice. Failure to understand the correct course of action to take may result in damage to the leader's reputation, continuance of the offence and the loss of valuable evidence.
- Create an environment where team members feel valued and respected and where professional misconduct of any kind is seen as totally unacceptable.
- Make sure that any person the subject of misconduct proceedings is treated fairly and without prejudice and discrimination, justly and with respect at all times. This helps to maintain the requirements of an unbiased and professional investigation and gathers the support of non-affected team members.

In all cases, act promptly to call a halt to the misconduct and to gather evidence before it becomes lost to the proceedings.

- Take notice of Home Office Guidance—Conduct, Efficiency and Effectiveness: Statutory Guidance on Professional Standards, Performance and Integrity in Policing (Version 1 February 2020). Section 2.9 notes that Standards of Professional Behaviour must be applied reasonably, transparently, objectively, proportionately and fairly. Procedures are designed to encourage a culture of learning and development for individuals and the police service. Disciplinary action has a part to play where necessary, but all outcomes should include learning opportunities.

An important caveat is that both management action and disciplinary action should satisfy the confidence needs of the police service and the public.

- Note that disciplinary proceedings do not apply to matters of unsatisfactory performance, unsatisfactory attendance or gross incompetence.

Disciplinary proceedings should only be used when there is a breach of the Standards of Professional Behaviour that justifies at least a written warning and constitutes what can be considered misconduct. This is distinct from dealing with less serious breaches or low-level conduct issues that can be addressed by line managers and supervisors, for example as Practice Requiring Improvement through the Reflective Practice Review Process.

Checklist 22—Leader's communication skills

(See Chapter 17, 'Communications—general discussion')

Summary

It cannot be overstated how important both personal and police communications are to creating a motivated and energetic workforce able to satisfy business plans. To make things even harder, the acquiring of sophisticated communication skills requires training, practice and a lot of experience.

A leader unable to communicate well with those people he or she comes into contact with both within and outside the police service, including members of the public, is likely to experience problems in carrying out his or her role.

A leader has to be aware of how difficult it is to transmit a message in any form; this is because different people have different perspectives on life and this can lead to different interpretations of even the simplest of messages.

The communications network of interactions is very complex. However, a leader has to deal with, among other considerations, two broad levels of workplace communications that operate at an 'official' business level and at a 'social' personal level, which can be both motivational and harmful in sometimes equal measure.

Creating a communications plan helps to manage and control information but also utilise it to great advantage.

Toolkit

(1) A leader needs to be aware that:

- first-class communications are difficult to achieve; this is because of their complexity and there are many obstacles to success;
- great care needs to be taken over the construction of messages, their clarity, method of delivery and their likely interpretation by recipients. Where possible, checking that a message has been received as intended is helpful;
- acquiring sophisticated communications skills takes time, training, practice and experience. The conscientious leader should always review the value of his or her transactions by way of outcomes and in a non-defensive way with others so as to bring about improvement;
- police communications operate at two main levels—that is, at an 'official' level and at a 'social' level. The official level deals with business considerations; for example, planning, policy, directions, information, compliance and aims and objectives. The 'social' level operates at a personal level through the everyday contact team members have with each other. Unrelated work matters are discussed but so too are vexatious work concerns;
- leaders should ensure that team members are fully conversant with business requirements. Naturally occurring social communications between team members can be motivational but also destructive if the leader fails to identify issues and deal with them. Therefore, the leader needs to sensitively penetrate the social level by identifying with its positive aspects whilst dealing with its negative connotations by encouraging people to express worries and concerns without fear and recrimination.

(2) To prevent confusion and ensure that individual and police needs are satisfied, the leader should create a communications plan to cater for the following:

Team needs:

- designed to cover the inward flow of information to the team and the outward flow of information from the team to others (e.g. to and from senior management);
- intended to review performance, monitor progress, receive and give feedback, solve problems, benefit from team creativity and make adjustments.

Individual needs:

- making provision for a forum to discuss all manner of business and personal concerns that elude meeting agendas but are nonetheless important and may be very useful for avoiding latent problems.

(3) It is necessary to gauge the success of any communications plan. A leader can do this by visiting and talking to police staff to see if, for example, information and

directions have been implemented in the workplace. Individual discussions should also reveal difficulties and problems and solutions. Team discussions will help also and so will critical feedback from seniors, peers, juniors and members of the public. In the final analysis, team success and contentment will speak volumes for the communication process.

(4) The effective leader should never be complacent but strive at all times to improve existing communications to make them even better.

Checklist 23—Leader's interpersonal skills

(See Chapter 18, 'Communications—interpersonal skills')

Summary

Good communications are the 'lifeblood' of any organisation. A failure to communicate well is likely to result in a failure to complete tasks and objectives satisfactorily.

The effective leader has to communicate at many different levels in widely differing circumstances. He or she may, for example, have to communicate with colleagues, senior managers and outside agencies. Also, he or she may have to present ideas, gain cooperation from others, negotiate for resources, deal with misconduct and attend potentially hostile public meetings. The list is almost endless, and each situation is likely to demand a separate approach. This all makes on-the-job learning, practice and self-development in communication techniques very important.

Toolkit

(1) The leader should recognise that:

- excellent communications skills are required in the leadership role because of the many different situations that a leader is likely to experience when working with team members, colleagues, external organisations and members of the public;
- the acquisition of sophisticated communication skills is an accumulative lifetime experience which means that there is always scope for learning and improvement;
- it is necessary to acquire basic interpersonal skills to which additional complementary skills may be added later; for example, assertiveness and transactional

analysis skills. Critical self-analysis, feedback and formal training courses are likely to assist in this regard.

(2) The interpersonal skills identified and explained:

- *Empathy* is at the very heart of good communications. Empathy involves trying to understand how a person might feel given their personal circumstances or situation no matter what that situation entails. Also, empathy involves exploring those circumstances through sensitive questioning and by building an affinity with the person or persons involved. Empathy helps to build bridges to true understanding.

- *Words* are the bedrock upon which good communication rests. A narrow vocabulary or a misunderstanding of words or subtle differences between words can limit the ability to communicate effectively.

  The leader should actively seek to increase his or her word capacity through conscientiously picking up and understanding new words through, for instance, reading books and newspapers, consulting dictionaries and listening to others.

- *Body language* is a natural part of being human and is central to human feelings, behaviours and communications. It is essential that a good leader watches body language closely to see whether it appears to support what is being said or implied.

  It is very difficult to mask body language especially for any length of time. However, it can be controlled in certain situations so as not to betray what a person is really thinking or feeling. Therefore, instant interpretations should not be assumed but checked where appropriate by the use of open questions.

  A leader can use his or her own body language (along with voice tone) to convey messages; for example, seriously, enthusiastically or empathetically.

- *Voice tone* helps to punctuate and enliven oral communications. For example, a raised voice may be used to emphasise determination or it may be used to overwhelm opposition. A quiet voice may indicate passivity and an inability to combat more aggressive personalities. However, a quiet voice may underpin a steely determination to succeed. However, all assumptions should be checked to ascertain the truth.

- *Listening* is necessary to properly understand communications from others and to show interest in what is being said. Listening involves:

  - remaining silent while others talk;

  - concentrating hard, focusing and listening intently to what is being said;

  - showing that listening is taking place through, for example, good eye contact, nodding the head and asking questions and seeking clarification;
  - checking that a message has been correctly received by repeating back important pieces of information and summarising where appropriate (see later).

- *Note-taking* is a writing skill but it is a useful aid to listening. It is difficult during a long discussion to remember everything that is said. Therefore, notes amount to a valuable aide-memoire. However, notes should be as brief as possible otherwise listening may suffer.

  Note-taking should take place openly and preferably in agreement with the other party (who should also be invited to keep notes if they wish to do so).

- *Questioning* is a very important skill to acquire. Questions can be asked to gain information, clarify issues and interrogate the facts.
- *Open questions*—using, for example, the words *what, why* and *how*—are good for gaining information. This is because they leave matters open for a full answer whereas closed questions do not. When interrogating the facts, in many different situations one of the most common mistakes made is not to pursue answers with more open questions to establish deeper meanings.
- *Closed questions* are good for gaining specific answers and verifying facts but their use invites limited responses. An example of a closed question would be: 'Are you a member of blue team?' This encourages a one-word response: 'Yes' or 'No' but it does establish a fact that may be further pursued. They often act as a good prelude to open questions and may be used in conjunction with them.
- *Silence* can be both helpful and coercive. Silence is helpful when a speaker is giving someone time to reflect upon what has been said. It is coercive when it is prolonged, making a person feel uncomfortable and therefore prone to say something that he or she might later regret.
- *Clarifying* involves establishing whether a listener has heard correctly and is in command of the facts. Sometimes, for example, a person delivering information might realise through body language that a person has not understood a particular message. Then he or she should seek to clarify the situation by reissuing the message. When doubt exists, matters should be clarified through the use of questions and by inviting (ideally) or delivering summaries (see the following point).
- *Summarising* is a very important and useful communications skill because it helps to ensure that a message has been correctly delivered in the manner in which it was intended.

  By asking someone to repeat a delivered message, the leader can find out whether they have fully understood it and its implications. When checked, any inaccuracies can be removed and a true understanding of what has to be done established. Equally, this process can be reversed by the recipient of a message asking the leader to summarise his or her own response in return.

Summarising is essential when people have been asked to take a particular course of action after the issuing of important operational directions or after, for example, corrective misconduct actions.

Checklist 24—Leader's assertiveness skills

(See Chapter 19, 'Positive communications—assertiveness')

Summary

Learning how to behave assertively is one of the most important things that a leader can do and assertiveness skills are absolutely essential to establishing good relationships with others. Being assertive should never be interpreted as being either aggressive or passive both of which can have negative consequences.

Assertiveness principles are easily understood but the skills are difficult to apply successfully without a great deal of practice. They are based upon respect for self and for others, openness, honesty and being forthright and they can yield considerable advantages for all concerned in a transaction.

Toolkit

(1) The tips that follow are designed to help the assertive leader:

- be clear about what you want to achieve—have clear objectives;
- know your 'rights' and 'responsibilities' (what you can do and the obligations that you have);
- be aware of the other party's 'rights' and 'responsibilities' and consider the position they are likely to adopt;

- plan what you are going to say and the points you must cover;
- acquire a positive state of mind and do not be put off by issues which you could find useful as excuses for inaction;
- choose the right time and place to act—sometimes you may wish to consider issues more deeply before responding and you may want to consult with others;
- rehearse before entering into a transaction as this should offer you an immediate advantage in terms of articulacy and preparedness;
- treat other parties with respect—do not belittle them;
- state how a particular action makes you feel (a matter of fact) if appropriate, for example: 'This incident has made me feel angry' or 'I am really upset that you should swear at me in that way';
- do not seek to excuse the bad behaviour of others although you may wish to draw their attention to it;
- ask people to justify apparently unfounded remarks and allegations;
- point out the consequences of certain behaviours (e.g. aggression) or suggestions proposed where necessary;
- try to reach an agreement through compromise—concede your position if appropriate and do not battle on regardless of the merits of your case;
- review your performance through critical self-analysis, results achieved and feedback from others.

(2) In trying circumstances it is necessary to pluck up courage and behave with determination so as to be able to tackle difficult people and difficult situations. However, a leader may be surprised by how far he or she can get with the facts, a good case, prior planning and a little bit of boldness. Success builds confidence for those occasions in the future when a positive approach is required.

Checklist 25—Leader's modes of behaviour and transactional analysis

(See Chapter 20, 'Communications—modes of behaviour and transactional analysis')

Summary

Transactional analysis (Berne 1968) is a positive communications tool and should not be used in a manipulative way. It is a useful addition to sound interpersonal and assertiveness skills. It is important because it allows a leader to look closely at his or her own behaviour and the effect he or she is likely to have on others including, for example, team members and the general public. Equally important, however, is gaining an insight into the behaviours of other people including members of the public as this allows for flexible communications leading to successful transactions between individuals and groups.

Toolkit

(1) A leader should be aware that:

- transactional analysis should never be manipulated and used maliciously.

(2) There are three main '*Ego States*':

- *Parent State*—split into two modes; that is, *Nurturing Parent* who, for example, is loving and concerned with protection and development and *Critical Parent* who, for instance, exercises control, sets rules and governs morality and behaviours;
- *Adult State*—with a rational, factual, reasoned evidence-based approach;
- *Child State*—split into two main modes including the *Adapted Child* who is, for example, submissive and non-confrontational but who can be rebellious, hostile and difficult to manage and the *Free Child* who may be, for instance, fun loving, untroubled, inquisitive, creative and able to do things instinctively.

(3) The *Little Professor* state is reminiscent of the *Free Child* in that Little Professors are inquisitive and creative and are often inspired to do things. However, the downside is that despite these benefits a Little Professor can be deviously manipulative. Although the positive aspects of this mode should be used to advantage, leaders should be alert to the possibility of behaviour which might seek to undermine their position.

(4) Experiencing the modes:

- People may dwell more in one particular mode than another but staying stuck in a particular mode may not be helpful. Imagine a sergeant who is nearly always in a *Parent* mode or an inspector who more often than not is in a *Child* mode: how would team members react and what would be the effect on the team?
- However, we do have choices which we should exercise to meet changing circumstances. For instance, it is not hard to see that when a police officer is enforcing the law he or she is likely to be initially at least in the *Critical Parent* mode whilst also slipping into the *Adult* mode when dealing with *Adult* responses or trying to raise the difficult *Adapted Child* response to an *Adult* level;
- The leader should try to be aware of which mode he or she prefers and the effect his or her own behaviour has on others. Equally, being cognisant of the modes being adopted by other people is important. For example, when leading their teams police sergeants and inspectors will meet all three of the Ego States and will have to choose which mode to adopt to meet particular situations. To assist, the mode an individual is adopting should be fairly obvious although this can be tested through questioning and regular contact.

(5) There are four 'Life Positions':

- I'm not OK but you're OK.
- I'm OK and you're OK.
- I'm not OK and you're not OK.
- I'm OK and you're not OK.

The best situation is: I'm OK and you're OK. The frame of mind that supports this position ensures respect for oneself and for others. This is likely to lead to good relationships and positive results. However, the leader should be aware of all the other positions so as to make appropriate motivational and problem-solving interventions where necessary. Other than the best position, all the other positions require investigation and the *I'm not OK and you're not OK* position is particularly worrying. On occasions expert help may be necessary, perhaps in the first instance in the form of human resources personnel. Leaders must not stray into areas that they are not competent to deal with, for example, medical matters.

(6) Practising transactional analysis skills—the leader should practise transactional analysis skills with outcomes then being subjected to critical self-analysis and feedback from others.

Checklist 26—Leader's communications feedback

(See Chapter 21, 'Communications—feedback')

Summary

A good leader should regard feedback as an essential communication tool. Feedback helps greatly with learning, self-development, problem solving, motivation, spreading good practice and efficiency and effectiveness.

Leaders should endeavour to ensure that feedback is regarded as a natural everyday process within the team. Where this is the case and where the leader is subjected to the same process of feedback, team members are far more likely to accept feedback as a natural part of their work. Acceptance reduces personal anxiety and helps to increase the likelihood of success.

Toolkit

When offering feedback a leader should ensure the following:

- Remember that feedback is a non-confrontational method of communication and exploration. It is never negative in that it looks for positive outcomes even when things appear to have gone wrong. It should be delivered in a non-judgemental way concentrating on facts, evidence and behaviours and not a person's personality.

- Offer praise where this is due. It recognises those things that a person has done well and sets the positive aspects against the negative ones. Positive features may heavily outweigh the negative aspects. Additionally, praise at the outset will help to create an atmosphere conducive to the reception of the elements that are harder to accept.
- Give feedback of a critical nature in privacy. Where feedback is offered as a result of team performance it may be delivered, diplomatically, to the team as a whole and not to individuals, although individuals may identify themselves with issues.
- Never seek to subject the person receiving feedback to personal abuse. Any remarks must rely on observable behaviour and aspects of performance for which there is evidence. Concentrate on what has taken place and not who a person is.
- Invite the person receiving feedback to comment on its validity. The leader should be prepared to change his or her position and, if necessary, act upon the information offered in response to the feedback.
- Where appropriate, ask the person gaining feedback to consider the consequences of what they have done.
- Ask the person who is the subject of the feedback to generate solutions to any perceived problem. This action empowers individuals to solve problems themselves and helps to build up confidence and self-esteem. When a person is able to generate solutions they are more likely to implement them because they are owned by them and not imposed upon them.
- Provide any appropriate help or training that the individual concerned requires to deal with problems identified.
- Invite the person receiving feedback to summarise what has taken place along with any remedial measures that need to be taken. This will help to ensure that a person knows what exactly is required of them.
- Make sure that the person receiving feedback fully understands the likely outcome of a failure to correct mistakes.
- Monitor what then takes place so as to be certain that errors or problems are eliminated, efficiency and effectiveness are achieved and the person concerned learns from the experience.
- Where appropriate, record what has been learned in writing and spread good practices identified to all team members, other teams and individuals who would benefit from the knowledge acquired.

Checklist 27—Leader's briefing skills

(See Chapter 22, 'Communications—briefing skills')

Summary

It is a leader's job to ensure that people are properly briefed at all times, whether in the workplace, on an individual or team basis or on major operations. If staff do not know what to do or how to do it or they are afraid to ask questions about what is required of them, success will surely be denied.

An efficient briefing requires clarity of purpose (if a planner is unclear then his or her messages will also be unclear), careful preparation and an awareness of how difficult it is to deliver a message effectively because of different perceptions and interpretations. First-class interpersonal skills are essential.

The National Decision Model devised by the College of Policing can be used in spontaneous incidents and planned operations, and by individuals or teams engaged with both operational and non-operational situations. Further, the model can be used as the basis for planning and debriefing events.

Toolkit

Adopting large-scale operations as an adaptable template, leaders should ensure the following:

- Remember that it can be difficult to deliver a message effectively because of different perceptions and interpretations.

- Choose a suitable briefing location devoid of noise and interruption that takes into account seating, lighting, general comfort and briefing aids such as PowerPoint and flip charts.
- Invite for briefing key players whose roles are essential to successful operations. The key players will have a responsibility to cascade information down to their staff making it doubly important that they are properly briefed. (With small-scale operations it may be possible to ask all participants to attend for a briefing.)
- Prepare and be totally familiar with the material to be used at the briefing. This includes being clear about objectives, difficulties and desired outcomes.
- Reinforce messages with voice tone, body language, summaries at regular intervals but particularly at the conclusion, written instructions and visual displays. Also, those being briefed should be encouraged to take notes.
- Ensure that those being briefed are made fully aware of what the objectives are and what success will mean.
- Acquaint individuals being briefed with what they and their colleagues are being required to do, why they are doing it and how what each person has been assigned to do fits in with the responsibilities of each person being briefed. Remind individuals of the ethical attitudes and behaviours required by the police service.
- Emphasise the desired ethical and professional behaviours that are required from officers at all times no matter what the circumstances are.
- Make sure that people being briefed are aware of difficulties and risks and how these might be overcome or brought to the attention of the leader if seemingly insurmountable. However, individual initiative where important should be encouraged as plans never seem to cater for all eventualities.
- Make certain that those being briefed are fully aware of the command and communication structure including where the main control point is, who the controller is and how communications as a whole will work.
- Watch the body language of persons receiving messages. Body language may indicate, for example, approval, disapproval, discomfiture at certain instructions or a failure to listen properly (e.g. lack of eye contact or talking to a neighbour while the briefing is in progress). Listen intently to questions, ideas, suggestions and doubts and where appropriate adjust plans accordingly.
- Where practicable, invite those key players being briefed to summarise what they are being required to do.
- Remember that every effort should be made to ensure that people are properly briefed before they leave the briefing area as a failure to absorb correct instructions

could prove disastrous. The leader should emphasise that *where people are in doubt they must ask for clarification.*

- Test the effectiveness of briefing skills by the results of operations and through a thorough debriefing process including comment on the briefing session which set up the operation in the first place.

Checklist 28—Leader's debriefing skills

(See Chapter 23, 'Communications—debriefing skills')

Summary

Running effective debriefing sessions following individual, small or major operations allows a leader to evaluate the worth of the original briefing and ascertain whether objectives have been satisfactorily completed; identify good practice and things that did not go so well so as to learn from experience and invest knowledge gained in the future.

Failure to run debriefing sessions bars the way to future progress and exposes poor leadership. This is because a good leader must always have an eye to the future and the changes that improve police efficiency and service to the public.

The National Decision Model devised by the College of Policing can be used in spontaneous incidents and planned operations, and by individuals or teams engaged with both operational and non-operational situations. Further, the model can be used as the basis for planning and debriefing events.

Toolkit

Based upon large-scale operations but adaptable to suit other circumstances, when debriefing people leaders should ensure the following:

- Plan debriefing sessions in advance taking into account pre-agreed objectives, performance standards and measures and desired outcomes.

- Choose a debriefing venue that is comfortable, well lit, devoid of noise and distractions. Make arrangements for refreshments if required and install debriefing aids such as flip charts.
- Invite to debriefing sessions all those people who contributed to the task or operation under review including specialists and outside agencies. Feedback from the public should be considered where appropriate.
- People who actually perform tasks are among those best able to suggest improvements to activities and procedures.
- Exercise first-class interpersonal skills, for example by using voice tone and body language to make things interesting and emphasise points, listening intently, showing empathy, asking open, probing questions, clarifying and summarising.
- Impartially, and concentrating on performance rather than personality, ascertain the degree to which events ran (or did not run) to plan.
- Do not embarrass individual officers but explore with fellow supervisors whether or not desirable attitudes and behaviours prevailed (these may well come out voluntarily from officers during a debriefing). Take any opportunity to offer praise to hard-pressed officers who acted professionally (e.g. were polite, helpful and calm under pressure). Poor behaviour (i.e. being over- zealous, rude and aggressive) can be dealt with separately and discretely.
- In a non-defensive way, seek from those assembled feedback on how well the operation as a whole went and what could be done better in the future. Solicit ideas and suggestions for improvement.
- Offer praise where this is due.
- Make immediate adjustments to work or operational procedures where appropriate.
- Utilise knowledge gained in future events and occurrences and spread new knowledge to areas that would benefit from receiving them, for example other police forces, training units and other emergency services and agencies.
- Finally, seek feedback on the quality of the original briefing session as well as the debriefing session and act upon information gained.

Checklist 29—Leader's influencing skills

(See Chapter 24, 'Communications—influencing skills')

Summary

Influencing skills are particularly relevant to the role of a police leader as a significant part of a leader's role concerns persuading people (e.g. team members, peers, seniors, agencies and members of the public) to adopt certain courses of action. Influencing may centre on, for example, administrative or operational matters or public concerns.

Influencing others is not easy and requires careful planning and the use of a sophisticated bundle of interpersonal skills among which empathy and sensitivity to the needs of others are of paramount importance. Exercising flexibility is essential. Further, listening carefully to the views, ideas and suggestions of others may well lead to the achievement of goals but also the development of a much better outcome than was originally planned or envisaged.

Toolkit

To gain influence a leader should ensure the following:

- Be fully competent in the topic, subject matter or area in which it is necessary to persuade others to take on ideas, suggestions and plans. Relevant detailed research is essential.
- Carefully plan what needs to be achieved. This entails having written objectives with clear outcomes. Risks should be identified and dealt with without necessarily abandoning a particular aspect of the plan.

- Be cognisant of possible difficulties and likely objections with prepared responses and identified areas for negotiation and concession. Appreciating the sensitivities and needs of others is of the greatest importance.
- Remain in a professional, courteous and polite mode that respects others. Do not become emotionally involved with content but deal with matters in a factual way although empathy with the positions of others is always a major consideration.
- Be assertive (honest, open and forthright) but never confrontational or aggressive or passive. Deploy interpersonal skills to full advantage. This includes listening intently, adopting the right voice tone and body language and watching the body language of others. Questioning is really important—using, in particular, open questions and probing with follow-up questions.
- Challenge unfounded remarks and allegations with a request for facts and evidence.
- Be open to criticism and admit fault where this is appropriate. This shows strength not weakness and reassures people that their contributions are valued.
- Adopt a flexible approach to negotiations, being prepared to modify or alter or abandon aspects of plans in favour of other valid and more attractive ideas and suggestions. Point out the strengths and merits of a particular case but do not shy away from possible difficulties to which solutions should be sought.
- Offer praise and encouragement where merited.
- Draw strength and support from people who show that they are interested in proposals and build upon their ideas and enthusiasm. This may entice more reticent people to join in discussions. Even contrary views are valid and they are useful for stimulating discussion and creative alternatives.
- Avoid 'hard selling' or making exaggerated claims which may make people suspicious or hostile, especially if eventually executed plans do not come up to perceived expectations. Failure may lead to a lack of cooperation in the future.
- Where possible encourage a cooperative approach, inviting people to join in the planning or execution process where possible.
- Share success with all participants involved in fulfilling a plan.
- Evaluate the exercise of influence in a self-critical way by results and seek feedback from others.

Checklist 30—Leader's report-writing skills

(See Chapter 25, 'Influencing skills—report writing')

Summary

It is essential that a leader should have good oral and writing skills. This is in order to express him- or herself clearly so as to be able to gain influence and desired results. Poorly written, confusing and unattractive reports which frustrate a reader may lead to rejection of the report and the serious messages that the writer is trying to convey to the reader.

Toolkit

The guidelines that follow should be adapted to suit local requirements and different types of report. When writing a report the leader should ensure the following:

- Be clear about what the report is intended to achieve. This means creating writing objectives and planning the structure of the report.
- Take into account the needs of the reader and what he or she already knows about the subject matter. Repetition of known facts may not be appreciated by the busy reader.
- Encourage the reader to pick up the report by making it attractive and easy to read and explore. Considerations in this regard would include, for example: the quality of paper

used, the report cover and binding, the typeface used and the use of space, which enables the reader to cope with content.

- Introduce an eye-catching but not fussy front cover as this is the first thing a reader sees and first impressions are lasting. A cover should be simple and contain the report title, the date of publication and the writer's details (including rank and professional and academic qualifications).
- Recognise that exploration by the reader requires 'signposts'. Signposting includes headings, subheadings, emboldened and underlined words, bullet points and italics. The use of colour should be considered where appropriate along with graphs, diagrams and pie charts.
- Include an executive summary following the title page. The summary should amount to a brief but clear précis of the report's contents. This is an important 'trailer' to the report itself. The hard-pressed reader will judge from the summary whether the report is worth reading at all. A précis should be as brief as possible and ideally not exceed half a sheet of A4 paper and only in *exceptional circumstances* one full page.
- Create a table of contents to help the reader to find his or her way around the document. The contents page should include page numbers, report headings and subheadings and appendices or annexes.
- Number all pages to assist with navigation. The writer may decide not to number the executive summary. But many people number the index pages in the following way: (i), (ii), (iii), etc. These small 'Roman numerals' in brackets draw a distinction between the nature of the contents and the numbering of the report pages, which should ideally (for clarity) be in 'Arabic numerals', for example: 1, 2, 3, etc. (Some people do not number the title page, with the number 2 appearing on the second page (number 1 being omitted).)
- Note that the report's subject headings should be emboldened and numbered consecutively with Arabic numerals, for example: 1, 2, 3, etc. Ensuing paragraphs should be numbered to follow the subject headings thus: 1.1, 1.2, 1.3 and 2.1, 2.2, 2.3, etc. Some people further subdivide numbers, for instance: 2.1.1 and 2.1.2 and this is acceptable, but it may appear a little complicated.
- Try to acquire a wide vocabulary to increase the ability to put over information with subtlety and in the most descriptive and effective way. Bad spelling will damage the writer's credibility and the credibility of the report. Additionally, to assist ease of reading the writer should use simple rather than complicated words although sometimes these are very necessary.
- Use a variety of sentence lengths to create interest. However, shorter rather than longer sentences enable the reader to absorb information more quickly without the need to reread a sentence because of its undue length.

- Consider using 'active' rather than 'passive' verbs wherever possible, although the choice of how verbs are used is always open to the writer. 'Active' verbs tend to make sentences more direct and shorter, resulting perhaps in a considerable word saving.
- To aid simplicity avoid the construction of overly long paragraphs as these can become confusing. Confine a paragraph to the subject under discussion. When the subject changes, a new paragraph is needed. Where paragraphs are necessarily fairly long a concluding summarising sentence at the end of the paragraph will help comprehension.
- Acquire a good understanding of grammar and the conventions and understanding it brings to writing.
- Understand that punctuation helps to create sense of what is written and gives life and meaning to prose. Unpunctuated short sentences enable rapid reading whereas heavily punctuated work slows the reader down. But punctuation can also be used to pose questions, create suspense and add excitement.
- Consider a report's structure, for example:

An *introduction*, which should include:

- why the report has been written, what in brief terms it covers and what it is intended to achieve;
- terms of reference and sponsor (if any);
- research methodology;
- any other additional information deemed necessary.

The *main body of the report* should contain facts and evidence but not supposition or conjecture. It should be based upon reason, with the merits of particular pieces of information being discussed in full. The report should not stray from its writing objectives or terms of reference. The content of the report should be produced in a logical and chronological form.

The report's *conclusions*—the facts of the report should lead to logical conclusions, which should be expressed in simple but very clear terms. Individual conclusions should be cross-referenced with the appropriate paragraphs in the main body of the report.

The report's *recommendations* should follow on logically from the *conclusions*, which themselves should follow on logically from the facts. Recommendations should be cross-referenced with the conclusions.

Appendices or annexes should be included where appropriate. Appendices and annexes are used to remove information from the main body of the report to the back of the document. Information removed amounts to additional material that can be examined later at the reader's leisure. If it is of critical importance, material should remain with the main body of the report. Appendices or annexes are usually produced in alphabetical order, for example: Appendix A, Appendix B, etc. They should be recorded in the report's table of contents after the main subject headings.

Checklist 31—Leader's meeting skills

(See Chapter 26, 'Meeting skills')

Summary

Meetings can be very frustrating, expensive time-wasters and should only be called when absolutely necessary to assist with the promotion of efficiency and effectiveness and public service. The chair of a meeting amounts to a leader directing and benefiting from the creative power of meeting members.

Chairing a meeting well requires a mixture of sophisticated planning, problem-solving, time-management and interpersonal skills. It also involves close cooperation with the minute secretary.

Toolkit

The advice offered here covers formal chaired meetings but can be adapted to include other meetings.

(1) The chair (leader) of a meeting should:

- only convene a meeting when it is absolutely necessary to do so and alternatives are unlikely to achieve the desired results;
- appoint a minute secretary;
- set the agenda for the meeting;
- agree the date, time and place and frequency of meetings;

- decide who will attend meetings;
- agree the conditions for the submission of papers to be discussed at meetings;
- lay down the conditions for visiting speakers including time allocations (uncontrolled speakers can, for example, cause real time-management problems through overly long and irrelevant discourses);
- give directions on the time limit for meeting minutes to be published after the conclusion of meetings;
- issue instructions covering instances where people attending meetings have failed to prepare properly; for example, by failing to read pre-meeting briefing notes or the minutes of the last meeting (depending upon the circumstances, a meeting member may be denied the time to read papers and minutes at a meeting);
- lay down the procedure for excluding meeting members for bad behaviour or disorderly conduct.

(2) *Setting an agenda using SMART objectives* (Doran 1981) (see also Chapter 10, 'Planning', section 10.2.6)—a good way of being clear about outcomes and managing time effectively is to link agenda items to SMART objectives adapted for the purpose. SMART objectives are:

S	Specific and stretching
M	Measurable
A	Achievable
R	Realistic, relevant and reviewable
T	Time-based or time-bound

(3) *Agenda format*—an agenda tends to follow a time-honoured format and this is reproduced below. However, there is no reason why a chair should not create a different format provided that it enables a meeting to proceed efficiently.

Day, Date, Time, Place

1. Apologies for absence
2. Minutes of previous meeting
3. Matters arising
4. Item one—subject or topic
5. Item two—subject or topic
6. Item three—subject or topic
7. Any other business

8. Date of next meeting

(4) *The role of a minute secretary* is a particularly onerous one. The interpersonal skills the minute secretary uses most are in conflict with each other. The minute secretary is required to listen intently but also take down notes, which detract from the listening process. Where necessary the minute secretary should seek clarification of statements through the chair.

It is the job of the minute secretary to:

- circulate the agenda to meeting members along with any briefing papers and other directions (it is not the responsibility of the minute secretary to prepare the agenda—that is the chair's job. However, he or she may prepare the agenda under the chair's guidance and it is the chair's task to approve the content of the agenda before circulation);
- book meeting venues and manage any consequent administrative tasks;
- write and circulate meeting minutes;
- file meeting papers.

(5) *Chair: specific* responsibilities—the chair of a meeting should:

- introduce each agenda item separately, supplying background information, progress and facts, as appropriate;
- use his or her interpersonal skills to manage behaviours assertively, encourage participation, suggestions and ideas while curtailing excessive or aggressive contributions and asking people to substantiate what appear to be spurious arguments and allegations;
- as a general rule listen more than talk, watching reaction through body language and noting the use of voice tone to illustrate doubt, concern, commitment or opposition;
- use closed questions to verify facts and open questions to gain more detail—using a series of probing, open questions in particular is important. For example: what is to be done, why is it to be done, what are the benefits, who should do it, who will help to do it, what resources are required, how long will it take, how much will it cost, when will it be completed, what are the measurements for success, how will the police service and the public benefit;
- allocate tasks for completion and ensure that they are in fact completed and not put aside;
- not allow 'Any other business', which is intended for urgent or immediately important items only, to become a vehicle for ill-prepared and unstructured debate.

Often 'Any other business' can take almost as long as the substantial meeting itself;

- ensure that meetings run to strict time limits. Short time limits tend to be constructive rather than destructive for it helps to concentrate minds. Hold back some time in reserve—it does not matter if it is not used;
- with meeting members, evaluate and validate the worth of the meeting and its outcomes, which can only be judged in the final analysis in the workplace itself. It is possible to have a 'good meeting' and poor workplace consequences;
- the worth of a meeting may also be judged by its costs; that is, the salaries of meeting members and other expenses including accommodation, travelling and refreshment, etc. Examining 'opportunity costs' (i.e. what people would have been able to do if they had not attended the meeting) is particularly important;
- abandon unproductive and unsuccessful meetings in favour of other methods of exploring issues.

Checklist 32—Leader's self-development skills for others

(See Chapter 27, 'Self-development for the leader and encouraging leadership skills in others')

Summary

A leader has a responsibility for developing him- or herself in the leadership role. Additionally, whilst having a duty to develop all team members to improve their competence and satisfy their aspirational needs, the leader should also seek to develop the latent talents of individuals showing signs of leadership potential for the future.

The desire to motivate oneself to do anything is a matter of individual preference and choice. However, leaders can offer encouragement, counselling and support and make meaningful practical interventions.

Toolkit

(1) Leaders (and aspiring leaders) wishing to develop themselves should ensure the following:

- Consider what their aspirations and ambitions are and what they want to achieve. In other words, what will success entail?

- Take stock of past and present experiences. What competences have been acquired and what will those competences contribute (exactly) to the desired outcomes?
- Place existing competences and experience gained against the competences required for improvement or a new position. What additional competences are required and how will they be gained?
- Ascertain what resources are required and who might be willing to help with the fulfilling of self-development objectives. These might include, for example, peers, team members, other colleagues, senior officers (who could act as mentors), trainers and, most importantly, family members—particularly spouses and partners.
- Create a self-development plan based upon SMART objectives (Doran 1981) (see also Chapter 10, 'Planning', section 10.2.6):

S	Specific and stretching
M	Measurable
A	Achievable
R	Realistic, relevant and reviewable
T	Time-based or time-bound

- Create a learning log to profit from an analysis of current meaningful events that help to stimulate thought and improve competence. A log is not a daily diary nor should it become a chore that detracts from content and satisfaction. Entries in the log should be short, clear and meaningful. Briefly, in practice significant events should be recorded, analysed and evaluated to find out what can be done differently to improve future performance.
- Seek and act upon feedback as another part of the developmental process.
- Critical self-analysis is also important.

(2) To develop leadership in others the leader, in addition to the above, should:

- provide potential leaders with opportunities to enhance skills through formal training programmes and on-the-job workplace coaching and perhaps even mentoring;
- offer openings to develop skills and competence; for example, through delegating tasks with leadership connotations, including deputising for the actual leader, together with the responsibility for carrying out certain actions without necessarily referring back to the leader continuously. This will encourage independent action. A leader can also offer potential leaders (and indeed all staff) opportunities to take on additional new skills to increase their competence;

- be approachable when problems occur or difficulties are experienced;
- keep performance under continuous review and monitor progress giving advice and help where appropriate;
- offer encouragement, particularly when the potential leader is under pressure, and provide praise for things done well.

Index

For the benefit of digital users, indexed terms that span two pages (e.g., 52–53) may, on occasion, appear on only one of those pages.